THE
STRUCTURE
of the
SIDDUR

THE

STRUCTURE

of the

S I D D U R

STEPHEN R. SCHACH

JASON ARONSON INC.
Northvale, New Jersey
London

This book was set in 10 pt. Times by FASTpages of Nanuet, NY.

Copyright © 1996 by Stephen R. Schach

10 9 8 7 6 5 4 3 2 1

Library of Congress Cataloging-in-Publication Data

Schach, Stephen R.
    The Structure of the Siddur / Stephen R. Schach.
      p. cm.
    Includes indexes.
    ISBN 1-56821-974-1 (alk. paper)
      1. Siddur.   2. Judaism—Liturgy—Outlines, syllabi, etc.
    I. Title.
    BM674.39.S33   1997
    296.4'5—dc21   96–37005
                                          CIP

Manufactured in the United States of America. Jason Aronson Inc. offers books and cassettes. For information and catalog write to Jason Aronson Inc., 230 Livingston Street, Northvale, New Jersey 07647.

To
Sharon,
David,
and
Lauren

Contents

Preface

A Jewish religious service does not consist of an arbitrary collection of prayers, thrown together in some random order. On the contrary, every service has the same underlying structure. It is hard to understand an individual prayer without first understanding the structure of the service of which it is a part. My purpose in writing "The Structure of the *Siddur*" is to use computer graphics to illustrate the structure of the *Siddur* (prayer book), that is, to harness modern technology to help explain and understand a book that is centuries old.

There are many truly excellent *Siddurim* with English translations and detailed commentaries. These *Siddurim* carefully explain the **content** of every prayer. Unfortunately, I have yet to find a *Siddur* that gives the **context** of the prayers. In other words, there is generally no problem in finding the meaning of a word or phrase in a prayer; up to now, however, there has been no way of understanding how that prayer relates to the other prayers in the overall service. That need is addressed in this book.

The emphasis in "The Structure of the *Siddur*" is on the structure of the service. In order to simplify explanations, I have relied heavily on the use of diagrams. The primary item on virtually every page is a diagram that illustrates some aspect of the structure of the service; the words on the page are essentially an explanation of that diagram.

A second expository technique I have used is top-down presentation. Each chapter begins with a diagram showing the overall structure of its topic, for example, the *Amidah*. This initial diagram highlights the major components of the *Amidah*. Next, each major component in turn is presented in terms of its constituent subcomponents. Then, each of these subcomponents is presented and so on. Thus, by starting with the "big picture" and working down toward the details, the reader can clearly see how each part of the *Amidah* fits together.

One problem that I faced in writing this book is that there are many different *Siddurim*, corresponding to the different Jewish religious traditions and liturgies. For example, the *Ashkenazi* (Central and Eastern European) *Siddur* is different from the *Sephardi* (Spanish, North African, and Levantine) *Siddur*. The *Siddur* used by *Chassidim* is different from that of *Mitnagdim*. To compound the issue, many subgroups of these larger groups have their own *Siddurim*. Furthermore, the liturgy in Israel is different from that of the Diaspora.

One alternative was to show all variants. However, the purpose of this book is to highlight structure. The inclusion of all variants would have led to the structure being stifled by the many details. The solution I adopted instead was to choose one *Siddur* as a basis, namely, the *Ashkenazi Siddur* for the Diaspora, because I believe that the majority of the readers of this book use some version of that *Siddur*. I apologize to anyone who is slighted by this choice. Furthermore, because I have indicated only a few of the countless differences between the *Ashkenazi* liturgy and the many other liturgies, I also apologize to any reader whose religious traditions I have omitted in the preparation of this work.

Acknowledgments

I should like to thank two good friends for their assistance. I am grateful to Rabbi Ronald S. Roth and Rabbi Dr. Peter Haas for giving freely of their advice and encouragement.

Bruce Bromberg Seltzer meticulously checked the manuscript and made a number of excellent suggestions. I thank Bruce for his help and also for his enthusiasm.

I developed the manuscript by giving adult education courses on the structure of the *Siddur*. I am appreciative of the many questions and frank comments of the participants in those courses; their opinions helped shape this book.

Finally, I should like to thank my family. As a consequence of having to integrate text and graphics, writing "The Structure of the *Siddur*" has proved to be far more complex than any of my previous books. Without the constant support of my family, this book would never have been completed. In addition to their encouragement, they carefully read the manuscript and provided many suggestions; this was a true family project. Accordingly, I dedicate this book, with love, to my wife, Sharon, and my children, David and Lauren.

Stephen R. Schach
May 1996

1
What Is Structure?

At first sight, a Jewish religious service seems to consist of a totally random collection of prayers. Furthermore, every service, be it the Evening Service on a weekday, the Morning Service on *Shabbat* (the Sabbath), or the Additional Service on Pesach (Passover), seems to be completely different from and to have nothing in common with any other service.

In reality, every service without exception has the same structure. And if we understand that structure, we understand the service. It's just that simple!

A service consists of a number of components, such as the *Amidah*, the *Sh'ma*, and the *Kaddish*, put together in a specific order. In this book, we examine the underlying structure of each service in order to be able to understand the component items. In the early chapters, the various components are described. Then, toward the end of the book, the structure of each service as a whole is described in terms of the structures of these components.

Before we investigate the structure of the service or its components, we must first examine the concept of "structure" itself.

For the Maven

The Yiddish word *maven* (meaning an expert or a connoisseur) has become a part of everyday English. Not only do newspapers use it, but it can now be found in standard English dictionaries. Some readers of the first draft of this book claimed that there was not enough material for *m'vinim* (plural of *maven*, believe it or not). So the lower half of some of the pages of this book contains advanced material—heaven forbid that I should be accused of discrimination against *m'vinim*!

Consider human beings. Every human being is different, but each of us has the same basic structure.

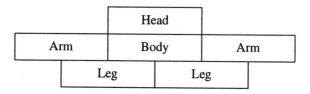

This diagram reflects the fact that every human being has a head. It is true that each head is different. For example, some people have red hair, some have blond hair (and some of us have no hair at all!), but everyone has a head. In the same way, we each have a body, two arms, and two legs.

For the Maven

Here is a puzzle that will keep even a maven awake at night (I first heard this posed by Dr. Max Peisach):

The service is different each day. For example, on Monday morning we read the Psalm of the Day for Monday and skip the psalms for the other six days. On some occasions we recite _Hallel_, on others we omit it. Everyday between Sukkot (or more precisely, _Sh'mini Atzeret_) and Pesach we pray for rain in Israel, but not during the rest of the year. The prayer for agricultural produce in Israel that we recite on weekdays also comes in two versions, namely, summer (from Pesach through December 4th) and winter (December 5th through Pesach). Different _Torah_ readings compound the issue—for example, seven different readings are possible for the (first) _Shabbat_ of Chanukah. And the different permutations for the _Hoshanot_ on Sukkot must also be counted.

Now for the question: How many different services are there?

I do not know the correct answer—I gave up after finding 3,000 different services, with many more to come. But the key point is this: every one of those 3,000 different services has the identical structure.

We can take this further. The structure of a leg can be broken down into a thigh, knee, calf, ankle, and foot.

Thigh
Knee
Calf
Ankle
Foot

We could take this even further, but we will resist the temptation to note that a foot has components of its own, such as the five toes. Instead, we will consider the structure of something completely different.

The next diagram depicts the structure of a typical television situation comedy or "sitcom."

Opening credits
Program
Commercial break
Program
Commercial break
Program
Commercial break
Program
Closing credits

The sitcom begins with the opening credits and ends with the closing credits. Program sections are interspersed with commercial breaks. This diagram depicts the structure of every sitcom, irrespective of the channel on which the sitcom is shown.

Now that we fully comprehend the meaning of the word "structure," it seems that we are ready to look at the structure of the service. However, there is one more preliminary item we have to cover, translation and transliteration of the Hebrew text.

2
Translation, Transliteration, and Terminology

Translation

There are two extremes in translating the *Siddur* from Hebrew into English. One approach is a literal, word-for-word translation; the other is a figurative approach. A literal translation is sometimes difficult for the modern reader to understand, whereas a figurative approach hampers the reader who is trying to comprehend the meaning of a specific Hebrew word.

The purpose of this book is to explain the **structure** of the *Siddur*. In order to explain where in the *Siddur* a specific prayer begins and ends, I have quoted a few Hebrew words from the beginning and the end of that prayer.* Thus, my translations are not of complete sentences, only of short phrases. In this context, a literal translation seems to be more appropriate. On a few occasions, however, I have given a more idiomatic translation when I felt that a literal translation would be misleading.

---

* In Appendix B, I have given the page numbers of three popular *Siddurim* for each prayer in this book to assist the reader in locating the prayer in his or her *Siddur*.

Transliteration

The difficulty of coming up with a translation that is both correct and clear to the modern reader pales into insignificance when compared to the problem of transliteration of Hebrew words into English characters. There is no one "correct" way to pronounce liturgical Hebrew. There are two basic pronunciation systems, namely, the *Ashkenazi* and the *Sephardi*, plus numerous variants within each. In addition, there appears to be a trend in some circles in Israel to use the modern Israeli pronunciation. Thus, there is no way to transliterate liturgical Hebrew without insulting someone's tradition.

On the basis of a totally unscientific survey, I determined that the majority of the readers of this book are likely to use the *Sephardi* pronunciation system. Accordingly, that is what I have used for transliterating Hebrew words.

I have used three special symbols in my transliterations:

ch	Guttural, pronounced like the last sound of the Scottish word "loch" or the composer "Bach"
' (apostrophe)	Vowel, pronounced "*uh*"
- (hyphen)	Used (as sparingly as possible) to resolve ambiguities, such as *be-emet* or *uvinvi-ei*

All transliterated Hebrew words appear in *italics*; the corresponding English translation is parenthesized.

Examples

To see how all this works, consider the *b'rachah* (blessing) before drinking wine:

Baruch Attah Adonai, Eloheinu Melech ha-olam, Borei p'ri hagafen
(Blessed are You, O Lord our God, King of the universe, Who creates the fruit of the vine)

We observe the use of the *ch* in the words *Baruch* and *Melech*.

Next, consider the first word of the Call to Worship. It is sometimes transliterated *Barchu*, but that overlooks the fact that the word is actually pronounced *Ba-ruh-chu*. In order to indicate the *uh* sound in the middle of the word and the break after the *Ba*, I transliterate it *Ba-r'chu*.

Now look at one of the responses of the *K'dushah*:

Baruch k'vod Adonai mi-m'komo (Blessed be the glory of the Lord from His place)

The apostrophe in *mi-m'komo* tells us that there is an *uh* sound between the second *m* and the *k*. The hyphen is needed because the word is not pronounced *mim'komo*.

For the Maven

I use *ch* for transliterating the Hebrew consonants *chaf* and *chet*. I do not attempt to distinguish between them. Similarly, *k* is used for both *kaf* and *kuf;* nor do I attempt to differentiate between *aleph* and *ayin*, *vet* and *vav*, *tet* and *tav*, or *sin* and *samech*. These issues can easily be resolved by referring to the Hebrew text.

I use ' (apostrophe) to denote the *sh'va na*.

Exceptions

The transliteration of three Hebrew words, *Ashkenazi, Sephardi,* and *Halleluyah,* has become virtually standardized. The correct pronunciation of those words is well-known, so there is nothing to be gained by using our transliteration scheme. Thus, the standard transliteration is used in this book.

Standard transliteration	More accurate transliteration
Ashkenazi	*Ashk'nazi*
Halleluyah	*Ha-l'luyah*
Sephardi	*S'faradi*

Pronunciation of Hebrew Vowels

All the seven different transliterated vowels I use are found in the first seven words of the *b'rachah* said before eating bread, namely, *Baruch Attah Adonai Eloheinu Melech ha-olam, Hamotzi lechem min ha-aretz* (Blessed are You, O Lord our God, King of the universe, Who brings forth bread from the earth).

Hebrew Word	Vowel	Pronounced as in
Baruch (Blessed)	u	put
Attah (You)	a	ah
Adonai (Lord)	ai	aisle
Eloheinu (our God)	ei	rein
Melech (King)	e	set
ha-Olam (the universe)	o	for
Hamotzi (Who brings forth)	i	see

Capitalization

Whenever a word refers to God, I have capitalized it in both the Hebrew and its English translation. To some, usage like "You" or "Who" might seem excessively pietistic. However, this capitalization is often necessary to clarify the meaning of a short phrase that would otherwise be obvious from the context of the complete prayer.

For the sake of clarity, I have written words like "God" and "Lord" in full, rather than "G-d" or "L-rd." Also, I have also spelled out *Adonai* rather than use *Hashem* or some other synonym. I apologize if this usage is offensive to some.

Terminology: Festivals

The following terminology is used in this book regarding the Festivals:

Festivals	
Yamim Nora-im (Days of Awe)	Rosh haShanah (New Year) Yom Kippur (Day of Atonement)
Chagim (sing. *Chag*)	First two days of Sukkot (Feast of Booths) *Sh'mini Atzeret* (Eighth Day of the Assembly) *Simchat Torah* (Rejoicing of the Law) First two and last two days of Pesach (Passover) Shavuot (Feast of Weeks)
Minor Festivals	*Rosh Chodesh* (New Month Festival) *Chol haMo-ed Sukkot* (Intermediate Days of Feast of Booths) Chanukah (Festival of Dedication) Tu b'Shvat (Fifteenth day of *Shvat*) Purim (Festival of Lots) *Shushan Purim* (Purim celebrated in Shushan) *Purim Katan* (Minor Purim) *Chol haMo-ed Pesach* (Intermediate Days of Passover) *Pesach Sheni* (Second Pesach) *Yom haSho-ah* (Holocaust Day) *Yom ha-Atzma-ut* (Independence Day) *Lag ba-Omer* (Thirty-third Day of the *Omer*) *Yom Y'rushalayim* (Jerusalem Day) *Tu b'Av* (Fifteenth of *Av*)

For the Maven

Some of the Minor Festivals, such as *Tu b'Av* or *Pesach Sheni*, may seem to be relatively obscure. The reason that they are included here is that they have an impact on the liturgy. For example, *Tachanun* is not said on *Tu b'Av* (or, in some liturgies, on *Pesach Sheni*). Also, *La-m'natze-ach* (Psalm 20) is not said, inter alia, on *Shushan Purim* or *Purim Katan*.

Terminology: Fasts

Fasts	
	Tish-ah b'Av (Ninth of *Av*)
Minor Fasts	*Tzom G'dalyah* (Fast of Gedaliah) *Assarah b'Tevet* (Tenth of *Tevet*) *Ta-anit Ester* (Fast of Esther) *Tzom l'B'chorim* (Fast for the Firstborn) *Shiv-ah Assar b'Tammuz* (Seventeenth of *Tammuz*)

Now that all the preliminaries are complete, we are ready to appreciate the structure of the service.

For the Maven

Even a M.I.T. (maven-in-training) will have noticed the omission of Yom Kippur from the list of Fasts! The reason is that, from a liturgical viewpoint, Yom Kippur is essentially a Festival. That is, the structure of the service for Yom Kippur is that of a Festival and bears little resemblance to the structure of the services for the other Fasts listed on this page.

3
The Structure of Every Service

Every single service, without exception, has the following structure:

Section before the *Amidah*
Amidah section
Section after the *Amidah*

That is, every service consists of three sections: the section before the *Amidah*, the *Amidah* itself and its associated prayers, and the section after the *Amidah*. The *Amidah* (literally, prayer to be recited while standing) is so important a prayer that it is frequently referred to as *Ha-T'filah*, literally, "**The** Prayer."

Here is a more detailed view of the previous diagram:

Section before the *Amidah*	Preliminary material
	[Morning and Evening Service only] *Sh'ma* section
Amidah Section	*Amidah*
Section after the *Amidah*	[Most weekday Morning and Afternoon Services] *Tachanun* (supplication)
	[Prescribed occasions] *Torah* reading
	Additional material
	Aleinu
	Kaddish Yatom (Mourner's *Kaddish*)

As shown in the diagram, the section before the *Amidah* begins with pre-liminary material of some kind. During the Morning and the Evening Services, this is followed by the *Sh'ma* section; that section is shown in detail below.

Then comes the *Amidah* section, shown in more detail in Chapter 5 (*Shabbat*), Chapter 6 (weekdays), and Chapter 7 (Festivals).

During the Morning and Afternoon Services on most weekdays, this is followed by *Tachanun* (see Chapter 9), and then by the reading from the *Torah* when prescribed (Chapter 11). The service concludes with *Aleinu* and the mourner's *Kaddish*, both described in detail in Chapter 9.

Now we look in more detail at the structure of the *Sh'ma* section.

Ba-r'chu (Call to Worship)
B'rachot before *K'riat Sh'ma*
K'riat Sh'ma (reading the *Sh'ma*)
B'rachot after *K'riat Sh'ma*

This diagram shows that the *Sh'ma* section, in turn, consists of four pieces. *Ba-r'chu,* the call to worship, comes first. Then we say the *b'rachot* (blessings—plural of *b'rachah*) before the *Sh'ma*. Next we read the three paragraphs of the *Sh'ma* and conclude with the *b'rachot* after the *Sh'ma*. We will investigate the *Sh'ma* section in greater detail in Chapter 8.

Next we show more details of the *Amidah* section.

First section
Second section
Third section

There are many different versions of the *Amidah*, such as the *Amidah* for the Evening Service for weekdays, the *Amidah* for the Additional Service on Rosh haShanah, and the *Amidah* for the Morning Service on Pesach. Notwithstanding their differences, all versions of the *Amidah* have the same overall structure, namely, that depicted above.

The first section of the *Amidah* is essentially the same for every *Amidah*. The last section is also essentially the same for every *Amidah*. It is in the middle section where the major differences are to be found. But before we can investigate this, we must first understand the structure of *b'rachot*, because the structure of the *Amidah* is that of a *b'rachah*. Thus, in order to understand the structure of the *Amidah*, we first need a thorough introduction to the structure of *b'rachot*. A bonus is that there are numerous other *b'rachot* in other parts of the service; therefore, the next chapter will help us to understand other parts of the service as well.

4

The Structure of *B'rachot*

B'rachot (blessings or benedictions) form an intrinsic part of the liturgy. Thus, in order to get a full understanding of the structure of the service, the next step is to conduct a detailed investigation of the structure of *b'rachot*.

All *b'rachot* begin with the same three-word phrase *Baruch Attah Adonai* (Blessed are You, O Lord). That is, if a prayer begins with those three Hebrew words, then there is no doubt that it is a *b'rachah* (singular of *b'rachot*). As we will see, although all *b'rachot* begin the same way, they can have many different endings.

An example of a *b'rachah* is the prayer recited before we eat bread, otherwise known as *Hamotzi*.

Box 1	*Baruch Attah Adonai* (Blessed are You, O Lord)
Box 2	*Eloheinu Melech ha-olam* (our God, King of the universe)
Box 3	*Hamotzi lechem min ha-aretz* (Who brings forth bread from the earth)

It begins with the three-word phrase with which every *b'rachah* begins, *Baruch Attah Adonai* (Blessed are You, O Lord) (Box 1). Then comes the phrase *Eloheinu Melech ha-olam* (our God, King of the universe) (Box 2). The *b'rachah* ends with the words *Hamotzi lechem min ha-aretz* (Who brings forth bread from the earth) (Box 3).

17

Short Form *B'rachah*

Hamotzi is one example of a Short Form *b'rachah*. Here is the general structure:

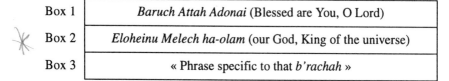

Box 1	*Baruch Attah Adonai* (Blessed are You, O Lord)
Box 2	*Eloheinu Melech ha-olam* (our God, King of the universe)
Box 3	« Phrase specific to that *b'rachah* »

A Short Form *b'rachah* begins with the three-word phrase with which every *b'rachah* begins, *Baruch Attah Adonai* (Blessed are You, O Lord) (Box 1). Next we have the phrase *Eloheinu Melech ha-olam* (our God, King of the universe) (Box 2). The Short Form *b'rachah* ends with a phrase that is specific to the *b'rachah* in question (Box 3).

If we compare this general structure with that of *Hamotzi* on the previous page, we see that *Hamotzi* is indeed a Short Form *b'rachah*.

Let us now examine another Short Form *b'rachah*. Consider the structure of the *Kiddush* for Friday evening. It begins with biblical verses from the story of the Creation (Gen. 1:31–2:3). The second paragraph is the *b'rachah* recited before drinking wine or grape juice. We have seen it previously (on page 6), but that was before we knew that it was a Short Form *b'rachah*, so here it is again:

Box 1	*Baruch Attah Adonai* (Blessed are You, O Lord)
Box 2	*Eloheinu Melech ha-olam* (our God, King of the universe)
Box 3	*Borei p'ri hagafen* (Who creates the fruit of the vine)

As in the case of *Hamotzi*, the structure of this *b'rachah* is precisely that of the Short Form *b'rachah* on the top of this page. The *b'rachah* begins *Baruch Attah Adonai* (Box 1), continues *Eloheinu Melech ha-olam* (our God, King of the universe) (Box 2), and ends *Borei p'ri hagafen* (Who creates the fruit of the vine) (Box 3).

For the Maven

A maven with a taste for grammar will have noticed that this *b'rachah* begins in the second person ("You . . . our God") but switches to the third person in the middle of Box 2 ("King . . . Who creates"). In fact, this feature is common to all *b'rachot* and, indeed, to Hebrew prayer in general. It reflects the tensions between approaching God directly by using the second person and keeping a respectful distance by using the third person.

Long Form *B'rachah*

Now look at the third paragraph of the *Kiddush*.

Box 1	*Baruch Attah Adonai* (Blessed are You, O Lord)
Box 2	*Eloheinu Melech ha-olam* (our God, King of the universe)
Box 3	*Asher kid'shanu b'mitzvotav . . . v'Shabbat kod-sh'cha b'ahavah uvratzon hinchaltanu* (Who has sanctified us with His commandments . . . and has lovingly and willingly given us Your holy Sabbath as a heritage)
Box 4	*Baruch Attah Adonai* (Blessed are You, O Lord)
Box 5	*M'kadesh haShabbat* (Who sanctifies the Sabbath)

It begins with the by now familiar three-word phrase, so it must be a *b'rachah*. But the rest of the paragraph does not fit the structure of the diagram on the top of page 18. In particular, the three-word phrase *Baruch Attah Adonai* (Blessed are You, O Lord) occurs twice, first in Box 1 and then again in Box 4.

What we have here is a Long Form *b'rachah*.

Here is the structure of a Long Form *b'rachah*:

Box 1	*Baruch Attah Adonai* (Blessed are You, O Lord)
Box 2	*Eloheinu Melech ha-olam* (our God, King of the universe)
Box 3	« Body of *b'rachah* »
Box 4	*Baruch Attah Adonai* (Blessed are You, O Lord)
Box 5	« Ending of *b'rachah* »

The Long Form *b'rachah*, like all *b'rachot*, begins with the standard three-word phrase (Box 1), followed by *Eloheinu Melech ha-olam* (our God, King of the universe) (Box 2). The body of the *b'rachah* comes next (Box 3). Then, because this is a Long Form *b'rachah*, the three-word phrase *Baruch Attah Adonai* (Box 4) is repeated a second time. The *b'rachah* ends with a short phrase (Box 5) that is specific to the *b'rachah* in question.

We now re-examine the third paragraph of the *Kiddush* to convince ourselves that it is indeed a Long Form *b'rachah*. Here is the paragraph again, copied from the top of this page.

Box 1	*Baruch Attah Adonai* (Blessed are You, O Lord)
Box 2	*Eloheinu Melech ha-olam* (our God, King of the universe)
Box 3	*Asher kid'shanu b'mitzvotav . . . v'Shabbat kod-sh'cha b'ahavah uvratzon hinchaltanu* (Who has sanctified us with His commandments . . . and has lovingly and willingly given us Your holy Sabbath as a heritage)
Box 4	*Baruch Attah Adonai* (Blessed are You, O Lord)
Box 5	*M'kadesh haShabbat* (Who sanctifies the Sabbath)

The third paragraph of the *Kiddush* begins with the standard three-word phrase (Box 1), followed by *Eloheinu Melech ha-olam* (our God, King of the universe) (Box 2). The body of the *b'rachah* comes next (Box 3). The body begins *Asher kid'shanu b'mitzvotav* (Who has sanctified us with His commandments) and concludes with the words *v'Shabbat kod-sh'cha b'ahavah uvratzon hinchaltanu* (and has lovingly and willingly given us Your holy Sabbath as a heritage). Then the three-word phrase *Baruch Attah Adonai* (Box 4) is repeated. The *b'rachah* ends with the phrase *M'kadesh haShabbat* (Who sanctifies the Sabbath) (Box 5).

We see that this is indeed a Long Form *b'rachah*.

A second example of a Long Form *b'rachah* is to be found in the *Havdalah* (*Havdalah* is the ceremony that marks the conclusion of *Shabbat* or a Festival; it is described in detail in Chapter 9).

Havdalah begins with a series of Biblical verses. Then three Short Form *b'rachot* are recited: the *b'rachah* over wine, the *b'rachah* over spices, and the *b'rachah* over the *Havdalah* candle. Finally, the *b'rachah* on the separation between sacred time (Sabbath or Festival) and secular time (weekday) is said.

Box 1	*Baruch Attah Adonai* (Blessed are You, O Lord)
Box 2	*Eloheinu Melech ha-olam* (our God, King of the universe)
Box 3	*Hamavdil bein kodesh l'chol . . . l'sheshet y'mei hama-aseh* (Who makes a distinction between sacred and secular . . . from the six working days)
Box 4	*Baruch Attah Adonai* (Blessed are You, O Lord)
Box 5	*Hamavdil bein kodesh l'chol* (Who makes a distinction between sacred and secular)

This Long Form *b'rachah* begins with the standard three-word phrase (Box 1), followed by *Eloheinu Melech ha-olam* (our God, King of the universe) (Box 2). Next comes the body of the *b'rachah,* beginning with the phrase *Hamavdil bein kodesh l'chol* (Who makes a distinction between sacred and secular) and ending with *l'sheshet y'mei hama-aseh* (from the six working days) (Box 3). Then the three-word phrase *Baruch Attah Adonai* (Box 4) is repeated and finally the *b'rachah* ends with *Hamavdil bein kodesh l'chol* (Who makes a distinction between sacred and secular) (Box 5).

Series Form *B'rachah*

There is yet another structure for a *b'rachah* and that is the Series Form. The next diagram depicts a Series Form consisting of two *b'rachot.*

Box 1	*Baruch Attah Adonai* (Blessed are You, O Lord)
Box 2	« Body of first *b'rachah* »
Box 3	*Baruch Attah Adonai* (Blessed are You, O Lord)
Box 4	« Ending of first *b'rachah* »
Box 5	« Body of second *b'rachah* »
Box 6	*Baruch Attah Adonai* (Blessed are You, O Lord)
Box 7	« Ending of second *b'rachah* »

Boxes 1 through 4 are the same as Boxes 1, 3, 4, and 5 on the bottom of page 19, that is, the Series Form begins like a Long Form *b'rachah* but without the phrase *Eloheinu Melech ha-olam* (our God, King of the universe). Then, the last three boxes of the Series Form above (Boxes 5 through 7) resemble the last part of a Long Form *b'rachah,* that is, Boxes 3 through 5 on the bottom of page 19. In other words, this Series Form *b'rachah* essentially consists of two Long Form *b'rachot* that share the same three-word introductory phrase (Box 1).

Now consider the following structure:

Box 1	*Baruch Attah Adonai* (Blessed are You, O Lord)
Box 2	« Body of first *b'rachah* »
Box 3	*Baruch Attah Adonai* (Blessed are You, O Lord)
Box 4	« Ending of first *b'rachah* »
Box 5	« Body of second *b'rachah* »
Box 6	*Baruch Attah Adonai* (Blessed are You, O Lord)
Box 7	« Ending of second *b'rachah* »
Box 8	« Body of third *b'rachah* »
Box 9	*Baruch Attah Adonai* (Blessed are You, O Lord)
Box 10	« Ending of third *b'rachah* »
Box 11	« Body of fourth *b'rachah* »
Box 12	*Baruch Attah Adonai* (Blessed are You, O Lord)
Box 13	« Ending of fourth *b'rachah* »

Here we have a Series Form *b'rachah* with four component *b'rachot*. Again, this essentially consists of four Long Form *b'rachot*, with the last three component *b'rachot* (Boxes 5 through 7, 8 through 10, and 11 through 13) sharing the three-word introductory phrase (Box 1) of the first Long Form *b'rachah* (Boxes 1 through 4).

We will see in Chapter 8 that this is precisely the structure of *K'riat Sh'ma* (reading the *Sh'ma*) for the Evening Service for *Shabbat*. There are two *b'rachot* before *K'riat Sh'ma* and two *b'rachot* after *K'riat Sh'ma*, and the structure of the four *b'rachot* is exactly what is shown on this page.

The next diagram shows the structure of a Series Form *b'rachah* with seven component *b'rachot*.

Baruch Attah Adonai (Blessed are You, O Lord)
« Body of first *b'rachah* »
Baruch Attah Adonai (Blessed are You, O Lord)
« Ending of first *b'rachah* »
« Body of second *b'rachah* »
Baruch Attah Adonai (Blessed are You, O Lord)
« Ending of second *b'rachah* »
. . .
« Body of seventh *b'rachah* »
Baruch Attah Adonai (Blessed are You, O Lord)
« Ending of seventh *b'rachah* »

This is the structure of the *Shabbat Amidah*. There are four different *Amidot* on *Shabbat* (one for the Evening Service, Morning Service, Additional Service, and Afternoon Service) and each one has exactly this structure. In order to understand the *Shabbat* service, we have to appreciate this structure.

Finally, we come to a Series Form *b'rachah* with nineteen (yes, nineteen!) component *b'rachot*.

Here is the structure of a Series Form *b'rachah* with nineteen component *b'rachot:*

Baruch Attah Adonai (Blessed are You, O Lord)
« Body of first *b'rachah* »
Baruch Attah Adonai (Blessed are You, O Lord)
« Ending of first *b'rachah* »
« Body of second *b'rachah* »
Baruch Attah Adonai (Blessed are You, O Lord)
« Ending of second *b'rachah* »
. . .
« Body of nineteenth *b'rachah* »
Baruch Attah Adonai (Blessed are You, O Lord)
« Ending of nineteenth *b'rachah* »

You may be wondering where in the *Siddur* such a Series Form *b'rachah* occurs. The answer is that the weekday *Amidah* has precisely this structure. Whether it be the weekday *Amidah* for the Evening, Morning, or Afternoon Service, its structure is that of a Series Form *b'rachah* with nineteen components.

Again, if we want to understand the weekday service, we have to be familiar with this structure.

Mitzvah Form *B'rachah*

Before we leave the topic of the structure of *b'rachot*, there is one special version of the Short Form *b'rachah* that has to be mentioned and that is the *b'rachah* recited before performing a *mitzvah*. The structure of this is shown below.

Baruch Attah Adonai (Blessed are You, O Lord)
Eloheinu Melech ha-olam (our God, King of the universe)
Asher kid'shanu b'mitzvotav, v'tzivanu (Who has sanctified us with His commandments, and has commanded us)
« Description of *mitzvah* »

Such a *b'rachah* begins with the phrases *Baruch Attah Adonai, Eloheinu Melech ha-olam, Asher kid'shanu b'mitzvotav, v'tzivanu* (Blessed are You, O Lord, our God, King of the universe, Who has sanctified us with His commandments, and has commanded us), followed by a description of the specific *mitzvah* that is about to be performed.

An example of a *Mitzvah* Form *b'rachah* is the *b'rachah* recited before lighting the *Shabbat* candles:

Baruch Attah Adonai (Blessed are You, O Lord)
Eloheinu Melech ha-olam (our God, King of the universe)
Asher kid'shanu b'mitzvotav, v'tzivanu (Who has sanctified us with His commandments, and has commanded us)
l'hadlik ner shel Shabbat (to light the Sabbath candles)

A second example of a *Mitzvah* Form *b'rachah* is the *b'rachah* recited before counting the *Omer*:

Baruch Attah Adonai (Blessed are You, O Lord)
Eloheinu Melech ha-olam (our God, King of the universe)
Asher kid'shanu b'mitzvotav, v'tzivanu (Who has sanctified us with His commandments, and has commanded us)
al s'firat ha-Omer (concerning the counting of the *Omer*)

After this *b'rachah* has been recited, the appropriate day of the *Omer* is counted.

A final example of a *Mitzvah* Form *b'rachah* is the *b'rachah* recited before taking the *lulav*:

Baruch Attah Adonai (Blessed are You, O Lord)
Eloheinu Melech ha-olam (our God, King of the universe)
Asher kid'shanu b'mitzvotav, v'tzivanu (Who has sanctified us with His commandments, and has commanded us)
al n'tilat lulav (concerning the taking of the *lulav*)

Now that we are familiar with the structure of *b'rachot*, we are ready to understand the structure of the *Sh'ma* and the *Amidah*. Because, as described on page 13, the *Amidah* is found in every service, we start with the *Amidah*. In the next chapter we examine the *Amidah* for *Shabbat*. The weekday *Amidah* is described in Chapter 6 and the *Amidah* for *Chagim* in Chapter 7.

5
The Structure of the
Shabbat Amidah

There are four services on *Shabbat*, namely, the Evening Service, Morning Service, Additional Service, and Afternoon Service, and hence there are four corresponding *Amidot*. Each *Amidah* is structured as a Series Form *b'rachah* with seven component *b'rachot*.

Baruch Attah Adonai (Blessed are You, O Lord)
« Body of first *b'rachah* »
Baruch Attah Adonai (Blessed are You, O Lord)
« Ending of first *b'rachah* »
« Body of second *b'rachah* »
Baruch Attah Adonai (Blessed are You, O Lord)
« Ending of second *b'rachah* »
.
.
.
« Body of seventh *b'rachah* »
Baruch Attah Adonai (Blessed are You, O Lord)
« Ending of seventh *b'rachah* »

These seven *b'rachot* can be grouped into three sections.

First section	First three *b'rachot*	Praises
Second section	Intermediate *b'rachah*	*Shabbat* themes
Third section	Last three *b'rachot*	Thanksgiving

The first section consists of three *b'rachot* of praises; this part of the *Amidah* is essentially the same for every *Amidah*, be it *Shabbat*, a weekday, a Festival, or whatever. The third section also consists of three *b'rachot*, largely devoted to thanksgiving. Again, this material hardly varies from *Amidah* to *Amidah*. It is the middle section of the *Amidah* that differs widely from service to service. The number of *b'rachot* in this middle section can be one, three, or thirteen. In the case of the four *Shabbat Amidot*, there is exactly one middle *b'rachah* and the contents of each *b'rachah* reflects a different aspect of *Shabbat*.

We now examine the structure of the *Shabbat Amidah* in more detail. We first describe the structure of the basic *Amidah* and then those pieces that are added on special occasions and when the *Amidah* is repeated by the Reader.

First Section of the Basic *Shabbat Amidah*: Praises

The first section of the basic *Amidah* consists of three *b'rachot*, all of which praise God. Here are the three *b'rachot:*

1. *Avot* (praising the God of the Patriarchs)
     Baruch Attah Adonai (Blessed are You, O Lord)
     Eloheinu Velohei avoteinu ... (our God and God of our fathers ...)
          Baruch Attah Adonai, (Blessed are You, O Lord,)
     Magen Avraham (Shield of Abraham)

2. *G'vurot* (praising God's powers)
          Attah gibor l'olam Adonai ... (You, O Lord, are mighty forever ...)
          Baruch Attah Adonai, (Blessed are You, O Lord,)
     M'chayei hametim (Who revives the dead)

3. *K'dushat haShem* (sanctification of God's Name)
          Attah kadosh v'Shimcha kadosh ... (You are holy and Your Name is holy ...)
          Baruch Attah Adonai, (Blessed are You, O Lord,)
     ha-El hakadosh (the holy God)

We now look at each of these *b'rachot* in more detail.

First *B'rachah*

1. *Avot* (praising the God of the Patriarchs)
   Baruch Attah Adonai (Blessed are You, O Lord)
   Eloheinu Velohei avoteinu ... (our God and God of our fathers ...)
   Baruch Attah Adonai, (Blessed are You, O Lord,)
   Magen Avraham (Shield of Abraham)

The first *b'rachah, Avot* (Patriarchs), praises God as the great, mighty, and revered Creator and God of History. He is the God of Abraham, Isaac, and Jacob; He will bring a redeemer to us, their descendants.

Second *B'rachah*

2. *G'vurot* (praising God's powers)
   Attah gibor l'olam Adonai ... (You, O Lord, are mighty forever ...)
   Baruch Attah Adonai, (Blessed are You, O Lord,)
   M'chayei hametim (Who revives the dead)

The second *b'rachah, G'vurot* (powers or might), praises God Who sustains the living, revives the dead, and heals the sick.

Third *B'rachah*

3. *K'dushat haShem* (sanctification of God's Name)
   Attah kadosh v'Shimcha kadosh ... (You are holy and Your Name is holy ...)
   Baruch Attah Adonai, (Blessed are You, O Lord,)
   ha-El hakadosh (the holy God)

The third *b'rachah, K'dushat haShem* (sanctification of God's Name), praises the holiness of God.

Second Section of the Basic *Shabbat Amidah: Shabbat* Themes

Each instance of the middle (fourth) *b'rachah, K'dushat haYom* (holiness of the day), expresses a different aspect of *Shabbat.*

Service	Opening Words	Theme
Evening Service	*Attah kidashta et yom ha-sh'vi-i liShmecha* (You sanctified the seventh day for Your Name's sake)	Creation
Morning Service	*Yismach Moshe b'mat'nat chelko* (Moses rejoiced at the gift of his destiny)	Revelation
Additional Service	*Tikanta Shabbat ratzita kor-b'no-teha* (You instituted the Sabbath and prescribed its offerings)	Temple sacrifices
Afternoon Service	*Attah Echad v'Shimcha Echad* (You are One and Your Name is One)	Redemption

Now we consider the fourth *b'rachah* for each *Shabbat Amidah* in detail.

Fourth *B'rachah:* Evening Service

First we consider *Arvit (Ma-ariv) l'Shabbat* (Evening Service for the Sabbath). Here, the theme of the middle *b'rachah, K'dushat haYom,* is Creation.

Attah kidashta et yom ha-sh'vi-i liShmecha ... v'chen katuv b'Toratecha (You sanctified the seventh day for Your Name's sake ... and so it is written in Your *Torah*)
Va-y'chulu hashamayim v'ha-aretz v'chol tz'va-am ... asher bara Elohim la-asot (Thus the heavens and the earth and all they contain were finished ... which God had created)
Eloheinu Velohei avoteinu, r'tzei vimnuchatenu ... Baruch Attah Adonai, M'kadesh haShabbat (O God and God of our fathers, be pleased with our rest ... Blessed are You, O Lord, Who sanctifies the Sabbath)

The *b'rachah* begins *Attah kidashta et yom ha-sh'vi-i liShmecha* (You sanctified the seventh day for Your Name's sake). This paragraph expresses the fact that God made the seventh day holy, holier than any other day or time of the year.

To back up this statement, next come three biblical verses, beginning *Va-y'chulu hashamayim v'ha-aretz v'chol tz'va-am* (Thus the heavens and the earth and all they contain were finished) (Gen. 2:1–3). These verses state that on the seventh day God rested from His work of creation, and He blessed and sanctified the Sabbath. (The practice of citing a "proof text," usually from the *Torah,* to support a statement is common to almost all Jewish religious writings, including the *Siddur*.)

The final paragraph is the prayer, *Eloheinu Velohei avoteinu, r'tzei vimnuchatenu* (O God and God of our fathers, be pleased with our rest), which expresses the holiness of *Shabbat*. The *b'rachah* ends with the words *Baruch Attah Adonai, M'kadesh haShabbat* (Blessed are You, O Lord, Who sanctifies the Sabbath). In fact, the fourth *b'rachah* of all four *Shabbat Amidot* has the same concluding prayer.

Fourth *B'rachah:* Morning Service

Now we turn to the Morning Service. Here the theme of *K'dushat haYom* is revelation.

Yismach Moshe b'mat'nat chelko ... v'chen katuv b'Toratecha (Moses rejoiced at the gift of his destiny ... and so it is written in Your *Torah*)
V'sham'ru Vnei Yisra-el et haShabbat ... uva-yom ha-sh'vi-i shavat vayin-afash (The Children of Israel shall keep the Sabbath ... and on the seventh day He ceased from work and rested)
V'lo n'tato Adonai Eloheinu l'goyei ha-aratzot ... zecher l'ma-asei v'reshit (And You did not give it, O Lord our God, to the nations of the earth ... a remembrance of the act of Creation)
Eloheinu Velohei avoteinu, r'tzei vimnuchatenu ... Baruch Attah Adonai, M'kadesh haShabbat (O God and God of our fathers, be pleased with our rest ... Blessed are You, O Lord, Who sanctifies the Sabbath)

The *b'rachah* begins *Yismach Moshe b'mat'nat chelko* (Moses rejoiced at the gift of his destiny). This paragraph describes Moses receiving the Ten Commandments during the revelation on Mount Sinai.

Again, the reference to *Shabbat* observance is backed up by biblical verses, in this case *V'sham'ru Vnei Yisra-el et haShabbat* (The Children of Israel shall keep the Sabbath) (Exod. 31:16–17). These verses state that *Shabbat* is an everlasting covenant, a sign between God and Israel that He created the world in six days and rested on the seventh day.

Next follows *V'lo n'tato Adonai Eloheinu l'goyei ha-aratzot* (And You did not give it, O Lord our God, to the nations of the earth), in which it is pointed out that *Shabbat* was specifically given to the Jewish people and not the other peoples of the world.

The last paragraph in *K'dushat haYom*, as in the case of the other three *Shabbat Amidot*, is the prayer, *Eloheinu Velohei avoteinu, r'tzei vimnuchatenu* (O God and God of our fathers, be pleased with our rest).

Fourth *B'rachah:* Additional Service

Tikanta Shabbat ... mipi ch'vodecha ka-amur (You instituted the Sabbath ... from the mouth of Your glory, as it is said)
Uvyom haShabbat ... al olat hatamid v'niskah (On the Sabbath day ... in addition to the daily burnt offering and its libation)
Yis-m'chu v'malchu-t'cha ... zecher l'ma-asei v'reshit (They shall rejoice in Your kingdom ... as a remembrance of the work of the Creation)
Eloheinu Velohei avoteinu, r'tzei vimnuchatenu ... Baruch Attah Adonai, M'kadesh haShabbat (O God and God of our fathers, be pleased with our rest ... Blessed are You, O Lord, Who sanctifies the Sabbath)

Next we consider the Additional Service *(Musaf)*. This service marks the fact that additional sacrifices were offered on *Shabbat* and during Festivals in the Temple in Jerusalem. Accordingly, the theme of the fourth *b'rachah*, *K'dushat haYom*, is those very *Shabbat* sacrifices.

The first paragraph begins with the words *Tikanta Shabbat* (You instituted the Sabbath). The first twenty-two words of this prayer have the structure of a reverse acrostic. That is, successive words begin with successive letters of the Hebrew alphabet but in reverse order, first *Tav*, then *Shin*, and finally *Bet* and *Alef*. This is a common construct in Jewish liturgical writing. Not only does it give structure to a prayer, but it makes it easier to memorize, an important criterion at a time when the written word was ruinously expensive, beyond the means of all but the very rich.

Tikanta Shabbat begins with a description of the joys of *Shabbat* and points out that *Shabbat* was commanded to us, as were the sacrifices. This statement is, yet again, backed by biblical verses, *Uvyom haShabbat* (On the Sabbath day) (Num. 28:9–10), which describe the *musaf* (additional) sacrifices that were offered every *Shabbat* in the Temple.

Next comes the paragraph *Yis-m'chu v'malchu-t'cha* (They shall rejoice in Your kingdom), a description of the pleasures of *Shabbat*.

The last paragraph, as always, is *Eloheinu Velohei avoteinu, r'tzei vimnuchatenu* (O God and God of our fathers, be pleased with our rest), which expresses the holiness of *Shabbat*.

Fourth *B'rachah:* Afternoon Service

Finally, we turn to the Afternoon Service for *Shabbat*.

Attah Echad v'Shimcha Echad ... yakdishu et Sh'mecha (You are One and Your Name is One ... they will sanctify Your Name)
Eloheinu Velohei avoteinu, r'tzei vimnuchatenu ... Baruch Attah Adonai, M'kadesh haShabbat (O God and God of our fathers, be pleased with our rest ... Blessed are You, O Lord, Who sanctifies the Sabbath)

The first paragraph of the fourth *b'rachah* of the *Amidah* begins with the words *Attah Echad v'Shimcha Echad* (You are One and Your Name is One). Superficially, the theme of this prayer is rest. But what is referred to here is *m'nuchah sh'lemah* (perfect rest), that is, messianic times. In other words, as *Shabbat* draws to a close, our thoughts turn to the future. Accordingly, the theme of the *Amidah* for the Afternoon Service is redemption, as shown in the diagram on page 30.

The last paragraph of *K'dushat haYom*, as in the Evening, Morning, and Additional Services, is *Eloheinu Velohei avoteinu, r'tzei vimnuchatenu* (O God and God of our fathers, be pleased with our rest), which expresses the holiness of *Shabbat*. As with all other *Shabbat Amidot*, the middle *b'rachah* ends with the words *Baruch Attah Adonai, M'kadesh haShabbat* (Blessed are You, O Lord, Who sanctifies the Sabbath).

Third Section of the Basic *Shabbat Amidah:* Thanksgiving

The third section of every *Amidah* consists of three *b'rachot,* largely expressing thanksgiving to God.

---

5. *Avodah* (for restoration of the Temple service)
    R'tzei Adonai Eloheinu ... (Be pleased, O Lord our God ...)
        Baruch Attah Adonai, (Blessed are You, O Lord,)
    Hamachazir Sh'chinato l'Tziyon (Who returns the Divine Presence to Zion)

---

6. *Hoda-ah* (thanksgiving for God's mercy)
    Modim anachnu Lach ... (We give thanks to You ...)
        Baruch Attah Adonai, (Blessed are You, O Lord,)
    HaTov Shimcha uLcha na-eh l'hodot (Your Name is "The Good" and
      to You it is fitting to give thanks)

---

7. *Birkat Shalom* (petition for peace)
    [Morning, Additional Service]   *Sim shalom* ... (Grant peace ...)
    [Evening, Afternoon Service]   *Shalom rav* ... (Abundant peace ...)
        Baruch Attah Adonai, (Blessed are You, O Lord,)
    Ha-m'varech et ammo Yisra-el bashalom (Who blesses His people
      Israel with peace)

We now look at each of these three *b'rachot* in detail.

Fifth *B'rachah*

---

5. *Avodah* (for restoration of the Temple service)
    R'tzei Adonai Eloheinu ... (Be pleased, O Lord our God ...)
        Baruch Attah Adonai, (Blessed are You, O Lord,)
    Hamachazir Sh'chinato l'Tziyon (Who returns the Divine Presence to Zion)

The fifth *b'rachah, Avodah* (Temple worship), is an appeal for the restoration of the Temple service and the return of God's divine presence to Zion.

Sixth *B'rachah*

6. *Hoda-ah* (thanksgiving for God's mercy)
   Modim anachnu Lach ... (We give thanks to You ...)
   Baruch Attah Adonai, (Blessed are You, O Lord,)
   HaTov Shimcha uLcha na-eh l'hodot (Your Name is "The Good" and
   to You it is fitting to give thanks)

In the sixth *b'rachah, Hoda-ah* (thanksgiving), we thank God for all His mercies.

Seventh *B'rachah*

7. *Birkat Shalom* (petition for peace)
   [Morning, Additional Service]   *Sim shalom* ... (Grant peace ...)
   [Evening, Afternoon Service]   *Shalom rav* ... (Abundant peace ...)
   Baruch Attah Adonai, (Blessed are You, O Lord,)
   Ha-m'varech et ammo Yisra-el bashalom (Who blesses His people
   Israel with peace)

Finally, in the seventh *b'rachah, Birkat Shalom* (blessing of peace), we pray for peace.

There are two different prayers for peace. In the *Amidah* of the Morning Service and Additional Service, the prayer *Sim shalom* (Grant peace) is said, whereas the prayer for peace during the Evening Service and Afternoon Service is *Shalom rav* (Abundant peace). These two prayers express similar desires for peace. Both *b'rachot* end the same way, *Baruch Attah Adonai, Ha-m'varech et ammo Yisra-el bashalom* (Blessed are You, O Lord, Who blesses His people Israel with peace).

For the Maven

The two forms of the last *b'rachah* are related to *Birkat Kohanim*. On those occasions when *Birkat Kohanim* is not added during the repetition of the *Amidah*, namely, *Minchah* and *Ma-ariv*, the last *b'rachah* is *Shalom rav*. Conversely, we say *Sim shalom* during *Shacharit* and *Musaf* (and *Minchah* on Fast Days) because *Birkat Kohanim* is recited then.

Personal Prayers

Yi-h'yu l'ratzon imrei fi ... Adonai Tzuri v'Go-ali (May the expressions of my mouth be acceptable ... Lord, my Rock and Redeemer)

Elohai, n'tzor l'shoni merah ... v'al kol Yisra-el, v'imru Amen (My God, guard my tongue from evil ... and on all Israel, and let us say, Amen)

Y'hi ratzon mi-l'fanecha ... uchshanim kadmoniyot (May it be Your will ... and as in former years)

After the recitation of the seven *b'rachot*, personal prayers follow. The first is Psalm 19:15, *Yi-h'yu l'ratzon imrei fi* (May the expressions of my mouth be acceptable). This corresponds to Psalm 51:17, *Adonai s'fatai tiftach ufi yagid t'hilatechah* (O Lord, open my lips, and my mouth will declare Your praises), which is said as a personal prayer before the beginning of the *Amidah*. Thus, the body of the silent *Amidah* is sandwiched between these two verses from the Psalms.

Elohai, n'tzor l'shoni merah (My God, guard my tongue from evil) is written in the first person, unlike any other prayer in the *Amidah*. It asks God to help us in desisting from speaking evil and for strength against those who insult us or plan evil against us. The third personal prayer, *Y'hi ratzon mi-l'fanecha* (May it be Your will), asks for the Temple to be rebuilt.

It is permissible to add personal prayers to any of the *b'rachot*, provided that the theme of the personal prayer is generally appropriate to that *b'rachah*. In addition, at the very end of the *Amidah*, personal prayers of any nature may be added.

We have completed our description of the basic *Amidah*. Now we will examine the pieces that are added.

For the Maven

Traditionally, speaking is forbidden in the middle of a *b'rachah*. Because a Series Form *b'rachah* is essentially one large, single *b'rachah*, this means that no talking at all is permitted during the silent *Amidah*. During the Reader's repetition of the *Amidah* there are a restricted number of responses, such as the responses during the *K'dushah* (added to the third *b'rachah*). In particular, the response *Amen* is required at the end of each individual *b'rachah*.

Additions

Depending on the season, additional pieces are added to the basic *Amidah*. Furthermore, other pieces are added when the *Amidah* is repeated by the Reader.

Additions to First *B'rachah*

1. *Avot* (praising the God of the Patriarchs)
    Baruch Attah Adonai (Blessed are You, O Lord)
    Eloheinu Velohei avoteinu ... l'ma-an Sh'mo b'ahavah (our God and
        God of our fathers ... for the sake of His Name, in love)

[Between Rosh haShanah and Yom Kippur add] *Zochrenu l'chayim ... l'ma-ancha Elohim chayim* (Remember us for life ... for Your sake, O living God)

Melech Ozer uMoshia uMagen (King, Helper, and Savior, and Shield)
    Baruch Attah Adonai, (Blessed are You, O Lord,)
    Magen Avraham (Shield of Abraham)

During *Asseret Y'mei T'shuvah* (Ten Days of Repentance), from Rosh ha-Shanah until Yom Kippur, five additions are made to every *Shabbat Amidah*. These additions begin in the first *b'rachah* where we add the phrase beginning *Zochrenu l'chayim* (Remember us for life). We believe that our deeds are examined between Rosh haShanah and Yom Kippur and we pray accordingly that our names be written in the Book of Life, that is, that we may live for another year.

Additions to Second *B'rachah*

2. *G'vurot* (praising God's powers)
   Attah gibor l'olam Adonai ... rav l'hoshia (You, O Lord, are mighty forever ... mighty to save)

> [Between *Sh'mini Atzeret* and Pesach add]
> *Mashiv haru-ach umorid hagashem [hageshem]* (He causes the wind to blow and the rain to fall)

M'chalkel chayim b'chesed ... umatzmiach y'shu-ah (He sustains the living with loving kindness ... salvation to flourish)

> [Between Rosh haShanah and Yom Kippur add]
> *Mi chamocha Av harachamim ... b'rachamim* (Who is like You, merciful Father ... in mercy)

V'ne-eman Attah l'hachayot metim (And You are faithful to revive the dead)

> *Baruch Attah Adonai,* (Blessed are You, O Lord,)
> *M'chayei hametim* (Who revives the dead)

In winter (that is, between *Sh'mini Atzeret* and Pesach), we pray that there may be rain in Israel so that the harvest will not fail. More specifically, in the second *b'rachah* we praise God for bringing the wind and the rain with the words *Mashiv haru-ach umorid hagashem [hageshem]* (He causes the wind to blow and the rain to fall). In some traditions, the phrase *Morid hatal* (He causes the dew to fall) is substituted between Pesach and Sukkot.

Between Rosh haShanah and Yom Kippur we also add a phrase to the second *b'rachah*, beginning *Mi chamocha Av harachamim* (Who is like You, merciful Father).

Additions to Third *B'rachah*

Two additions (or, more correctly, substitutions) are made to this *b'rachah*.

---

3. *K'dushat haShem* (sanctification of God's Name)
   Attah kadosh v'Shimcha kadosh ... (You are holy and Your Name
   is holy ...)

   Baruch Attah Adonai, (Blessed are You, O Lord,)

---

ha-El hakadosh (the holy God)

[Between Rosh haShanah and Yom Kippur substitute]
haMelech hakadosh (the holy King)

First, during *Asseret Y'mei T'shuvah* (Ten Days of Repentance), from Rosh
haShanah to Yom Kippur, we end this *b'rachah* with the words *haMelech
hakadosh* (the holy King), as opposed to the ending *ha-El hakadosh* (the holy
God) that we use during the rest of the year. The reason is that the Kingship of
God is foremost in our minds at that time of the year.

When the *Amidah* is repeated (during the Morning, Additional, and Afternoon Services), the Reader replaces the third *b'rachah* with the *K'dushah:*

---

3. *K'dushat haShem* (sanctification of God's Name)
   Attah kadosh v'Shimcha kadosh ... (You are holy and Your Name
   is holy ...)

[During the repetition of the *Amidah* in the Morning, Additional, and Afternoon Services, substitute]
*... Kadosh, Kadosh, Kadosh ... Baruch k'vod Adonai mi-
m'komo ...* (... Holy, Holy, Holy, ... Blessed be the glory of
the Lord from His place ...)

Baruch Attah Adonai, (Blessed are You, O Lord,)

---

ha-El hakadosh (the holy God)

[Between Rosh haShanah and Yom Kippur substitute]
haMelech hakadosh (the holy King)

The *K'dushah* is constructed around verses from prophetic theophanies
(visions of God). Two prophets in particular saw visions of God.

One was Isaiah. In Isaiah 6:3, we read of angels calling to one another and praising God, beginning with the words *Kadosh, Kadosh, Kadosh* (Holy, Holy, Holy).

The prophet Ezekiel also saw a vision of God. In Ezekiel 3:12, it is stated that he heard a great voice saying *Baruch k'vod Adonai mi-m'komo* (Blessed be the glory of the Lord from His place). The rest of the *K'dushah* is constructed around these two angelic expressions of the holiness of God. A detailed description of the structure of the *K'dushah* is given in Chapter 9.

Additions to Fourth *B'rachah:*
Additional Service on *Shabbat Rosh Chodesh*

Tikanta Shabbat ... mipi ch'vodecha ka-amur (You instituted the Sabbath ... from the mouth of Your glory, as it is said)

> [On *Rosh Chodesh* substitute]
> *Attah yitzarta olamcha mikedem ... mipi ch'vodecha ka-amur* (You created Your world long ago ... from the mouth of Your glory, as it is said)

Uvyom haShabbat ... al olat hatamid v'niskah (And the Sabbath day ... in addition to the daily burnt offering and its libation)

> [On *Rosh Chodesh* substitute]
> *UvRashei Chodsheichem ... k'hilchatam* (And on New Month Festivals ... according to their law)

Yis-m'chu v'malchu-t'cha ... zecher l'ma-asei v'reshit (They shall rejoice in Your kingdom ... as a remembrance of the work of the Creation)

Eloheinu Velohei avoteinu, r'tzei vimnuchatenu ... Baruch Attah Adonai, M'kadesh haShabbat (O God and God of our fathers, be pleased with our rest ... Blessed are You, O Lord, Who sanctifies the Sabbath)

> [On *Rosh Chodesh* substitute drastically modified form]
> *Eloheinu Velohei avoteinu, r'tzei vimnuchatenu ... Baruch Attah Adonai, M'kadesh haShabbat v'Yisra-el v'Rashei Chodashim* (O God and God of our fathers, be pleased with our rest ... Blessed are You, O Lord, Who sanctifies the Sabbath and Israel and New Month Festivals)

When *Rosh Chodesh* (the New Month Festival, which is marked by the appearance of the new moon) falls on *Shabbat*, the middle *b'rachah* of the

Additional Service is greatly changed. First, the initial paragraph beginning *Tikanta Shabbat* (You instituted the Sabbath), is replaced by the paragraph beginning *Attah yitzarta olamcha mikedem* (You created Your world long ago), a prayer that alludes to both *Shabbat* and *Rosh Chodesh*. Its major theme is that, because of our sins, the Temple was destroyed and we were exiled from our land.

Then, as on every *Shabbat*, follows the description of the *Shabbat* sacrifices beginning *Uvyom haShabbat* (And on the Sabbath day) (Num. 28:9–10), which describes the specific sacrifices that were to be offered in the Temple on *Shabbat*.

Next follows a description of the *Rosh Chodesh* sacrifices beginning *UvRashei Chodsheichem* (And on New Month Festivals) (Num. 28:11). Then, as on a regular *Shabbat*, there is the paragraph *Yis-m'chu v'malchu-t'cha* (They shall rejoice in Your kingdom).

The last prayer in the fourth *b'rachah* is, as always, the *Shabbat* prayer, *Eloheinu Velohei avoteinu, r'tzei vimnuchatenu* (O God and God of our fathers, be pleased with our rest). However, on *Rosh Chodesh* this prayer is drastically modified to reflect *Rosh Chodesh* themes. Twelve phrases are used, including happiness, blessing, joy, and gladness. These twelve phrases allude to the twelve months of the year. However, in every sequence of nineteen years, seven years are leap years. A leap year has an additional (thirteenth) month. Thus, during a leap year, a thirteenth expression *ulchapparat pesha* (and for atonement of transgressions), is inserted. The prayer ends *Baruch Attah Adonai, M'kadesh haShabbat v'Yisra-el v'Rashei Chodashim* (Blessed are You, O Lord, Who sanctifies the Sabbath and Israel and New Month Festivals).

For the Maven

The twelve phrases are grouped into six pairs and, when the *Amidah* is repeated by the Reader, the congregation responds *Amen* after each pair (and after the thirteenth phrase in a leap year).

Additions to Fifth *B'rachah*

5. *Avodah* (for restoration of the Temple service)
   R'tzei Adonai Eloheinu ... avodat Yisra-el amecha (Be pleased,
   O Lord our God ... the service of Israel, Your people)

> [On *Rosh Chodesh* and *Chol haMo-ed* during the Evening,
> Morning, and Afternoon Services add]
>
> *Eloheinu Velohei avoteinu, ya-aleh v'yavo ... chanun
> v'rachum Attah* (Our God and God of our fathers, may [the
> remembrance] ascend and come ... for You are gracious and
> merciful)

> *V'techezenah eineinu ...* (May our eyes behold ...)
>   *Baruch Attah Adonai,* (Blessed are You, O Lord,)
> *Hamachazir Sh'chinato l'Tziyon* (Who returns the Divine Presence
> to Zion)

When *Shabbat* coincides with *Rosh Chodesh* (New Month Festival) or
Chol haMo-ed (Intermediate Days of Pesach or Sukkot), the prayer *Eloheinu
Velohei avoteinu, ya-aleh v'yavo* (Our God and God of our fathers, may [the
remembrance] ascend and come) is inserted in the fifth *b'rachah* of the *Shabbat Amidah* during the Evening, Morning, and Afternoon Services. The prayer
asks that we be granted life, well-being, and peace.

If the *Amidah* is repeated, the congregation responds *Amen* after the Reader
recites each of the three clauses toward the end of *Ya-aleh v'yavo* where we
ask for goodness, blessing, and life.

Additions to Sixth *B'rachah*

6. *Hoda-ah* (thanksgiving for God's mercy)
   Modim anachnu Lach ... me-olam kivinu lach (We give thanks to You ... we have always hoped in You)

> [When repeating the *Amidah*, substitute drastically modified form]
>
> *Modim anachnu Lach ... Baruch El hahoda-ot* (We give thanks to You ... Blessed is the God of thanksgiving)
>
> > [On Chanukah add]
> > *Al hanisim ... bayamim hahem ba-z'man hazeh* (For the miracles ... in those days at this season)
> >
> > *Bimei Matityahu ... l'Shimcha hagadol* (In the days of Mattathias ... to Your great Name)

V'al kulam ... tamid l'olam va-ed (For all of these ... forever and ever)

> [Between Rosh haShanah and Yom Kippur add]
>
> *Uchtov l'chayim tovim kol bnei v'ritecha* (And inscribe all the children of Your covenant for a good life)

V'chol hachayim yoducha Selah ... (And all living things will give thanks to you, *Selah ...*)
   Baruch Attah Adonai, (Blessed are You, O Lord,)
HaTov Shimcha uLcha na-eh l'hodot (Your Name is "The Good" and to You it is fitting to give thanks)

> [When repeating the *Amidah* of the Morning and Additional Services, add]
>
> *Y'varech'cha Adonai v'yishm'recha ... v'yasem l'cha sha-lom* (May the Lord bless you and protect you ... and grant you peace)

Recall that the sixth *b'rachah* is a prayer of thanksgiving to God. When the *Amidah* is repeated, the first paragraph of the *b'rachah, Modim anachnu Lach* (We give thanks to You), is replaced by a complete paragraph, the so-called *Modim d'Rabbanan* (the *Modim* of the Rabbis). This expression of thanksgiving is similar in content to the *Modim* of the Silent *Amidah. Modim d'Rabbanan* is recited by the congregation while the Reader says the *Modim* of the Silent *Amidah* in an undertone.

On *Shabbat* Chanukah, two paragraphs expressing our thanks for the miraculous deliverance of Chanukah are inserted.

The fourth addition between Rosh haShanah and Yom Kippur is inserted just before the end of the sixth *b'rachah*. We pray *Uchtov l'chayim tovim kol bnei v'ritecha* (And inscribe all the children of Your covenant for a good life).

During the repetition of the *Amidah* for the Morning and Additional Services, at the end of the sixth *b'rachah*, the Reader adds *Birkat Kohanim* (Priestly Blessing). In the Temple in Jerusalem, the *Kohanim* (priests) blessed the people with the three-part blessing beginning *Y'varech'cha Adonai v'yishm'recha* (May the Lord bless you and protect you) (Num. 6:24–26).

Additions to Seventh *B'rachah*

7. *Birkat Shalom* (petition for peace)
 	
    [Morning, Additional Service] *Sim shalom* ... (Grant peace ...)
    [Evening, Afternoon Service]   *Shalom rav* ... (Abundant peace ...)
    ... *uvchol sha-ah bishlomecha* (And in every hour with Your peace)

Baruch Attah Adonai, (Blessed are You, O Lord,) *Ha-m'varech et ammo Yisra-el bashalom* (Who blesses His people Israel with peace)

[Between Rosh haShanah and Yom Kippur substitute]   *B'Sefer Chayim* ... (In the Book of Life ...)

The final insertion for *Asseret Y'mei T'shuvah* (Ten Days of Repentance), between Rosh haShanah and Yom Kippur, appears here; we change the ending of the last *b'rachah* to a prayer for life as well as for peace. The passage begins *B'Sefer Chayim* (In the Book of Life).

This concludes our description of the structure of the *Shabbat Amidah*. We now consider the structure of the Weekday *Amidah*.

For the Maven

The *Arvit Amidah* is not repeated by the Reader. The original reason why the *Amidah* was repeated was to enable uneducated people, who did not know the *Amidah*, to fulfill the mitzvah of saying the *Amidah* every day by listening to the repetition and saying *Amen* at the end of each *b'rachah*. Originally, saying the evening *Amidah* was optional, so there was no need to repeat that prayer.

6
The Structure of the Weekday *Amidah*

As stated in Chapter 4, the weekday *Amidah* is a Series Form *b'rachah* with nineteen component *b'rachot*.

Baruch Attah Adonai (Blessed are You, O Lord)
« Body of first *b'rachah* »
Baruch Attah Adonai (Blessed are You, O Lord)
« Ending of first *b'rachah* »
« Body of second *b'rachah* »
Baruch Attah Adonai (Blessed are You, O Lord)
« Ending of second *b'rachah* »
.   .   .
« Body of nineteenth *b'rachah* »
Baruch Attah Adonai (Blessed are You, O Lord)
« Ending of nineteenth *b'rachah* »

All three *Amidot* for weekdays (Evening Service, Morning Service, and Afternoon Service) have this structure.

These nineteen *b'rachot* can be grouped into three sections, as shown in the diagram below:

First section	First three *b'rachot*	Praises
Second section	Thirteen intermediate *b'rachot*	Petitions
Third section	Last three *b'rachot*	Thanksgiving

The first section consists of three *b'rachot* of praises; this material is essentially identical to that of the first three *b'rachot* of the *Shabbat Amidah* as described in Chapter 5. With regard to the third section, the last three *b'rachot*, too, are essentially the same as their *Shabbat* counterparts. However, there are major differences in the second section. On *Shabbat* this consists of just one *b'rachah*, *K'dushat haYom* (holiness of the day), whereas during the week, the second section comprises thirteen petitions.

As in Chapter 5, we first describe the basic *Amidah*. Then we examine the parts added on special occasions and when the *Amidah* is repeated by the Reader.

First Section of the Basic Weekday *Amidah*: Praises

The first section of the basic weekday Morning Service *Amidah* consists of three *b'rachot*, all of which praise God. The diagram below (which is identical to the diagram on page 28) shows each *b'rachah*, its opening words, and the closing phrase.

1. *Avot* (praising the God of the Patriarchs) *Baruch Attah Adonai* (Blessed are You, O Lord) *Eloheinu Velohei avoteinu ...* (our God and God of our fathers ...) *Baruch Attah Adonai,* (Blessed are You, O Lord,) *Magen Avraham* (Shield of Abraham)
2. *G'vurot* (praising God's powers) *Attah gibor l'olam Adonai ...* (You, O Lord, are mighty forever ...) *Baruch Attah Adonai,* (Blessed are You, O Lord,) *M'chayei hametim* (Who revives the dead)

> 3. *K'dushat haShem* (sanctification of God's Name)
> *Attah kadosh v'Shimcha kadosh* ... (You are holy and Your Name is holy ...)
> *Baruch Attah Adonai,* (Blessed are You, O Lord,)
> *ha-El hakadosh* (the holy God)

In the basic *Amidah*, these three *b'rachot* are the same as on *Shabbat* (page 29). Accordingly, that material is not repeated here.

Second Section of the Basic Weekday *Amidah:* Petitions

The thirteen *b'rachot* that comprise this section fall neatly into three groups.

First set of six petitions (*b'rachot* 4 through 9)	Prayers for personal well-being
Second set of six petitions (*b'rachot* 10 through 15)	Prayers for national well-being
Last petition (*b'rachah* 16)	Prayer for God to accept our prayers

As reflected in the diagram, the first six petitions (*b'rachot* 4 through 9) are for personal well-being, whereas the second six petitions (*b'rachot* 10 through 15) are for national well-being. The last petition (*b'rachah* 16) asks God to accept our prayers.

We now examine in greater detail the structure of the thirteen *b'rachot* in these three groups.

Six Requests for Personal Well-Being (*B'rachot* 4 through 9)

---

4. *Binah* (petition for wisdom and understanding)
    Attah chonen l'adam da-at ... (You favor man with knowledge ...)
        Baruch Attah Adonai, (Blessed are You, O Lord,)
    Chonen hada-at (gracious Giver of knowledge)

---

5. *T'shuvah* (petition for repentance)
    Hashivenu, Avinu, l'Toratecha ... (Restore us, our Father, to Your Torah ...)
        Baruch Attah Adonai, (Blessed are You, O Lord,)
    Harotzeh bitshuvah (Who desires repentance)

---

6. *S'lichah* (petition for forgiveness of sin)
    S'lach lanu, Avinu ... (Forgive us, our Father ...)
        Baruch Attah Adonai, (Blessed are You, O Lord,)
    Chanun hamarbeh lislo'ach (Who graciously and abundantly forgives)

---

7. *G'ulah* (petition for freedom from problems)
    R'ei [na] v'onyenu ... (Look upon our afflictions ...)
        Baruch Attah Adonai, (Blessed are You, O Lord,)
    Go-el Yisra-el (Redeemer of Israel)

---

8. *R'fu-ah* (petition for healing)
    R'fa-enu, Adonai, v'nerafeh ... (Heal us, O Lord, and we shall be healed ...)
        Baruch Attah Adonai, (Blessed are You, O Lord,)
    Rofei cholei ammo Yisra-el (Who heals the sick of His people Israel)

---

9. *Birkat haShanim* (petition for freedom from want)
    Barech aleinu, Adonai Eloheinu ... (Bless for us, O Lord our God ...)
        Baruch Attah Adonai, (Blessed are You, O Lord,)
    M'varech hashanim (Who blesses the years)

We now examine each of these six *b'rachot* in detail.

Fourth *B'rachah*

4. *Binah* (petition for wisdom and understanding)
   Attah chonen l'adam da-at ... (You favor man with knowledge ...)
   Baruch Attah Adonai, (Blessed are You, O Lord,)
   Chonen hada-at (gracious Giver of knowledge)

The fourth *b'rachah, Binah* (understanding), is a prayer for wisdom and understanding. This petition comes first because knowledge of what is morally right and wrong is a fundamental underpinning of religion. Also, knowledge is a precursor to repentance, the subject of the next *b'rachah;* one cannot repent unless one knows right from wrong.

Fifth *B'rachah*

5. *T'shuvah* (petition for repentance)
   Hashivenu, Avinu, l'Toratecha ... (Restore us, our Father, to Your Torah ...)
   Baruch Attah Adonai, (Blessed are You, O Lord,)
   Harotzeh bitshuvah (Who desires repentance)

Now we consider the fifth *b'rachah, T'shuvah* (repentance). In this petition, we entreat God to cause us to return to the *Torah* and to His service.

Sixth *B'rachah*

6. *S'lichah* (petition for forgiveness of sin)
   S'lach lanu, Avinu ... (Forgive us, our Father ...)
   Baruch Attah Adonai, (Blessed are You, O Lord,)
   Chanun hamarbeh lislo'ach (Who graciously and abundantly forgives)

In the sixth *b'rachah, S'lichah* (forgiveness), we ask for forgiveness for all our sins. In other words, first we admit that we have sinned (fifth *b'rachah*) and then we ask for forgiveness (sixth *b'rachah*).

Seventh *B'rachah*

> 7. *G'ulah* (petition for freedom from problems)
> *R'ei [na] v'onyenu ...* (Look upon our afflictions ...)
> *Baruch Attah Adonai,* (Blessed are You, O Lord,)
> *Go-el Yisra-el* (Redeemer of Israel)

The seventh *b'rachah*, *G'ulah* (redemption), is a request to deliver us from our personal problems.

Eighth *B'rachah*

> 8. *R'fu-ah* (petition for healing)
> *R'fa-enu, Adonai, v'nerafeh ...* (Heal us, O Lord, and we shall be healed ...)
> *Baruch Attah Adonai,* (Blessed are You, O Lord,)
> *Rofei cholei ammo Yisra-el* (Who heals the sick of His people Israel)

The eighth *b'rachah*, *R'fu-ah* (healing), is a plea for recovery from sickness. The first sentence of this *b'rachah* is based on Jeremiah 17:14.

Ninth *B'rachah*

> 9. *Birkat haShanim* (petition for freedom from want)
> *Barech aleinu, Adonai Eloheinu ...* (Bless for us, O Lord our God ...)
> *Baruch Attah Adonai,* (Blessed are You, O Lord,)
> *M'varech hashanim* (Who blesses the years)

In the ninth *b'rachah*, *Birkat haShanim* (blessing for the years), we ask for an abundant harvest. That is, we plead that we should not be in need.

It is interesting to note that all six of these personal petitions are written in the plural. Thus, even if we ourselves are, say, in perfect health, we still pray for others who are sick.

Next we consider the six petitions for national well-being.

Six Requests for National Well-Being (*B'rachot* 10 through 15)

10. *Kibbutz Galuyot* (petition for the ingathering of the exiles in Israel) *T'kah b'shofar gadol l'cherutenu* ... (Sound the great *shofar* for our freedom ...)   *Baruch Attah Adonai,* (Blessed are You, O Lord,) *M'kabbetz nidchei ammo Yisra-el* (Who gathers the dispersed of His people Israel)
11. *Birkat haMishpat* (petition for justice and righteousness) *Hashivah shof'teinu k'varishonah* ... (Restore our judges as in former times ...)   *Baruch Attah Adonai,* (Blessed are You, O Lord,) *Melech ohev tz'dakah umishpat* (King Who loves righteousness and judgment)
12. *Birkat haMinim* (petition against heretics) *V'lamalshinim* ... (And as for the slanderers ...)   *Baruch Attah Adonai,* (Blessed are You, O Lord,) *Shover oy'vim umachnia zedim* (Who breaks the enemies and humbles the arrogant)
13. *Birkat haTzadikim* (petition for the righteous and the proselytes) *Al hatzadikim v'al hachasidim* ... (On the righteous and the pious ...)   *Baruch Attah Adonai,* (Blessed are You, O Lord,) *Mishan uMivtach latzadikim* (the Support and the Trust of the righteous)
14. *Birkat Y'rushalayim* (petition for the rebuilding of Jerusalem) *V'lirushalayim ir'cha* ... (And to Jerusalem Your city ...)   *Baruch Attah Adonai,* (Blessed are You, O Lord,) *Boneh Y'rushalayim* (Builder of Jerusalem)
15. *Birkat David* (petition for re-establishment of the Kingdom of David) *Et tzemach David avd'cha* ... (Cause the offspring of David Your servant ...)   *Baruch Attah Adonai,* (Blessed are You, O Lord,) *Matzmi'ach keren y'shu-ah* (Who causes salvation to flourish)

Again, we now examine each of these six *b'rachot* in detail.

Tenth *B'rachah*

10. *Kibbutz Galuyot* (petition for the ingathering of the exiles in Israel)
   T'kah b'shofar gadol l'cherutenu ... (Sound the great *shofar* for our freedom ...)
   Baruch Attah Adonai, (Blessed are You, O Lord,)
   M'kabbetz nidchei ammo Yisra-el (Who gathers the dispersed of His people Israel)

In the tenth *b'rachah*, *Kibbutz Galuyot* (ingathering of the exiles), we pray for the end of the dispersion of the Jewish people and for all Jews to be gathered together in Israel.

Eleventh *B'rachah*

11. *Birkat haMishpat* (petition for justice and righteousness)
   Hashivah shof'teinu k'varishonah ... (Restore our judges as in former times ...)
   Baruch Attah Adonai, (Blessed are You, O Lord,)
   Melech ohev tz'dakah umishpat (King Who loves righteousness and judgment)

The eleven *b'rachah*, *Birkat haMishpat* (blessing for justice), is a petition for God to restore righteous judges and for Him to reign over us.

Twelfth *B'rachah*

12. *Birkat haMinim* (petition against heretics)
   V'lamalshinim ... (And as for the slanderers ...)
   Baruch Attah Adonai, (Blessed are You, O Lord,)
   Shover oy'vim umachnia zedim (Who breaks the enemies and humbles the arrogant)

In the twelfth *b'rachah*, *Birkat haMinim* (blessing concerning heretics), we plead to God to destroy apostate Jews who turn against their former brethren.

For the Maven

For historical reasons, the wording of this prayer varies from liturgy to liturgy. First, the prayer has been modified in order to direct it against different groups of heretics. Second, although the prayer has always been directed against Jewish heretics and non-Jewish persecutors of Jews, during the Middle Ages it was interpreted as being anti-Christian. Thus, as a result of censorship, the wording of this *b'rachah* was changed in many parts of Europe.

Thirteenth *B'rachah*

13. *Birkat haTzadikim* (petition for the righteous and the proselytes)
Al hatzadikim v'al hachasidim ... (On the righteous and the pious ...)
Baruch Attah Adonai, (Blessed are You, O Lord,)
Mishan uMivtach latzadikim (the Support and the Trust of the righteous)

In the thirteenth *b'rachah, Birkat haTzadikim* (blessing for the righteous), we pray for the righteous and the pious, and for the sincere converts to Judaism.

Fourteenth *B'rachah*

14. *Birkat Y'rushalayim* (petition for the rebuilding of Jerusalem)
V'lirushalayim ir'cha ... (And to Jerusalem Your city ...)
Baruch Attah Adonai, (Blessed are You, O Lord,)
Boneh Y'rushalayim (Builder of Jerusalem)

In the fourteenth *b'rachah, Birkat Y'rushalayim* (blessing for Jerusalem), we ask God to rebuild the city of Jerusalem and for the dynasty of King David to rule there again.

For the Maven

The fourteenth and fifteenth *b'rachot* were formerly one single *b'rachah*, making eighteen *b'rachot* in all. This is the origin of the term *Sh'moneh Esrei,* "The Eighteen [*b'rachot*]." This term is frequently used by Hebrew speakers to refer to the *Amidah.* Similarly, we sometimes hear Yiddish speakers refer to the *Amidah* as the *Shimmenesra,* a corruption of the Hebrew *Sh'moneh Esrei.* However, in Talmudic times (around the fifth century C.E.), this single *b'rachah* was split into two, making the nineteen *b'rachot* we have today. However, the term *Sh'moneh Esrei* was so widely used by that time that the name did not change, and for the past fifteen centuries or so, we have referred to the **nineteen** *b'rachot* of the weekday *Amidah* as "The Eighteen." In fact, the seven *Shabbat b'rachot* are also sometimes referred to as the *Sh'moneh Esrei;* the latter term is, nowadays, simply a synonym for *Amidah.*

Fifteenth *B'rachah*

---

15. *Birkat David* (petition for re-establishment of the Kingdom of David)
   Et tzemach David avd'cha ... (Cause the offspring of David Your
   servant ...)
              Baruch Attah Adonai, (Blessed are You, O Lord,)
   Matzmi'ach keren y'shu-ah (Who causes salvation to flourish)

In the fifteenth *b'rachah, Birkat David* (blessing for the House of David),
we pray for salvation and the re-establishment of the dynasty of King David.
The references to King David flow from the belief that the Messiah will be a
direct descendant of King David. Thus, both the fourteenth and the fifteenth
b'rachot express Messianic ideas.

The fifteenth *b'rachah* is the last in the second group of six petitions. We
now examine the sixteenth *b'rachah*.

Last Petition (Sixteenth *B'rachah*)

---

16. *Kabbalat T'filah* (petition for prayer to be accepted)
   Sh'ma kolenu, Adonai Eloheinu ... (Hear our voices, O Lord our
   God ...)
              Baruch Attah Adonai, (Blessed are You, O Lord,)
   Shome-ah t'filah (Who hears prayer)

The final *b'rachah* of the set of thirteen petitions, the sixteenth, *Kabbalat
T'filah* (acceptance of prayer), is extremely appropriate in that it is a petition
for our prayers to be accepted by God. In other words, the first twelve petitions ask for specific items, six personal and six national. Then, in the last
petition, we pray that the preceding requests be answered.

Third Section of the Basic Weekday *Amidah*: Thanksgiving

The third section of every *Amidah* consists of three *b'rachot,* largely expressing thanksgiving to God.

17. *Avodah* (for restoration of the Temple service) *R'tzei Adonai Eloheinu* ... (Be pleased, O Lord our God ...) *Baruch Attah Adonai,* (Blessed are You, O Lord,) *Hamachazir Sh'chinato l'Tziyon* (Who returns the Divine Presence to Zion)
18. *Hoda-ah* (thanksgiving for God's mercy) *Modim anachnu Lach* ... (We give thanks to You ...) *Baruch Attah Adonai,* (Blessed are You, O Lord,) *HaTov Shimcha uLcha na-eh l'hodot* (Your Name is "The Good" and to You it is fitting to give thanks)

19. *Birkat Shalom* (petition for peace)
[Morning, Additional Service; Afternoon Service on Fast Days]
                                   Sim shalom ... (Grant peace ...)
[Evening, Afternoon Service]   *Shalom rav* ... (Abundant peace ...)
        Baruch Attah Adonai, (Blessed are You, O Lord,)
Ha-m'varech et ammo Yisra-el bashalom (Who blesses His people Israel with peace)

Again, in the basic *Amidah* this material is the same as on *Shabbat* (pages 34–35).

Personal Prayers

Yih'yu l'ratzon imrei fi ... Adonai Tzuri v'Go-ali (May the expressions of my mouth be acceptable ... Lord, my Rock and Redeemer)
Elohai, n'tzor l'shoni merah ... v'al kol Yisra-el, v'imru Amen (My God, guard my tongue from evil ... and on all Israel, and let us say, Amen)
Y'hi ratzon mi-l'fanecha ... uchshanim kadmoniyot (May it be Your will ... and as in former years)

After the recitation of the nineteen *b'rachot,* personal prayers follow exactly as on *Shabbat* (page 36).

We have completed our description of the basic weekday *Amidah.* Now we examine the pieces that are added.

Additions

Depending on the season, additional pieces are added to the silent *Amidah.* Furthermore, other pieces are added when the *Amidah* is repeated by the Reader.

Additions to First, Second, and Third *B'rachot*

With regard to the first three *b'rachot* of the *Amidah,* namely, *Avot* (praising the God of the Patriarchs), *G'vurot* (praising God's powers), and *K'dushat haShem* (sanctification of God's Name), the weekday additions are similar to those of the *Shabbat* service. Accordingly, the material is not repeated here; the reader should consult pages 37 through 40 for details.

For the Maven

There is one difference between the additions to the first three *b'rachot* on weekdays and on *Shabbat,* namely, the contents of the *K'dushah* added to the third *b'rachah* when the *Amidah* is repeated by the Reader. This is described in detail in Chapter 9.

Additions to Fourth *B'rachah*

4. *Binah* (petition for wisdom and understanding) *Attah chonen l'adam da-at umlamed le-enosh binah* (You favor man with knowledge ... and teach understanding to humans)

[On Saturday night and the evening following the last day of a Festival add] *Attah chonantanu l'madah Toratecha ... umdubakim b'yiratecha. V'* (You have favored us with knowledge of Your *Torah* ... and cleave to fear of You. And)

chonenu me-it'cha de-ah binah v'haskel (grant us knowledge, understanding, and discernment from You) *Baruch Attah Adonai,* (Blessed are You, O Lord,) *Chonen hada-at* (gracious Giver of knowledge)

On *Motza-ei Shabbat* (the going out of the Sabbath, in other words, on Saturday night) and *Motza-ei Yom Tov* (the evening following the last day of a Festival), the fourth *b'rachah* of the Evening Service *Amidah* is drastically modified to incorporate *Havdalah*, that is, the separation between sacred time (the Sabbath or a Festival) and secular time (weekdays). After the first verse of the *b'rachah*, a paragraph is inserted that begins *Attah chonantanu l'madah Toratecha* (You have favored us with knowledge of Your *Torah*).

For the Maven

In fact, *Havdalah* is said twice at the end of *Shabbat*, once in the *Amidah* and then again (as explained on pages 107–108) in a separate ceremony. This is analogous to the way that *Shabbat* is "announced" twice, once in the fourth (intermediate) *b'rachah*, *K'dushat haYom* (holiness of the day), of the *Amidah* for the Evening Service for *Shabbat* (see pages 30–31) and then again in the *Kiddush* (Sanctification).

Additions to Seventh *B'rachah*

7. *G'ulah* (petition for freedom from problems)
   R'ei [na] v'onyenu ... (Look upon our affliction ...)
      Baruch Attah Adonai, (Blessed are You, O Lord,)
   Go-el Yisra-el (Redeemer of Israel)

> [On Fast Days, during the repetition of the *Amidah* in the Morning and Afternoon Services, add]
>
> *Anenu* ... *Baruch Attah Adonai, Ha-oneh b'et tzarah* (Answer us ... Blessed are You, O Lord, Who answers us in time of trouble)

During the repetition of the *Amidah* during the Morning and Afternoon Services on Fast Days (such as Tish-ah b'Av or *Shiv-ah Assar b'Tammuz*), the reader inserts *Anenu* between the seventh and eighth *b'rachot*. This is a prayer asking God to answer our supplications in times of trouble. This prayer is said on Fast Days during the silent *Amidah,* in the Afternoon Service only, as part of the sixteenth *b'rachah, Kabbalat T'filah.*

Additions to Eighth *B'rachah*

8. *R'fu-ah* (petition for healing)
   R'fa-enu, Adonai, v'nerafeh ... *l'chol makoteinu* (Heal us, O Lord, and we shall be healed ... for all our wounds)

> [During the silent *Amidah*, a prayer for one who is sick may be inserted]
>
> *Y'hi ratzon mi-l'fanecha* ... *cholei Yisra-el* (May it be Your will ... the sick of Israel)

   Ki El Melech Rofei ... (For [You are] God, King, Healer ...)
      Baruch Attah Adonai, (Blessed are You, O Lord,)
   Rofei cholei ammo Yisra-el (Who heals the sick of His people Israel)

During the silent *Amidah*, an individual may insert here the prayer for a specific sick person, *Y'hi ratzon mi-l'fanecha* (May it be Your will).

Additions to Ninth *B'rachah*

9. *Birkat haShanim* (petition for freedom from want)
Barech aleinu, Adonai Eloheinu ... kol minei t'vu-atah l'tovah (Bless for us, O Lord our God ... all kinds of produce for good)

[From December 5 until Pesach, add]	[From *Chol haMo-ed* Pesach to December 4, add]	
v'ten tal umatar livrachah (and grant dew and rain for a blessing)	*v'ten b'rachah* (and grant a blessing)	

al pnei ha-adamah ... (on the face of the earth) *Baruch Attah Adonai,* (Blessed are You, O Lord,) *M'varech hashanim* (Who blesses the years)

In this *b'rachah* we pray for abundant harvests, that is, for freedom from want. In Israel, there is no rain during the summer. Thus there are serious agricultural consequences if the winter rains fail. Accordingly, in winter (from December 5 until Pesach) we ask for dew and rain, *v'ten tal umatar livrachah* (and grant dew and rain for a blessing), whereas in summer (from *Chol haMo-ed Pesach* to December 4) we ask for a blessing on the earth, *v'ten b'rachah* (and grant a blessing). This prayer is tied to the agricultural system in Israel irrespective of where one lives.

Additions to Eleventh *B'rachah*

11. *Birkat haMishpat* (petition for justice and righteousness) *Hashivah shof'teinu k'varishonah* ... (Restore our judges as in former times ...) *Baruch Attah Adonai,* (Blessed are You, O Lord,)
Melech ohev tz'dakah umishpat (the King Who loves righteousness and judgment)

[Between Rosh haShanah and Yom Kippur, substitute] *haMelech hakadosh* (the holy King)

During *Asseret Y'mei T'shuvah* (Ten Days of Repentance), between Rosh haShanah and Yom Kippur, we conclude this *b'rachah* with the words *haMelech hakadosh* (the holy King). As was pointed out on page 39, this is because the Kingship of God is a major preoccupation between Rosh haShanah and Yom Kippur.

Additions to Fourteenth *B'rachah*

14. *Birkat Y'rushalayim* (petition for the rebuilding of Jerusalem)

V'lirushalayim ir'cha ... l'tochah tachin (And to Jerusalem Your city... establish in it)

Baruch Attah Adonai, (Blessed are You, O Lord,)
Boneh Y'rushalayim (Builder of Jerusalem)

[During the Afternoon Service on Tish-ah b'Av, substitute]

Nachem, Adonai Eloheinu, et avelei Tziyon ... Baruch Attah Adonai, M'nachem Tziyon uVoneh Y'rushalayim (Comfort, O Lord our God, those who mourn for Zion ... Blessed are You, O Lord, Comforter of Zion and Builder of Jerusalem)

During the Afternoon Service on Tish-ah b'Av (Ninth of Av), a special prayer is added to the fourteenth *b'rachah*, *Birkat Y'rushalayim* (blessing for Jerusalem). The Fast of Tish-ah b'Av commemorates the destruction of the First Temple and the Second Temple in Jerusalem, both of which occurred on the ninth day of the month of *Av*. Accordingly, it is appropriate that this passage, beginning *Nachem, Adonai Eloheinu, et avelei Tziyon* (Comfort, O Lord our God, those who mourn for Zion), is inserted into *Birkat Y'rushalayim*.

Additions to Sixteenth *B'rachah*

<table>
<tr><td colspan="2">16. Kabbalat T'filah (petition for prayer to be accepted)

Sh'ma kolenu, Adonai Eloheinu ... avodat Yisra-el amecha (Hear our voices, O Lord our God ... the service of Israel, Your people)</td></tr>
<tr><td></td><td>[On Fast Days, in the silent Amidah of the Afternoon Service, insert]

Anenu ... b'chol et tzarah v'tzukah (Answer us ... at all times of trouble and distress)</td></tr>
<tr><td colspan="2">Ki Attah shome'ah t'filat am'cha Yisra-el b'rachamim (Because You hear the prayer of Your people Israel in mercy)</td></tr>
<tr><td colspan="2" align="center">Baruch Attah Adonai, (Blessed are You, O Lord,)
Shome'ah t'filah (Who hears prayer)</td></tr>
</table>

As pointed out on page 58, in the silent *Amidah* of the Afternoon Service on Fast Days, we insert into the sixteenth *b'rachah* the prayer *Anenu*, asking God to answer our prayers in times of trouble.

Additions to Seventeenth *B'rachah*

<table>
<tr><td colspan="2">17. Avodah (for restoration of the Temple service)

R'tzei Adonai Eloheinu ... avodat Yisra-el amecha (Be pleased, O Lord our God ... the service of Israel, Your people)</td></tr>
<tr><td></td><td>[On Rosh Chodesh and Chol haMo-ed add]

Eloheinu Velohei avoteinu, ya-aleh v'yavo ... chanun v'rachum Attah (Our God and God of our fathers, may [the remembrance] ascend and come ... for You are gracious and merciful)</td></tr>
<tr><td colspan="2">V'techezenah eineinu ... (May our eyes behold ...)
    Baruch Attah Adonai, (Blessed are You, O Lord,)
Hamachazir Sh'chinato l'Tziyon (Who returns the Divine Presence to Zion)</td></tr>
</table>

On *Rosh Chodesh* (New Month Festival) and *Chol haMo-ed* (Intermediate Days of Pesach and Sukkot), the prayer *Eloheinu Velohei avoteinu, ya'aleh v'yavo* (Our God and God of our fathers, [may the remembrance] ascend and come) is inserted. The prayer asks that we be granted life, well-being, and peace on those days that were given to us for rejoicing.

Ya-aleh v'yavo (May [the remembrance] ascend and come) is inserted here to acknowledge the changes in the Temple service as noted in the Bible. It is added only on biblical festivals (such as *Rosh Chodesh*) and not on festivals added by the Rabbis, like Purim or Chanukah.

Additions to Eighteenth *B'rachah*

18. *Hoda-ah* (thanksgiving for God's mercy)
    Modim anachnu Lach ... me-olam kivinu Lach (We give thanks to You ... we have always hoped in You)

> [When repeating the *Amidah*, substitute drastically modified form]
>
> *Modim anachnu Lach ... Baruch El hahoda-ot* (We give thanks to You ... Blessed is the God of thanksgiving)
>
> > [On Chanukah and Purim add]
> >
> > *Al hanisim ... bayamim hahem ba-z'man hazeh* (For the miracles ... in those days at this season)
> >
> > | [On Chanukah add] | [On Purim add] |
> > |---|---|
> > | *Bimei Matityahu ... l'Shimcha hagadol* (In the days of Mattathias ... to Your great Name) | *Bimei Mord'chai ... v'et banav al ha-etz* (In the days of Mordechai ... and his sons on the gallows) |

V'al kulam ... tamid l'olam va-ed (For all of these ... forever and ever)

> [Between Rosh haShanah and Yom Kippur add]
>
> *Uchtov l'chayim tovim kol bnei v'ritecha* (And inscribe all the children of Your covenant for a good life)

V'chol hachayim yoducha Selah ... (And all living things will give thanks to you, *Selah ...*)
       Baruch Attah Adonai, (Blessed are You, O Lord,)
HaTov Shimcha uLcha na-eh l'hodot (Your Name is "The Good" and to You it is fitting to give thanks)

> [When repeating the *Amidah* of the Morning Service (and the Afternoon Service on Fast Days), add]
>
> *Y'varech'cha Adonai v'yishm'recha ... v'yasem l'cha shalom* (May the Lord bless you and protect you ... and grant you peace)

Recall that the eighteenth *b'rachah* is a prayer of thanksgiving to God. When the *Amidah* is repeated, the first paragraph of the *b'rachah*, *Modim anachnu Lach* (We give thanks to You) is replaced by a complete paragraph, the so-called *Modim d'Rabbanan* (the *Modim* of the Rabbis). This expression of thanksgiving is similar in content to the *Modim* of the silent *Amidah*. *Modim d'Rabbanan* is recited by the congregation while the Reader says the *Modim* of the silent *Amidah* in an undertone.

During Chanukah and Purim, a sentence, *Al hanisim* (For the miracles), expressing our thanks for the miraculous deliverance is inserted. This is followed by a paragraph specific to Chanukah or Purim. The Chanukah paragraph begins *Bimei Matityahu* (In the days of Mattathias), whereas the Purim paragraph starts with the words *Bimei Mord'chai* (In the days of Mordechai). Again, it is appropriate that these expressions of thanksgiving be inserted into the eighteenth *b'rachah*.

The fifth addition for *Asseret Y'mei T'shuvah* (Ten Days of Repentance)—between Rosh haShanah and Yom Kippur—is inserted just before the end of the eighteenth *b'rachah*. We pray *Uchtov l'chayim tovim kol bnei v'ritecha* (Inscribe all the children of Your covenant for a good life).

During the repetition of the *Amidah* for the Morning Service for weekdays (and the Afternoon Service for weekdays on Fast Days), the Reader adds *Birkat Kohanim* (Priestly Blessing) at the end of the eighteenth *b'rachah*. In the Temple in Jerusalem, the *Kohanim* (Priests) blessed the people with the three-part blessing beginning *Y'varech'cha Adonai v'yishm'recha* (May the Lord bless you and protect you) (Num. 6:24–26).

Additions to Nineteenth *B'rachah*

19. *Birkat Shalom* (petition for peace)
[Morning, Additional Service; Afternoon Service on Fast Days]
Sim shalom ... (Grant peace ...)
[Evening, Afternoon Service]   *Shalom rav* ... (Abundant peace ...)
... *uvchol sha-ah bishlomecha* (And in every hour with Your peace)

Baruch Attah Adonai, (Blessed are You, O Lord,)
Ha-m'varech et ammo Yisra-el bashalom (Who blesses His people Israel with peace)

[Between Rosh haShanah and Yom Kippur substitute]
B'Sefer Chayim ... (In the Book of Life ...)

The sixth and final insertion between Rosh haShanah and Yom Kippur appears here; we change the ending of the last *b'rachah* to a prayer for life as well as for peace. The passage begins *B'Sefer Chayim* (In the Book of Life).

We conclude our discussion of the weekday *Amidah* by examining specific aspects of the weekday *Amidah* for the Evening Service.

Weekday *Amidah* for the Evening Service

The weekday *Amidah* for the Evening Service is essentially the same as the *Amidah* for the Morning and Afternoon Services. However, there are some minor differences as a consequence of the fact that the *Amidah* for the Evening Service is not repeated by the Reader.

Morning and Afternoon Service	Evening Service
The *Amidah* is repeated (in the presence of a *minyan*)	The *Amidah* is never repeated

The original reason why the *Amidah* was repeated was to enable uneducated people who could not say the *Amidah* properly to fulfill the *mitzvah* of saying the *Amidah* by listening to the repetition and saying *Amen* (Amen) at the end of each *b'rachah*. Originally, the Evening Service (and hence the *Amidah* for the Evening Service) was optional, so the *Amidah* was not repeated. Because the *Amidah* for the Evening Service is never repeated, the prayer does not include any insertions added by the Reader, such as the *K'dushah* or *Birkat Kohanim* (Priestly Blessing).

There is another reason why there is no *Birkat Kohanim* in the weekday *Amidah* for the Evening Service. In the Temple in Jerusalem, the *Kohanim* blessed the people during the Morning Service and Additional Service only. That is also the reason why there is no *Birkat Kohanim* during the repetition of the *Amidah* for the Afternoon Service (except on Fast Days).

Havinenu

When we do not have time to recite the complete *Amidah*, we may say the paragraph *Havinenu* in place of the thirteen petitions (*b'rachot* 4 through 16); the first three and last three *b'rachot* are said as usual.

> *Havinenu Adonai Eloheinu* ... (Grant us, O Lord our God ...)
>
> *Baruch Attah Adonai,* (Blessed are You, O Lord,)
>
> *Shome-ah t'filah* (Who hears prayer)

This prayer is a summary of the thirteen weekday petitions in a single paragraph.

This concludes our discussion of the weekday *Amidah*. We now turn to the *Amidah* for Festivals.

7

The Structure of the
Amidah for Festivals

With one exception, the structure of every Festival *Amidah* is that of a Long Form *B'rachah* consisting of seven component *b'rachot*. These seven *b'rachot* are organized into three sections.

First section	First three *b'rachot*	Praises
Second section	Intermediate (fourth) *b'rachah*	Festival themes
Third section	Last three *b'rachot*	Thanksgiving

The first three *b'rachot* of the *Amidah* for Festivals are essentially identical to the first three *b'rachot* of the *Amidah* for *Shabbat*, and the last three *b'rachot* are also essentially the same. Accordingly, the major topic of this chapter is the intermediate *b'rachah*. We first consider the three *Chagim* (Pesach, Shavuot, and Sukkot). Then we consider *Chol haMo-ed* and *Rosh Chodesh*.

The *Amidot* for Rosh haShanah and Yom Kippur are not usually found in a *Siddur*, so they should not be included in this book. Nevertheless, the structure of the *Amidah* for the Rosh haShanah Additional Service, with its three intermediate *b'rachot,* is so interesting that it has been added as the final chapter (Chapter 18).

Amidah for *Chagim*

Here is the structure of the basic *Amidah* for the three *Chagim* (Pesach, Shavuot, and Sukkot):

	Evening, Morning, and Afternoon Services	Additional Service
First section	Same as on *Shabbat* (see Chapter 5)	
Section section	*Attah v'chartanu* ... (You have chosen us...) [Evening/Morning/Afternoon Service version]	*Attah v'chartanu* ... (You have chosen us...;) [Additional Service version]
Third section	Same as on *Shabbat* (see Chapter 5)	

We now consider the structure of *Attah v'chartanu*. This intermediate *b'rachah* is frequently referred to as *K'dushat haYom* (Holiness of the day) because that is the major theme of the second section of the *Amidah*.

Intermediate *B'rachah* for *Chagim*

The two forms of the intermediate *b'rachah* are shown in the diagram below.

Evening, Morning, and Afternoon Services	Additional Service
Attah v'chartanu ... (You have chosen us ...)	
[On Saturday night add] *Vatodi-enu* ... (You have made known to us ...)	—
[Modified appropriately for *Shabbat,* Pesach, Shavuot, Sukkot, and *Sh'mini Atzeret/Simchat Torah*] *Vatiten lanu* ... (And You have given us ...)	
[Modified appropriately for Pesach, Shavuot, Sukkot, and *Sh'mini Atzeret/Simchat Torah*] *Eloheinu Velohei avoteinu, ya-aleh v'yavo* ... (Our God and God of our fathers, may [the remembrance] ascend and come ...)	*Umi-p'nei chata-einu* ... (But because of our sins ...)
	Description of [*Shabbat* and] appropriate Festival sacrifice
	[On *Shabbat*] *Yis-m'chu v'malchu-t'cha* ... (They shall rejoice in Your kingdom ...)
	Eloheinu Velohei avoteinu, [r'tzei vimnuchatenu,] Melech rachaman ... (O God and God of our fathers, [be pleased with our rest,] merciful King ...)
[Modified appropriately for *Shabbat*] *V'hasi-enu* ... (Bestow on us ...)	

We first consider the intermediate *b'rachah* for the Evening, Morning, and Afternoon Services.

Intermediate *B'rachah* for Evening, Morning, and Afternoon Services

Evening, Morning, and Afternoon Services	Additional Service
Attah v'chartanu ... aleinu karata (You have chosen us ... proclaimed to us)	
[On Saturday night add] *Vatodi-enu ... bikdushatecha* (You have made known to us ... in Your holiness)	
[Modified appropriately for *Shabbat,* Pesach, Shavuot, Sukkot, and *Sh'mini Atzeret/Simchat Torah*] *Vatiten lanu ... zecher litziat Mitzraim* (And You have given us ... as a remembrance of the Exodus from Egypt)	
[Modified appropriately for Pesach, Shavuot, Sukkot, and *Sh'mini Atzeret/Simchat Torah*] *Eloheinu Velohei avoteinu, ya-aleh v'yavo ... chanun v'rachum Attah* (Our God and God of our fathers, may [the remembrance] ascend and come ... for You are gracious and merciful)	
[Modified appropriately for *Shabbat*] *V'hasi-enu ... Baruch Attah Adonai, M'kadesh [haShabbat v'] Yisra-el v'ha-z'manim* (Bestow on us ... Blessed are You, O Lord, Who sanctifies [the Sabbath and] Israel and the festive seasons.)	

The paragraph beginning *Attah v'chartanu* (You have chosen us) proclaims that the Jews are the Chosen People. This is followed, on Saturday night, by *Vatodi-enu* (You have made known to us), a *Havdalah* (separation) between the greater holiness of *Shabbat* and the lesser holiness of the *Chag* (see Chapter 9).

Next come two paragraphs, the contents of which are modified appropriately for the specific *Chag*. The paragraph beginning *Vatiten lanu* (And You have given us) describes why we have been given the specific *Chag* and proclaims the holiness of the day. This first paragraph is also modified for *Shabbat*. The second paragraph, *Eloheinu Velohei avoteinu, ya-aleh v'yavo* (Our God and God of our fathers, may [the remembrance] ascend and come) is a prayer asking that we be granted life, well-being, and peace on the *Chag*.

Finally, the paragraph beginning *V'hasi-enu* (Bestow on us) asks for the blessings of the *Chag*. It ends with the words, *Baruch Attah Adonai, M'kadesh [haShabbat v'] Yisra-el v'ha-z'manim* (Blessed are You, O Lord, Who sanctifies [the Sabbath and] Israel and the festive seasons).

Intermediate *B'rachah* for Additional Service

We now describe the four paragraphs that are specific to the Additional Service on *Chagim;* the other three paragraphs are described on pages 70 and 71.

Evening, Morning, and Afternoon Services	Additional Service
Attah v'chartanu ... aleinu karata (You have chosen us ... proclaimed to us)	
[Modified appropriately for *Shabbat,* Pesach, Shavuot, Sukkot, and *Sh'mini Atzeret/Simchat Torah*] *Vatiten lanu ... zecher litziat Mitzraim* (And You have given us ... as a remembrance of the Exodus from Egypt)	
	Umi-p'nei chata-einu ... mipi ch'vodecha ka-amur (But because of our sins ... from the mouth of Your glory, as it is said)
	Description of [*Shabbat* and] appropriate Festival sacrifices
	[On *Shabbat*] *Yis-m'chu v'malchu-t'cha ... zecher l'ma-asei v'reshit* (They shall rejoice in Your kingdom ... as a remembrance of the Creation)
	Eloheinu Velohei avoteinu, [r'tzei vimnuchatenu], Melech rachaman ... asher natan lach (O God and God of our fathers, [be pleased with our rest,] merciful King ... that He gave you)
[Modified appropriately for *Shabbat*] *V'hasi-enu ... Baruch Attah Adonai, M'kadesh [haShabbat v'] Yisra-el v'ha-z'manim* (Bestow on us ... Blessed are You, O Lord, Who sanctifies [the Sabbath and] Israel and the festive seasons.)	

The paragraph beginning *Umi-p'nei chata-einu* (But because of our sins) states the oft-repeated theme that we have been exiled because we have sinned.

Next come biblical quotations describing the relevant sacrifices. This material is shown in greater detail on the next two pages.

On *Shabbat, Yis-m'chu v'malchu-t'cha* (They shall rejoice in Your kingdom) is added. It is taken from the *Shabbat* Additional Service *Amidah* (page 32).

The paragraph beginning *Eloheinu Velohei avoteinu, [r'tzei vimnuchatenu,] Melech rachaman* (O God and God of our fathers, [be pleased with our rest,] merciful King) is a prayer for the restoration of the Temple and for the services that were conducted there.

Sacrificial Offerings

A central part of the *Musaf* (Additional Service) *Amidah* is a description of the corresponding *musaf* (additional) sacrifice that was offered in the Temple on that day, as shown in the tables below. In each case, the quotation is from the Book of Numbers (*Parshat Pinchas*).

Shabbat		
When a *Chag* falls on *Shabbat*	*Uvyom haShabbat* ... (And on the Sabbath day ...)	Numbers 28:9–10

Each of the following passages is followed by the additional material *Uminchatam v'niskeihem* (And their meal offerings and their libations) shown in the last box on the next page.

Pesach		
First two days	*Uvachodesh harishon* ... (And in the first month ...)	Numbers 28:16–19
Chol haMo-ed and last two days	*V'hikravtem isheh* ... (And you shall bring a burnt offering ...)	Numbers 28:19

Shavuot		
Both days	*Uvyom habikurim* ... (And on the day of the first fruits ...)	Numbers 28:26–27

Sukkot		
First two days	*Uvachamisha assar yom* ... (And on the fifteenth day ...)	Numbers 29:12–13
First day of *Chol haMo-ed*	*Uvayom hasheni* ... (And on the second day ...), *Uvayom hashlishi* ... (And on the third day ...)	Numbers 29:17, 20
Second day of *Chol haMo-ed*	*Uvayom hashlishi* ... (And on the third day ...), *Uvayom ha-r'vi-i* ... (And on the fourth day ...)	Numbers 29:20, 23
Third day of *Chol haMo-ed*	*Uvayom ha-r'vi-i* ... (And on the fourth day ...), *Uvayom hachamishi* ... (And on the fifth day ...)	Numbers 29:23, 26
Fourth day of *Chol haMo-ed*	*Uvayom hachamishi* ... (And on the fifth day ...), *Uvayom hashishi* ... (And on the sixth day ...)	Numbers 29:26, 29
Hoshana Rabba	*Uvayom hashishi* ... (And on the sixth day ...), *Uvayom ha-sh'vi-i* ... (And on the seventh day ...)	Numbers 29:29, 32
Sh'mini Atzeret, Simchat Torah	*Bayom ha-sh'mini* ... (On the eighth day ...)	Numbers 29:35–36

The following material is added after each of the specific Festival passages:

Uminchatam v'niskeihem ... *k'hilchatam* (And their meal offerings and their libations ... according to their law)

This additional passage is essentially a condensation of Numbers 28:12–15. It specifies the meal offerings and libations associated with animal sacrifices. It concludes with the requirement of sacrificing a he-goat for atonement, in addition to the two *tamid* (continual or daily) sacrifices.

For the Maven

In *Eretz Yisra-el,* only the first day of Sukkot is a *Chag,* so the first day of *Chol haMo-ed* corresponds to the second day of Sukkot. In the Diaspora, however, the first day of *Chol haMo-ed* coincides with the third day of Sukkot. Thus, the verses from *Parshat Pinchas* for the first day of *Chol haMo-ed* Sukkot deal with the second and third day of Sukkot (and similarly for the other days).

Amidah for *Chol haMo-ed*

	Evening, Morning, and Afternoon Services	Additional Service
Shabbat	Usual *Shabbat Amidah* (Chapter 5); paragraph beginning *Ya-aleh v'yavo* (May [the remembrance] ascend and come) is added to fifth *b'rachah* (see page 000)	*Amidah* for *Chagim,* with *Shabbat* additions
Weekdays	Usual weekday *Amidah* (Chapter 6); paragraph beginning *Ya-aleh v'yavo* (May [the remembrance] ascend and come) is added to seventeenth *b'rachah* (see pages 61–62)	*Amidah* for *Chagim*

When *Chol haMo-ed* falls on *Shabbat,* the *Amidah* for the Evening, Morning, and Afternoon Services is the usual *Shabbat Amidah* described in Chapter 5. The passage beginning *Ya-aleh v'yavo* (May [the remembrance] ascend and come) is added to the fifth *b'rachah,* as described on page 42. The *Amidah* for the Additional Service is the *Amidah* for *Chagim* described in this chapter, with the indicated additions for *Shabbat.*

When *Chol haMo-ed* falls on a weekday, the *Amidah* for the Evening, Morning, and Afternoon Services is the usual weekday *Amidah* (Chapter 6) with the passage beginning *Ya-aleh v'yavo* (May [the remembrance] ascend and come) added to the seventeenth *b'rachah* (see pages 61–62). The *Amidah* for the Additional Service is again the *Amidah* for *Chagim* described in this chapter.

In other words, the *Amidah* for the Evening, Morning, and Afternoon Services is the usual *Shabbat* or weekday *Amidah,* as the case may be, whereas the *Amidah* for the Additional Service is the *Amidah* for *Chagim.*

Amidah for *Rosh Chodesh*

	Evening, Morning, and Afternoon Services	Additional Service
Shabbat	Usual *Shabbat Amidah* (Chapter 5); paragraph beginning *Ya-aleh v'yavo* (May [the remembrance] ascend and come) is added to fifth *b'rachah* (see page 42)	*Shabbat Amidah* with greatly modified fourth *b'rachah* (Chapter 5)
Weekdays	Usual weekday *Amidah* (Chapter 6); paragraph beginning *Ya-aleh v'yavo* (May [the remembrance] ascend and come) is added to seventeenth *b'rachah* (see page 61)	Special fourth *b'rachah* for *Rosh Chodesh;* rest of *Amidah* same as for every other *Musaf*

When *Rosh Chodesh* falls on *Shabbat*, the *Amidah* is a modified form of the corresponding *Shabbat Amidah*. In the Evening, Morning, and Afternoon Services, the paragraph beginning *Ya-aleh v'yavo* (May [the remembrance] ascend and come) is added to the fifth *b'rachah* (see page 42). During the Additional Service, the intermediate (fourth) *b'rachah* of the *Shabbat Amidah*, *K'dushat haYom,* undergoes major changes, as described on page 40.

If *Rosh Chodesh* falls on a weekday, then the *Amidah* for the Evening, Morning, and Afternoon Services is the usual weekday *Amidah* described in Chapter 6; the passage beginning *Ya-aleh v'yavo* (May [the remembrance] ascend and come) is added to the seventeenth *b'rachah,* as described on page 61. With regard to the *Amidah* of the Additional Service, the first and third sections are the same as those of any other *Musaf Amidah.* The structure of the middle (fourth) *b'rachah, K'dushat haYom* (holiness of the day) is shown on the next page.

Intermediate *B'rachah* for Weekday
Additional Service on *Rosh Chodesh*

Rashei Chodashim ... mipi ch'vodecha ka-amur (New Month Festivals ... from the mouth of Your glory, as it is said)
UvRashei Chodsheichem ... k'hilchatam (And on New Month Festivals ... according to their law)
Eloheinu Velohei avoteinu, chadesh aleinu ... Baruch Attah Adonai, M'kadesh Yisra-el v'Rashei Chodashim (Our God and God of our fathers, renew for us ... Blessed are You, O Lord, Who sanctifies Israel and new month Festivals)

The passage beginning *Rashei Chodashim* (New Month Festivals) describes what used to happen in the Temple on *Rosh Chodesh,* and expresses the hope that the Temple will be rebuilt.

The second section, beginning *UvRashei Chodsheichem* (And on New Month Festivals) describes the specific *Rosh Chodesh Musaf* sacrifice (Num. 28:11), analogous to the sacrificial descriptions listed on pages 73 and 74. And like those listed there, it is concluded by the material beginning *Uminchatam v'niskeihem* (And their meal offerings and their libations), based on Num. 28:12–15.

The last section in the fourth *b'rachah* is the prayer beginning *Eloheinu Velohei avoteinu, chadesh aleinu* (Our God and God of our fathers, renew for us). This prayer reflects *Rosh Chodesh* themes using twelve phrases, including happiness, blessing, joy, and gladness. These twelve phrases allude to the 12 months of a regular year; a thirteenth expression, *ulchapparat pesha* (and for atonement of transgressions), is added during a leap year. The prayer ends *Baruch Attah Adonai, M'kadesh Yisra-el v'Rashei Chodashim* (Blessed are You, O Lord, Who sanctifies Israel and New Month Festivals). The corresponding prayer said during the Additional Service when *Rosh Chodesh* falls on *Shabbat* (page 40) is essentially the same as the weekday version described on this page but with additional phrases for *Shabbat.*

Prayer for Rain and Prayer for Dew

In Israel, there is no rain between Pesach and Sukkot. The only form of moisture for the parched fields is dew. Accordingly, on the first day of Pesach, a special prayer for dew is inserted into the first and second *b'rachot* during the Reader's repetition of the *Amidah* for the Additional Service. A similar prayer for rain is recited on *Sh'mini Atzeret* (Eighth Day of the Assembly), the beginning of the rainy season. The overall structure of the two prayers is shown below:

First Day of Pesach	Sh'mini Atzeret
1. *Avot* (praising the God of the Patriarchs)	
Baruch Attah Adonai (Blessed are You, O Lord)	
Eloheinu Velohei avoteinu ... Melech Ozer uMoshia uMagen (our God and God of our fathers ... King, Helper, and Savior, and Shield)	
First introduction to prayer for dew	First introduction to prayer for rain
Baruch Attah Adonai, (Blessed are You, O Lord,) *Magen Avraham* (Shield of Abraham)	

First Day of Pesach	Sh'mini Atzeret
2. *G'vurot* (praising God's powers)	
Attah gibor l'olam Adonai ... rav l'hoshia (You, O Lord, are mighty forever ... You are abundantly able to save)	
Second introduction to prayer for dew	Second introduction to prayer for rain
Prayer for dew	Prayer for rain
M'chalkel chayim b'chesed ... (He sustains the living with kindness ...) *Baruch Attah Adonai,* (Blessed are You, O Lord,) *M'chayei hametim* (Who revives the dead)	

Each of these components is now considered in greater detail.

Additions to First *B'rachah*

First Day of Pesach	Sh'mini Atzeret
1. *Avot* (praising the God of the Patriarchs)	
Baruch Attah Adonai (Blessed are You, O Lord)	
Eloheinu Velohei avoteinu ... Melech Ozer uMoshia uMagen (our God and God of our fathers ... King, Helper, and Savior, and Shield)	
B'Dato abiah chidut ... l'hagen l'toladot (With His agreement I shall speak of sophisms ... to protect the generations)	*Af-Bri utat shem sar matar ... sho-alei matar* (Af-Bri is designated as the name of the angel of rain ... those who pray for rain)
Baruch Attah Adonai, (Blessed are You, O Lord,) *Magen Avraham* (Shield of Abraham)	

An initial introduction to the prayer for dew and the prayer for rain is inserted into the first *b'rachah* of the *Musaf Amidah.* The paragraph beginning *B'Dato abiah chidut* (With His agreement I shall speak of sophisms) stresses the importance of dew. The corresponding sentiment is expressed in *Af-Bri utat shem sar matar* (Af-Bri is designated as the name of the angel of rain), the first introductory passage of the material on rain.

Additions to Second *B'rachah*

First Day of Pesach	*Sh'mini Atzeret*
2. *G'vurot* (praising God's powers) *Attah gibor l'olam Adonai ... rav l'hoshia* (You, O Lord, are mighty forever ... You are abundantly able to save)	
T'homot hadom ... n'kukei s'ifim (The depths of the earth... clefts of rocks)	*Yatriach l'faleg ... g'vurot hagashem* (May He burden [Af-Bri] to divide ... powers of the rain)
Eloheinu Velohei avoteinu, (Our God and God of our fathers)	
Tal ten ... b'tal (Grant dew ... with dew)	*Z'chor av ... maiyim* (Remember the patriarch ... water)
Sha-Attah Hu Adonai Eloheinu, Mashiv haru-ach umorid (For You are the Lord, our God, Who causes the blowing of the wind and the falling of)	
hatal (the dew)	*hagashem* (the rain)
Livrachah v'lo liklalah ... (For a blessing and not for a curse ...)	
M'chalkel chayim b'chesed ... (He sustains the living with kindness ...) *Baruch Attah Adonai,* (Blessed are You, O Lord,) *M'chayei hametim* (Who revives the dead)	

T'homot hadom (The depths of the earth) is the start of a second introductory passage to the prayer for dew; *Yatriach l'faleg* (May He burden [Af-Bri] to divide) is the corresponding passage for rain.

In both cases, next come the words *Eloheinu Velohei avoteinu* (Our God and God of our fathers). This is followed by the prayers for dew and rain, respectively. Both prayers are alphabetically arranged, and both comprise six stanzas, each consisting of four stiches. More specifically, the initial letters of the twenty-four stiches of *Tal ten* (Grant dew) constitute a reverse acrostic (the letters *bet* and *aleph* are repeated); the six stanzas each begin with the word *tal* (dew) and conclude with *b'tal* (with dew).

With regard to the prayer for rain, the initial letters of the twenty-four stiches of *Z'chor av* (Remember the patriarch) constitute a forward acrostic (the letters *shin* and *tav* are repeated). Each phrase ends with the word *maiyim* (water), sometimes with a prepositional prefix. The six stanzas each begin with the word *z'chor* (remember) and are followed by a congregational response, each response similarly ending with the word *maiyim* (water).

The prayer for dew is followed by the statement *Sha-Attah Hu Adonai Eloheinu, Mashiv haru-ach umorid hatal* (For You are the Lord, our God, Who causes the wind to blow and the dew to fall). The identical statement occurs in the prayer for rain, except that the last word, *hatal* (the dew), is changed to *hagashem* (the rain). A common three-verse plea beginning *Livrachah v'lo liklalah* (For a blessing and not for a curse) then concludes the prayer for dew and the prayer for rain; the congregation responds *Amen* to each verse.

For the Maven

The maven with knowledge of meteorology will no doubt be aware of the problems in the phrase *Mashiv haru-ach umorid hatal* (Who causes the wind to blow and the dew to fall). First, dew does not fall—it forms on the ground. Second, it has to be still for dew to form; when the wind blows, there is no dew. It would appear that the author of the statement had no farming experience!

More for the Maven

The prayers for dew and rain were written by arguably the greatest of the liturgical poets, Elazar Kallir. We do not know when he lived; scholars have suggested times varying from the second to the tenth century C.E. Even his name is shrouded in mystery; "Encyclopedia Judaica" gives no fewer than seventeen theories explaining "Kallir." The ArtScroll *Machzor* uses the name Elazar **ha**Kallir ("Elazar the cake [or cookie]"), citing the legend that he acquired his skills as a consequence of eating a cake or cookie on which certain Kabbalistic formulae had been written.

Birkat Kohanim

Immediately after the *tamid* (daily) offering in the Temple in Jerusalem, the *Kohanim* (priests) ascended a platform and blessed the people. In remembrance of this, during the repetition of the *Musaf Amidah* on Festivals in the *Ashkenazi* liturgy in the Diaspora, the *Kohanim* (now the descendants of the Temple priests) in the congregation ascend the platform in front of the Ark. They then bless the congregation. In many Diaspora liturgies, *Birkat Kohanim* (priestly blessing) is not performed when a Festival falls on *Shabbat*. In contrast, it is performed every *Shabbat* in Israel and daily in Jerusalem and other places. It is also performed daily in the *Sephardi* liturgy.

When the *Kohanim* bless the congregation, changes are made to both the fifth and sixth *b'rachot* of the *Musaf Amidah* as shown below:

5. *Avodah* (for restoration of the Temple service) *R'tzei Adonai Eloheinu ... avodat Yisra-el amecha* (Be pleased, O Lord our God ... the worship of Your people, Israel)
[Omit] *V'techezenah eineinu ... Baruch Attah Adonai, Hamachazir Sh'chinato l'Tziyon* ("May our eyes behold... Blessed are You, O Lord, Who returns the Divine Presence to Zion)

V'te-erav Alecha ... uchshanim kadmoniyot (May [our prayers] please You ... and as in former years)
Baruch Attah Adonai, She-otcha l'vad'cha b'yirah na-avod (Blessed are You, O Lord, Whom alone we worship with awe)

6. *Hoda-ah* (thanksgiving for God's mercy) *Modim anachnu Lach ...* (We give thanks to You ...) *Baruch Attah Adonai,* (Blessed are You, O Lord,) *HaTov Shimcha uLcha na-eh l'hodot* (Your Name is "The Good" and to You it is fitting to give thanks
[Omit] Priestly blessing recited by the Reader

Birkat Kohanim (priestly blessing)

We now examine these components in greater detail.

For the Maven

The Hebrew word for a platform (and specifically the platform from which the *Kohanim* blessed the people) is *duchan*. This is the origin of the Yiddish word *duchenen* for the Priestly Blessing.

Changes to Fifth *B'rachah*

5. *Avodah* (for restoration of the Temple service)
    R'tzei Adonai Eloheinu ... avodat Yisra-el amecha (Be pleased,
    O Lord our God ... the worship of Your people, Israel)

[Omit] *V'techezenah eineinu ... Baruch Attah Adonai, Hamachazir Sh'chinato l'Tziyon* (May our eyes behold... Blessed are You, O Lord, Who returns the Divine Presence to Zion)

V'te-erav Alecha ... uchshanim kadmoniyot (May [our
    prayers] please You ... and as in former years)
 	
    Baruch Attah Adonai, She-otcha l'vad'cha b'yirah na-avod
    (Blessed are You, O Lord, Whom alone we worship with awe)

After the *K'dushah* (see Chapter 9), inserted into the repetition of the third *b'rachah,* the *L'vi-im* (now the descendants of the Temple Levites) pour water over the hands of the *Kohanim.* Then, at the beginning of the repetition of the fifth *b'rachah,* the *Kohanim* remove their shoes and ascend the *duchan* and stand facing the Ark. The paragraph beginning *V'te-erav Alecha* (May [our prayers] please You) is recited by the congregation and *Kohanim* and is then repeated by the Reader. The latter then concludes the fifth *b'rachah* with the words *Baruch Attah Adonai, She-otcha l'vad'cha b'yirah na-avod* (Blessed are You, O Lord, Whom alone we worship with awe).

This material replaces the usual ending *V'techezenah eineinu ... Baruch Attah Adonai, Hamachazir Sh'chinato l'Tziyon* (May our eyes behold ... Blessed are You, O Lord, Who returns the Divine Presence to Zion). The new material expresses messianic themes similar to those of the weekday and *Shabbat* ending, but adds references to the Temple service.

Changes to Sixth *B'rachah*

6. *Hoda-ah* (thanksgiving for God's mercy)
    Modim anachnu Lach ... (We give thanks to You ...)
        Baruch Attah Adonai, (Blessed are You, O Lord,)
    HaTov Shimcha uLcha na-eh l'hodot (Your Name is "The Good"
    and to You it is fitting to give thanks)

<div align="center">[Omit] Priestly blessing recited by the Reader</div>

[Congregation] *Y'hi ratzon mi-l'fanecha* ... *v'ad olam* (May it be Your will ... and forever)
[Reader, in an undertone] *Eloheinu Velohei avoteinu, ba-r'chenu* ... *Aharon uvanav* (Our God and God of our fathers, bless us ... Aaron and his sons) <div align="center">[loudly] *Kohanim*</div>
[Congregation] *Am k'doshecha ka-amur* (Your holy people, as it is said)
[*Kohanim*] *Baruch Attah Adonai* ... *v'tzivanu l'varech et ammo Yisra-el b'ahavah* (Blessed are You, O Lord ... and has commanded us to bless His people Israel with love)
[Reader, followed word-for-word by *Kohanim*] *Y'varech'cha Adonai v'yishm'recha* ... *v'yasem l'cha shalom* (May the Lord bless you and protect you ... and grant you peace)
[Congregation] *Adir bamarom* ... (Mighty One on high ...)
[*Kohanim*] *Ribono shel olam* ... (Lord of the universe ...)

We now examine each of these components.

Y'hi Ratzon Mi-l'fanecha

> [Congregation] *Y'hi ratzon mi-l'fanecha ... v'ad olam*
> (May it be Your will ... and forever)

The paragraph beginning *Y'hi ratzon mi-l'fanecha* (May it be Your will) asks that the blessing about to be performed be perfect in every way. In some liturgies it is said by the congregation after the Reader has concluded the sixth *b'rachah* (as reflected on the previous page). In other liturgies, the *Kohanim* say it in an undertone while the Reader concludes the sixth *b'rachah*, ending at the same time so that the congregational *Amen* (Amen) will apply to their prayer as well.

Summoning the *Kohanim*

> [Reader, in an undertone] *Eloheinu Velohei avoteinu, ba-r'chenu ... Aharon uvanav* (Our God and God of our fathers, bless us ... Aaron and his sons)
>
> [loudly] *Kohanim*

The Reader now says the paragraph beginning *Eloheinu Velohei avoteinu, ba-r'chenu* (Our God and God of our fathers, bless us) in an undertone. Next, the Reader summons the *Kohanim* to bless the congregation by calling out loudly "*Kohanim*."

> [Congregation] *Am k'doshecha ka-amur* (Your holy people, as it is said)

The congregation responds by saying *am k'doshecha ka-amur* (Your holy people, as it is said).

B'rachah of the *Kohanim*

> [*Kohanim*] *Baruch Attah Adonai ... v'tzivanu l'varech et*
> *ammo Yisra-el b'ahavah* (Blessed are You, O Lord ... and
> has commanded us to bless His people Israel with love)

The *Kohanim* now recite a *Mitzvah* Form *b'rachah,* namely, *Baruch Attah Adonai ... v'tzivanu l'varech et ammo Yisra-el b'ahavah* (Blessed are You, O Lord ... and has commanded us to bless His people Israel with love).

Halfway through the *b'rachah* the *Kohanim* turn and face the congregation, their faces and hands covered by their *tallit.* Their hands are held at shoulder height, palms facing forward, with their fingers arranged in a special way. Specifically, the fifth and fourth fingers are touching one another, there is a wide gap between the fourth and third fingers, the third and second fingers are touching and there is another wide gap between the second fingers and thumbs. Finally, the tips of the two thumbs are touching one another.

For the Maven

Leonard Nimoy played Mr. Spock in the *Star Trek* series. During the filming of one episode, he was asked how he supposed a Vulcan greeting might look. Thinking quickly, he held up his right hand, palm forward. The fifth and fourth fingers were touching and so were the third and second fingers. Needless to say, Mr. Nimoy is a knowledgeable *Kohen* ...

Birkat Kohanim

> [Reader, followed word-for-word by *Kohanim*] *Y'varech'cha*
> *Adonai v'yishm'recha ... v'yasem l'cha shalom* (May the
> Lord bless you and protect you ... and grant you peace)

The *Kohanim* now bless the congregation in the words of Numbers 6:24–
26. That is, they use three phrases, the first of which is *Y'varech'cha Adonai*
v'yishm'recha (May the Lord bless you and protect you). The Reader acts as a
prompt, saying each word just loudly enough for the *Kohanim* to hear and
repeat aloud.

For the Maven

After each of the three phrases, the congregation responds *Amen* (Amen). In contrast, when the Priestly Blessing is inserted in the second to last *b'rachah* during the
repetition of the *Amidah*, the congregational response (in the *Ashkenazi* liturgy) is *Ken*
y'hi ratzon (May it be His will), thereby making it clear that the Reader is not actually
blessing the congregation, a task reserved for *Kohanim*.

Adir Bamarom

> [Congregation] *Adir bamarom* ... (Mighty One on high ...)

The *Kohanim* now once again face the Ark. The congregation recites *Adir bamarom* (Mighty One on high), asking for peace.

> [*Kohanim*] *Ribono shel olam* ... (Lord of the universe ...)

Then the *Kohanim* recite *Ribono shel olam* (Master of the universe), which asks God to keep His promise of giving us a land flowing with milk and honey.

In some liturgies, the practice is for the Reader to start the seventh *b'rachah*, *Sim shalom* (Grant peace). At that time the congregation says *Adir bamarom* (Mighty One on high) and simultaneously the *Kohanim* say *Ribono shel olam* (Master of the universe).

For the Maven

Many superstitions are associated with *Birkat Kohanim*. For example, there is a belief that anyone who looks at the hands of a *Kohen*, even if they are covered by a *tallit*, will instantly be struck blind. The origin of this is a statement in the *Talmud* (*Chagigah 16a*) that applied only to *Birkat Kohanim* in the Temple itself. Nevertheless, there are otherwise highly educated people who carefully envelop their heads and those of their children in a *tallit* out of fear that they will lose their sight by accidentally gazing at the hands of the *Kohanim*. A further reason for this bizarre superstition is that, traditionally, the correct practice is to avert one's eyes during *Birkat Kohanim*. First, it is a token of respect. Second, it is to indicate that the blessing, though pronounced by the *Kohanim*, actually emanates from God.

Another superstition associates *Birkat Kohanim* with the prevention of bad dreams, again as a consequence of a Talmudic statement (*B'rachot 55b*). In some liturgies, the Reader recites a chant before the *Kohanim* say the last word of each phrase to give the congregation time to say a prayer beginning *Ribono shel olam* (Master of the universe), which asks that bad dreams be averted.

8
The Structure of
K'riat Sh'ma

The *Sh'ma* expresses the central core of Jewish belief. The first verse, *Sh'ma Yisra-el, Adonai Eloheinu, Adonai Echad* says it all: "Hear, O Israel, the Lord is our God, the Lord is One." The entire *Sh'ma* is recited daily during the Morning and the Evening Services.

The overall structure of *K'riat Sh'ma* (reading the *Sh'ma*) is shown below:

Ba-r'chu (call to worship)
B'rachot before *K'riat Sh'ma*
K'riat Sh'ma (reading of *Sh'ma*)
B'rachot after *K'riat Sh'ma*

The *Sh'ma* itself consists of three paragraphs from the *Torah:* Deuteronomy 6:4–9, Deuteronomy 11:13–21, and Numbers 15:37–41. These three paragraphs are preceded by *b'rachot* and followed by *b'rachot*.

More precisely, the three paragraphs of the *Sh'ma* are embedded within a Series Form *b'rachah*. This is shown in the diagram on the next page.

Morning Service	Evening Service
Ba-r'chu (call to congregational worship)	
First *B'rachah* before *K'riat Sh'ma* ... *Yotzer ha-m'orot* (... Creator of lights)	First *B'rachah* before *K'riat Sh'ma* ... *Hama-ariv aravim* (... Who brings on the evening)
Second *B'rachah* before *K'riat Sh'ma* *Ahavah rabbah* ... (With great love ...)	Second *B'rachah* before *K'riat Sh'ma* *Ahavat olam* ... (With everlasting love ...)
First paragraph of the *Sh'ma* *Sh'ma Yisra-el, Adonai Eloheinu, Adonai Echad* ... *V'ahavta et Adonai Elohecha* ... (Hear, O Israel, the Lord is our God, the Lord is One ... You shall love the Lord your God ...)	
Second paragraph of the *Sh'ma* *V'hayah im shamo-a tishme-u* ... (If you will earnestly hearken ...)	
Third paragraph of the *Sh'ma* *Va-yomer Adonai el Moshe leimor* ... (The Lord said to Moses ...)	
First *B'rachah* after *K'riat Sh'ma* *Emet v'yatziv* ... (True and certain ...)	First *B'rachah* after *K'riat Sh'ma* *Emet ve-emunah* ... (True and faithful ...)
—	[Slight differences between *Shabbat* and weekday form] Second *B'rachah* after *K'riat Sh'ma* *Hashkivenu* ... *(Grant us to lie down ...)*
	[On Weekdays only] Third *B'rachah* after *K'riat Sh'ma* *Baruch Adonai l'olam* ... (Bless the Lord for ever ...)

We now examine each of these components in turn.

Ba-r'chu

Ba-r'chu is the call to congregational worship.

Morning Service	Evening Service
[Reader] *Ba-r'chu et Adonai Ha-m'vorach* (Bless the Lord, Who is to be blessed)	
[Congregation, then Reader] *Baruch Adonai Ha-m'vorach l'olam va-ed* (Blessed be the Lord Who is to be blessed forever and ever)	

The structure of *Ba-r'chu* consists of the actual call to worship, *Ba-r'chu et Adonai Ha-m'vorach* (Bless the Lord, Who is to be blessed). The congregation responds *Baruch Adonai Ha-m'vorach l'olam va-ed* (Blessed be the Lord Who is to be blessed forever and ever). The Reader then repeats the congregational response.

Next follow the *B'rachot* before *K'riat Sh'ma,* which we now examine.

For the Maven

Why does the Reader repeat the congregational response to *Ba-r'chu*? Some scholars felt that the verb form of the word *"Ba-r'chu"* (third person plural) excluded the Reader from the call to worship! Therefore, in order to ensure that the Reader was also included, they ordained that the Reader should repeat the congregational response, thus including the Reader beyond all doubt.

B'rachot before K'riat Sh'ma: Morning Service

First *B'rachah* before *K'riat Sh'ma:* Morning Service

Morning Service	Evening Service
Baruch Attah Adonai, Eloheinu Melech ha-olam, Yotzer or uvorei choshech, oseh shalom uvorei et hakol ... (Blessed are You, O Lord our God, King of the Universe, Who makes light and creates darkness, Maker of peace and Creator of everything ...)	
K'dushah d'Yotzer	
... *Baruch Attah Adonai, Yotzer ha-m'orot* (... Blessed are You, O Lord, Creator of lights)	

The first component in the Series Form *b'rachah, Birkat Yotzer* (blessing the Creator), begins *Baruch Attah Adonai, Eloheinu Melech ha-olam, Yotzer or uvorei choshech, oseh shalom uvorei et hakol* (Blessed are You, O Lord our God, King of the universe, Who makes light and creates darkness, Maker of peace and Creator of everything).

This *b'rachah* is interrupted by a *K'dushah* (see Chapter 9), the so-called *K'dushah d'Yotzer* (which takes its name from *Birkat Yotzer* in which it is embedded) described in the following pages.

After the *K'dushah d'Yotzer,* the *b'rachah* concludes with the words *Baruch Attah Adonai, Yotzer ha-m'orot* (Blessed are You, O Lord, Creator of lights).

K'dushah d'Yotzer

There are two forms of *K'dushah d'Yotzer*, one for the Morning Service for Shabbat, the other for the Morning Service for weekdays (including Festivals falling on weekdays).

Shabbat Morning Service	Weekday Morning Service and Festivals falling on weekdays
Hakol yoducha v'hakol y'shab'chucha ... (All will thank You and all will praise You ...)	*Hame-ir la-aretz* ... (He Who illuminates the earth ...)
El Adon al kol hama-asim ... (God, Master of all creation ...)	—
La-El Asher shavat mikol hama-asim ... (To God Who rested from all the work ...)	
Titbarach Tzurenu ... (May You be blessed, our Rock ...)	
Et Shem ha-El haMelech hagadol ... (To the Name of God, the great King ...)	

We sit during *K'dushah d'Yotzer* because it describes the actions of angels, not the holiness of God (we stand during the *K'dushah* during the repetition of the *Amidah*). For this reason, *K'dushah d'Yotzer* is sometimes called *K'dushah d'Y'shivah* (seated *K'dushah*).

We now examine the six components of *K'dushah d'Yotzer,* starting with the weekday version. Once that is complete, we will examine the second *b'rachah* before *K'riat Sh'ma*.

Hame-ir La-aretz

Weekday Morning Service and Festivals falling on weekdays
Hame-ir la-aretz ... misgav ba-adenu (He Who illuminates the earth ... a stronghold for us)
El baruch, g'dol de-ah ... y'fa-arucha. Selah (The blessed God, great in knowledge ... will glorify You. *Selah*)

This two-part prayer praises God as the powerful Creator of the universe, including the sun and the other sources of light.

The second part starts with the words *El baruch, g'dol de-ah* (The blessed God, great in knowledge). This is an acrostic; the first twenty-two words begin with the twenty-two letters of the *aleph bet* (Hebrew alphabet), in order.

We now examine the *Shabbat* version of *K'dushah d'Yotzer.*

For the Maven

The psalms contain a number of technical terms whose meaning is unclear. *Selah* is one of those technical terms.

Hakol Yoducha

Shabbat Morning Service
Hakol yoducha v'hakol y'shab'chucha ... b'midat rachamim (All will thank You and all will praise You ... in the attribute of mercy)
Hame-ir la-aretz ... misgav ba-adenu (He Who illuminates the earth ... a stronghold for us)
Ein ker-k'cha ... lit-chiyat hametim (There is none like You ... to the revival of the dead)

Hakol yoducha consists of three parts. The first part describes how every part of the universe will praise God. The second part is the same paragraph, *Hame-ir la-aretz* (He Who illuminates the earth), recited on weekdays (see previous page). The third part, beginning *Ein ker-k'cha* (There is none like You), describes the uniqueness of God.

El Adon

Shabbat Morning Service
El Adon al kol hama-asim ... v'Chayot hakodesh (God, Master of all creation ... and the holy Chayot)

The contents of the hymn *El Adon* (God, Master) parallel that of *El Baruch*, its weekday counterpart. *El Adon* is another acrostic; in this case, the first letter of each stich begins with the next letter of the Hebrew alphabet. The origin of this hymn is not certain; it has been ascribed to *Yordei Merkavah*, a group of eighth century mystics.

For the Maven

El Adon alludes explicitly to the sun and moon, and probably to the five planets known at that time. The initial letters of the phrase *SHevach Notnim Lo Kol TZ'va Marom* (all the hosts of heaven give praise to Him) may allude to the five planets *SHabtai* (Saturn), *Nogah* (Venus; literally brightness), *Kochav* (Mercury; literally star), *TZedek* (Jupiter; literally righteousness), and *Ma-adim* (Mars) [Birnbaum, p. 339].

La-El Asher Shavat

Shabbat Morning Service
La-El Asher shavat ... y'fa-arucha. Selah (To God Who rested ... will glorify You. Selah)

The Creation having being discussed, the paragraph beginning *La-El Asher shavat* (To God Who rested) describes the first *Shabbat* that occurred after the Creation. It connects the institution of the *Shabbat* to God's completion of Creation.

This concludes the material specific to the *Shabbat* Morning Service.

Titbarach Tzurenu

Shabbat Morning Service	Weekday Morning Service
Titbarach Tzurenu ... umakdishim umamlichim: (May You be blessed, our Rock ... and sanctify and declare the kingship:)	
Et Shem ha-El ... Baruch kavod Adonai mi-m'komo (To the Name of the God ... Blessed be the glory of the Lord from His place)	

Titbarach Tzurenu (May You be blessed, our Rock) describes the angels' praise of God. It is followed by a section that continues this theme, beginning *Et Shem ha-El* (To the Name of the God).

This constitutes a *K'dushah,* as described in detail in Chapter 9. For convenience, we mention here only that a *K'dushah* is constructed around two prophetic theophanies (visions of God), namely, those of Isaiah and Ezekiel. Isaiah 6:3 begins *Kadosh, Kadosh, Kadosh* (Holy, Holy, Holy), whereas Ezekiel 3:12 states *Baruch k'vod Adonai mi-m'komo* (Blessed be the glory of the Lord from His place). These two verses are embedded in this section of *K'dushah d'Yotzer.*

We now consider the second *b'rachah* before *K'riat Sh'ma* of the Morning Service.

Second *B'rachah* before *K'riat Sh'ma:* Morning Service

Morning Service	Evening Service
Ahavah rabbah ... (With great love ...) *Baruch Attah Adonai, Habocher b'ammo Yisra-el b'ahavah* (Blessed are You, O Lord, Who chose His people Israel in love)	

The second *b'rachah* before *K'riat Sh'ma* begins *Ahavah rabbah* (With great love). We thank God for having given us His teachings and we pray for assistance in understanding the *Torah*. Finally, we thank God for having chosen us, with the words *Baruch Attah Adonai, Habocher b'ammo Yisra-el b'ahavah* (Blessed are You, O Lord, Who chose His people Israel in love).

Next we consider the two *B'rachot* of *K'riat Sh'ma* for the Evening Service.

B'rachot before K'riat Sh'ma: Evening Service

First B'rachah before K'riat Sh'ma: Evening Service

Morning Service	Evening Service
	Baruch Attah Adonai Eloheinu Melech ha-olam, Asher bidvaro ... (Blessed are You, O Lord our God, King of the universe, Who by His word ...) *Baruch Attah Adonai, Hama-ariv aravim* (Blessed are You, O Lord, Who brings on the evenings)

Just as the first *b'rachah* before *K'riat Sh'ma* in the Morning Service praises God as creator of light, so the corresponding *b'rachah* in the Evening Service, *Birkat Ma-ariv* (blessing the evening), praises God Who brings on the night. The *b'rachah* concludes *Baruch Attah Adonai, Hama-ariv aravim* (Blessed are You, O Lord, Who brings on the evenings).

Second B'rachah before K'riat Sh'ma: Evening Service

Morning Service	Evening Service
	Ahavat olam ... (With everlasting love ...) *Baruch Attah Adonai, Ohev ammo Yisra-el* (Blessed are You, O Lord, Who loves His people Israel)

The second *b'rachah* in the Evening Service begins *Ahavat olam* (With everlasting love). It expresses themes similar to those of its Morning Service counterpart, *Ahavah rabbah* (With great love), which appears on the previous page. It concludes with the phrase *Baruch Attah Adonai, Ohev ammo Yisra-el* (Blessed are You, O Lord, Who loves His people Israel).

Now we consider the *Sh'ma* itself. It consists of three paragraphs from the *Torah*.

The *Sh'ma*

First Paragraph of the *Sh'ma*

Morning Service	Evening Service
Sh'ma Yisra-el, Adonai Eloheinu, Adonai Echad (Hear, O Israel, the Lord is our God, the Lord is One)	
[In an undertone] *Baruch Shem k'vod malchuto l'olam va-ed* (Blessed is the Name of His glorious kingdom forever and ever)	
V'ahavta et Adonai Elohecha ... beitecha uvisharecha (You shall love the Lord your God ... your house and your gates)	

The first paragraph of the *Sh'ma* (referred to as *V'ahavta*) is Deuteronomy 6:4–9. It begins *Sh'ma Yisra-el, Adonai Eloheinu, Adonai Echad* (Hear, O Israel, the Lord is our God, the Lord is One). That is, in the first verse of the *Sh'ma* (Deut. 6:4) we affirm the unity of God.

This is followed by a response inserted into the biblical passage, namely, *Baruch Shem k'vod malchuto l'olam va-ed* (Blessed is the Name of His glorious kingdom forever and ever). This is recited in an undertone to show that it is not part of the *Sh'ma* itself. In fact, it is not even a biblical verse, although it is similar to Psalm 72:19.

The rest of the paragraph (Deut. 6:5–9) follows, beginning *V'ahavta et Adonai Elohecha* (You shall love the Lord your God). The theme of this paragraph is that we should love God with all our ability. This paragraph of the *Sh'ma* is often referred to as *Kabbalat ol malchut shamayim* (acceptance of the yoke of the kingdom of heaven), that is, acceptance of the absolute sovereignty of God.

Second Paragraph of the *Sh'ma*

Morning Service	Evening Service
V'hayah im shamo-a tishme-u ... al ha-aretz (If you will earnestly hearken ... on the earth)	

V'hayah, the second paragraph of the *Sh'ma*, is Deuteronomy 11:13–21. It begins *V'hayah im shamo-a tishme-u* (If you will earnestly hearken). The theme here is reward and punishment. If we obey God's commandments we will be rewarded; if not, we will be punished.

Third Paragraph of the *Sh'ma*

Morning Service	Evening Service
Va-yomer Adonai el Moshe leimor ... Ani Adonai Eloheichem (The Lord said to Moses ... I am the Lord, your God)	

Va-yomer, the third and last paragraph of the *Sh'ma* (Num. 15:37–41), begins *Va-yomer Adonai el Moshe leimor* (The Lord said to Moses). It instructs us to put *tzitzit* (fringes) on the corners of our garments in order to remind us of the *Mitzvot* (commandments). The *Sh'ma* ends with the words *Ani Adonai Eloheichem* (I am the Lord, Your God). However, the first word of the next paragraph, *Emet* (True), is appended when saying the *Sh'ma.*

Next we consider the *B'rachot* after *K'riat Sh'ma.*

For the Maven

When reciting the *Sh'ma* privately, we add the three words *El Melech ne-eman* (God, the faithful King) before beginning the recitation. The reason for this is that the number of words in the *Sh'ma* is 245, whereas traditionally the human body consists of 248 parts. When praying with a *minyan* (quorum of ten), the Reader concludes the *Sh'ma* by saying aloud the last two words of the *Sh'ma* followed by the first word of the next *b'rachah,* yielding the phrase *Adonai Eloheichem emet* (The Lord your God is true). These three words bring the total number of words to 248, symbolizing that every part of our body affirms the unity of God. Therefore when praying alone, we add the three-word phrase *El Melech ne-eman* (God, the faithful King) before saying the *Sh'ma* to bring the total number of words up to the symbolic 248.

More for the Maven

The first two paragraphs of the *Sh'ma* allude to the *mitzvah* of *mezuzah* and to the *mitzvah* of *tefillin.* As mentioned above, the third paragraph is largely concerned with the *mitzvah* of *tzitzit.* Thus, the three paragraphs of the *Sh'ma* contain references to three *Mitzvot* that remind us about the *Mitzvot.*

B'rachot after *K'riat Sh'ma:* Morning Service

First and Only *B'rachah* after *K'riat Sh'ma:* Morning Service

Morning Service	Evening Service
Emet v'yatziv ... zera Yisra-el ava-decha (True and certain ... the descendants of Israel, your servants)	
Al harishonim ... ein Elohim zulate-cha (On the first generations ... there is no God beside You)	
Ezrat avoteinu ... Baruch Attah Adonai, Ga-al Yisra-el (The Help of our fathers ... Blessed are You, O Lord, Who has redeemed Israel)	

This *b'rachah, Birkat G'ulah* (blessing of redemption), consists of three parts. The first part, which begins with the words *Emet v'yatziv* (True and certain), stresses the enduring nature of God. The second part, *Al harishonim* (On the first generations) continues this theme.

The third and final part, beginning *Ezrat avoteinu* (The Help of our fathers) and concluding *Baruch Attah Adonai, Ga-al Yisra-el* (Blessed are You, O Lord, Who has redeemed Israel), describes God's role in the Exodus from Egypt and our redemption through that event.

This is the only *b'rachah* recited after the *Sh'ma* during the Morning Service. Consequently, *K'riat Sh'ma* for the Morning Service is a Series Form *b'rachah* with three component *B'rachot*.

During the Evening Service, however, there are three *b'rachot* after *K'riat Sh'ma* on weekday evenings (two on *Shabbat* and Festivals). This is now described.

B'rachot after *K'riat Sh'ma:* Evening Service

First *B'rachah* after *K'riat Sh'ma:* Evening Service

Morning Service	Evening Service
	Emet ve-emunah ... Baruch Attah Adonai, Ga-al Yisra-el (True and faithful ... Blessed are You, O Lord, Who has redeemed Israel)

Although the precise words of *Birkat G'ulah* (blessing of redemption) for the Evening Service are different from those of the third part of *Birkat G'ulah* for the Morning Service, both *B'rachot* express the same theme, namely, the redemption from Egypt. This *b'rachah* begins *Emet ve-emunah* (True and faithful) and ends, like its Morning Service counterpart, *Baruch Attah Adonai, Ga-al Yisra-el* (Blessed are You, O Lord, Who has redeemed Israel).

Second *B'rachah* after *K'riat Sh'ma:* Evening Service for *Shabbat* and Festivals

Morning Service	Evening Service
	Hashkivenu ... Baruch Attah Adonai, Hapores sukkat shalom aleinu v'al kol ammo Yisra-el, v'al Y'rushalayim (Grant us to lie down ... Blessed are You, O Lord, Who spreads the shelter of peace over us and over all His people Israel, and over Jerusalem)

The second and final *b'rachah* after *K'riat Sh'ma* during the Evening Service for *Shabbat* and Festivals is *Hashkivenu* (Grant us to lie down), a prayer for protection during the night which was considered to be a dangerous time. This *b'rachah* ends with the words *Baruch Attah Adonai, Hapores sukkat shalom aleinu v'al kol ammo Yisra-el, v'al Y'rushalayim* (Blessed are You, O Lord, Who spreads the shelter of peace over us and over all His people Israel, and over Jerusalem).

We see that for the Evening Service for *Shabbat* and Festivals, *K'riat Sh'ma* is a Series Form *b'rachah* with four component *B'rachot,* two recited before *K'riat Sh'ma* and two recited after.

Second *B'rachah* after *K'riat Sh'ma:* Evening Service for Weekdays

Morning Service	Evening Service
	Hashkivenu ... (Grant us to lie down ...)
	[Delete this sentence] *Ufros aleinu sukkat sh'lomecha* (Spread over us the shelter of Your peace)
	[Different concluding phrase] *Baruch Attah Adonai, Shomer ammo Yisra-el la-ad* (Blessed are You, O Lord, Who guards His people Israel forever)

On weekdays, one sentence is deleted from the end of *Hashkivenu* (the second *b'rachah* after the *Sh'ma*), namely, *Ufros aleinu sukkat sh'lomecha* (Spread over us the shelter of Your peace). Also, the ending of this *b'rachah* on weekdays is *Baruch Attah Adonai, Shomer ammo Yisra-el la-ad* (Blessed are You, O Lord, Who guards His people Israel forever).

Third *B'rachah* after *K'riat Sh'ma:* Evening Service for Weekdays

Morning Service	Evening Service
	Baruch Adonai l'olam ... Baruch Attah Adonai, haMelech ... v'al kol ma-asav (Bless the Lord forever ... Blessed are You, O Lord, the King ... and on all His works)

During the Evening Service for weekdays, a third *b'rachah* is recited after *K'riat Sh'ma*. This third *b'rachah* is *Baruch Adonai l'olam* (Bless the Lord forever). It consists of eighteen sentences and was composed at the time when the evening *Amidah* was optional; this prayer could therefore take the place of the *Amidah*. However, this prayer is clearly inappropriate for *Shabbat* and Festivals because the *Amidah* for *Shabbat* and Festivals consists of seven and not eighteen *b'rachot*. It ends with the phrase *Baruch Attah Adonai, haMelech ... v'al kol ma-asav* (Blessed are You, O Lord, the King ... and on all His works).

This concludes our discussion of *K'riat Sh'ma.*

For the Maven

In Talmudic times, many Babylonian rulers would not allow synagogues inside their towns; synagogues had to be built in the fields. However, it was dangerous to walk alone at night outside the towns. Thus, one reason why this prayer was originally included in the service was to give late-comers, who had put in a long day's work, the time to complete their prayers. They could then walk back to the town in safety together with the rest of the congregation. On Saturday night, however, there was no need for this. Thus, the prayer was omitted on Saturday night; in some liturgies it is omitted on Saturday night to this day.

In other liturgies (such as the *Sephardi* liturgy and the *Ashkenazi* liturgy in Israel), the prayer is omitted because the authorities in Israel had declared that the *Amidah* of the Evening Service was compulsory; therefore, this prayer was not needed.

More for the Maven

As has previously been pointed out, traditionally speech is not permitted in the middle of a *b'rachah*. Because a Series Form *b'rachah* is essentially one single large *b'rachah,* this means that speech is not allowed from the word *Ba-r'chu* until the words *v'al Y'rushalayim*. In particular, the response *Baruch Hu uvaruch Sh'mo* (Blessed be He and blessed be His Name) is not made after the words *Baruch Attah Adonai* at the end of each *b'rachah* in the Series. The only response permitted is the obligatory *Amen* at the end of each *b'rachah.*

9
The Structure of Commonly Occurring Components

In this chapter we examine various components that are found in a number of different services. These components include *Havdalah, Kiddush, K'dushah, Aleinu,* and *Ashrei.*

We begin with *Havdalah,* although it might seem more natural to start with *Kiddush.* After all, *Kiddush* ushers in *Shabbat* on Friday evening, whereas *Havdalah* ushers out *Shabbat* on Saturday night.

The reason we describe the structure of *Havdalah* first is that the *Kiddush* for a Festival that falls on Saturday evening includes two *Havdalah b'rachot.* By treating *Havdalah* first, we can explain the structure of those two *b'rachot* of *Kiddush* in terms of the material on *Havdalah.*

Havdalah

Havdalah was originally recited in the synagogue for those who could not afford to do it at home. The custom has persisted and to this day it is recited in the synagogue at the end of the service on *Motza-ei Shabbat* (the going out of the Sabbath), that is, on Saturday night, and on *Motza-ei Yom Tov* (the going out of the Festival), that is, on the night following the Festival. It is also recited on returning home from the synagogue on both of these occasions.

[*Motza-ei Shabbat* only; omitted in the synagogue] Biblical verses *Hinei El y'shu-ati* ... (Behold, God is my salvation ...)
B'rachah over wine ... *Borei p'ri hagafen* (... Who creates the fruit of the vine)
[*Motza-ei Shabbat* only] *B'rachah* over spices ... *Borei minei v'samim* (... Who creates various kinds of spices)
[*Motza-ei Shabbat* only] *B'rachah* over braided candle with two or more wicks ... *Borei m'orei ha-esh* (... Who creates the lights of the fire)
Long Form *Havdalah b'rachah* ... *Hamavdil bein kodesh l'chol* (... Who distinguishes between the sacred and the secular)

We now examine the structure of each component in more detail.

Biblical Verses

[*Motza-ei Shabbat* only; omitted in the synagogue] *Hinei El y'shu-ati* ... *uvShem Adonai ekra* (Behold, God is my salvation ... and I shall call on the Name of the Lord)

In the *Ashkenazi* liturgy, when *Havdalah* is said in the home on Saturday night, it is preceded by eight biblical verses, namely, Isaiah 12:2–3; Psalms 3:9, 46:12, 84:13, 20:10; Esther 8:16; and Psalm 116:13. These verses were supposed to bring good fortune in the coming week.

First *Havdalah B'rachah*

[Over wine or grape juice] *Baruch Attah Adonai Eloheinu Melech ha-olam, Borei p'ri hagafen* (Blessed are You, O Lord our God, King of the universe, Who creates the fruit of the vine)

The first Short Form *b'rachah,* which ends with the phrase *Borei p'ri hagafen* (Who creates the fruit of the vine), is said over wine (or grape juice). If wine is not available, a liquid other than water is substituted. In this case, the *b'rachah* that ends *Shehakol niyeh bidvaro* (by Whose word all things come into being) is said; see page 115.

Second *Havdalah B'rachah*

[*Motza-ei Shabbat* only]

[Over spices] *Baruch Attah Adonai Eloheinu Melech ha-olam, Borei minei v'samim* (Blessed are You, O Lord our God, King of the universe, Who creates various kinds of spices)

Next, but only on *Motza-ei Shabbat* (Saturday night), the Short Form *b'rachah* ending *Borei minei v'samim* (Who creates various kinds of spices) is recited, after which the contents of the spice box are smelled.

For the Maven

A number of reasons have been put forward for the spices. One suggestion is that a Jew is accompanied by a *n'shamah y'terah* (additional soul) on *Shabbat* and smelling the spices reinvigorates the individual as the additional soul leaves at the start of the work week. Another is that the fires of *G'hinnom* (vaguely, hell) die down over *Shabbat.* As the week starts, the souls of sinners are tormented again and the pain of knowing this is eased by the smell of the spices.

Third *Havdalah B'rachah*

[*Motza-ei Shabbat* only]

[Over braided candle with two or more wicks] *Baruch Attah Adonai Elo-heinu Melech ha-olam, Borei m'orei ha-esh* (Blessed are You, O Lord our God, King of the universe, Who creates the lights of the fire)

The third Short Form *b'rachah* is said over a braided, multiwick *Havdalah* candle (or two candles with their flames touching). The *b'rachah* ends with the phrase *Borei m'orei ha-esh* (Who creates the lights of the fire).

This *b'rachah* is said on *Motza-ei Shabbat* (Saturday night). It is also said on *Motza-ei Yom Kippur* (the night following Yom Kippur), but traditionally only if the candle can be kindled from a flame that has burned throughout Yom Kippur.

For the Maven

Not only is there uncertainty over the reason for the spices, but also for the candle. One possible explanation is that it indicates that *Shabbat* is now over and work (includ-ing lighting a fire, expressly prohibited in Exodus 35:3) may now commence. A multi-wick candle is used because the *b'rachah* uses the plural form, *m'orei ha-esh* (lights of the fire).

Fourth *Havdalah B'rachah*

> *Baruch Attah Adonai Eloheinu Melech ha-olam, Hamavdil bein kodesh l'chol* ... *Baruch Attah Adonai, Hamavdil bein kodesh l'chol* (Blessed are You, O Lord our God, King of the universe, Who distinguishes between the sacred and the secular ... Blessed are You, O Lord, Who distinguishes between the sacred and the secular)

Finally, there is a Long Form *b'rachah,* the *Havdalah b'rachah* itself. It ends with the words *Baruch Attah Adonai, Hamavdil bein kodesh l'chol* (Blessed are You, O Lord, Who distinguishes between the sacred and the secular).

For the Maven

In order to remember the order of the four *b'rachot,* the mnemonic *YiBaNeH* (He will build) is used. It is constructed from the initial letters of the words *Yayin* (wine), *B'samim* (spices), *Ner* (candle), and *Havdalah* (separation).

More For the Maven

When Tish-ah b'Av falls on Saturday night, *Havdalah* is split into two pieces. On Saturday night only the *b'rachah* over the candle is recited. Then, at the conclusion of the Fast (on Sunday night), the *b'rachah* over wine and the final Long Form *b'rachah* are recited; the *b'rachah* over the spices is omitted because it is said exclusively on Saturday night.

Kiddush

Kiddush is recited over wine, on *Shabbat* and Festivals. The word is derived from the root *kof-dalet-shin* (K-D-SH), meaning "holy." Other words in the *Siddur* derived from this root include *Kadosh, K'dushah, Kiddush,* and *Kiddushin.*

Term	Meaning	Comment
Kaddish	Sanctification	Group of five similar prayers (see page 123)
Kadosh	Holy	Word occurs frequently in the *Siddur*
K'dushah	Holiness	Prayer inserted during the repetition of the *Amidah* (see page 119)
Kiddush	Sanctification	Prayer recited over wine on *Shabbat*, evening and morning, in the synagogue and at home; the topic of this section
Kiddushin	Sanctities	A term for betrothal (marriage)

One form of the *Kiddush* is recited before the evening meal on *Shabbat* and Festivals and another before the midday meal the next day. In addition, in the *Ashkenazi* liturgy outside Israel, the evening version is recited in the synagogue toward the end of the Evening Service with the initial biblical verses omitted.

Evening *Kiddush* for *Shabbat*	Evening *Kiddush* for Festivals (including Festivals occurring on *Shabbat*)	Morning *Kiddush* for *Shabbat* and/or Festivals
[Omitted in the synagogue] Biblical verses	[On *Shabbat* only, omitted in the synagogue] Biblical verses	Biblical verses relating to *Shabbat* and/or the Festival
B'rachah over wine or bread		*B'rachah* over wine, other liquid, or bread
Long Form *b'rachah* sanctifying *Shabbat*	Long Form *b'rachah* sanctifying [*Shabbat* and] the Festival	—
—	[Saturday night only] Two *Havdalah b'rachot*	
	[On Sukkot] *B'rachah* on dwelling in the *Sukkah*	
	[Omitted on last two nights of Pesach] *Shehecheyanu*	

We now examine each of these components.

For the Maven

The morning *Kiddush* was introduced later than the evening *Kiddush* and is considered to be of lesser importance. The morning *Kiddush* is accordingly called *Kiddusha Rabba* (The Great *Kiddush*)—who says that the sages had no sense of humor?

Biblical Verses

[Friday evening, omitted in Evening Service]

Va-y'hi erev va-y'hi voker yom hashishi. Va-y'chulu hashamayim v'ha-aretz ... asher bara Elohim la-asot (And it was evening and it was morning on the sixth day. Thus the heavens and the earth were finished ... which God had created)

[*Shabbat* morning]

V'sha-m'ru Vnei Yisra-el et haShabbat ... uva-yom ha-sh'vi-i shavat vayin-afash (The Children of Israel shall keep the Sabbath ... and on the seventh day He ceased from work and rested)

Zachor et yom haShabbat l'ko-d'sho ... Al ken berach Adonai et yom haShabbat va-y'kad'sheihu (Remember the Sabbath day to keep it holy ... Accordingly God blessed the Sabbath day and sanctified it)

[Festival morning]

Eleh mo-adei Adonai ... b'mo-adatam (These are the Festivals of the Lord ... at their appointed times)

Va-y'daber Moshe et mo-adei Adonai el Bnei Yisra-el (Moses announced the Festivals of the Lord to the Children of Israel)

[Rosh haShanah morning]

Tiku vachodesh shofar ... mishpat Leilohei Ya-akov (Sound the *shofar* on the new moon ... an ordinance for the God of Jacob)

On Friday evening, four verses explaining *Shabbat* are given; God created the world in six days and rested on the seventh day, *Shabbat*. These verses, Genesis 1:31–2:3, are omitted from the Evening Service because the last three verses, beginning *Va-y'chulu*, have just been recited (page 215).

On *Shabbat* morning, Exodus 31:16–17, beginning *V'sha-m'ru Vnei Yisra-el* (The Children of Israel shall keep the Sabbath) is said, followed by Exodus 20:8–11. The latter is the fourth commandment, beginning *Zachor et yom haShabbat l'ko-d'sho* (Remember the Sabbath day to keep it holy). In some liturgies only the last verse, beginning *Al ken berach Adonai* (Accordingly God blessed), is recited; in others, only one of the two biblical passages is said.

Two verses are recited on Festival mornings, Leviticus 23:4, beginning *Eleh mo-adei Adonai* (These are the Festivals of the Lord) and Leviticus 23:44, beginning *Va-y'daber Moshe* (Moses announced).

On Rosh haShanah morning, two additional verses (Ps. 81:4–5) are said, beginning *Tiku vachodesh shofar* (Sound the *shofar* on the new moon).

B'rachah over Wine, Other Liquids, or Bread

> [Over wine or grape juice]
>
> *Baruch Attah Adonai Eloheinu Melech ha-olam, Borei p'ri hagafen* (Blessed are You, O Lord our God, King of the universe, Who creates the fruit of the vine)

> [Over other alcoholic beverages or the "national drink"]
>
> *Baruch Attah Adonai Eloheinu Melech ha-olam, Shehakol niyeh bidvaro* (Blessed are You, O Lord our God, King of the universe, by Whose word all things come into being)

> [Over bread]
>
> *Baruch Attah Adonai Eloheinu Melech ha-olam, Hamotzi lechem min ha-aretz* (Blessed are You, O Lord our God, King of the universe, Who brings forth bread from the earth)

In the evening, *Kiddush* is said over wine (or grape juice); if wine is not available, two loaves of bread may be substituted.

In the morning, however, any alcoholic beverage or the "national drink" may be substituted for wine (or bread).

For the Maven

The custom of reciting *Kiddush* as part of the Friday Evening Service arose in Eastern Europe because travelers were lodged and fed at the synagogue on *Shabbat*. In order for them to hear *Kiddush* as required before their evening meal, it was incorporated into the service itself. Even though the reason for the custom no longer exists, the custom itself persists in the *Ashkenazi* liturgy. That is also why *Kiddush* is not part of the *Sephardi* Friday Evening Service, nor is it part of the service in Israel.

Long Form *B'rachah*

Next comes the body of the *Kiddush*, a Long Form *b'rachah* sanctifying the Sabbath and/or Festival.

[On *Shabbat*]

Baruch Attah Adonai Eloheinu Melech ha-olam, Asher kid'shanu b'mitzvotav ... Baruch Attah Adonai, M'kadesh haShabbat (Blessed are You, O Lord our God, King of the universe, Who has sanctified us with His commandments ... Blessed are You, O Lord, Who sanctifies the Sabbath)

[On *Chagim*, including *Chagim* occurring on *Shabbat*]

Baruch Attah Adonai Eloheinu Melech ha-olam, Asher bachar banu mikol am ... Baruch Attah Adonai, M'kadesh [haShabbat v'] Yisra-el v'ha-z'manim (Blessed are You, O Lord our God, King of the universe, Who has chosen us from all nations ... Blessed are You, O Lord, Who sanctifies [the Sabbath and] Israel and the Festivals)

[On Rosh haShanah, including on *Shabbat*]

Baruch Attah Adonai Eloheinu Melech ha-olam, Asher bachar banu mikol am ... Baruch Attah Adonai, M'kadesh [haShabbat v'] Yisra-el v'Yom haZikaron (Blessed are You, O Lord our God, King of the universe, Who has chosen us from all nations ... Blessed are You, O Lord, Who sanctifies [the Sabbath and] Israel and the Day of Remembrance)

The long *b'rachah* for *Shabbat* explains that *Shabbat* was given to us *zecher litziat Mitzraim* (as a remembrance of the Exodus from Egypt), that is, the Exodus gave us the freedom to observe *Shabbat*. The long *b'rachah* for each Festival expresses the same thought, together with a reason for the specific Festival.

This concludes the discussion of the *Kiddush* on *Shabbat*. On Festivals, however, there are additional components.

Havdalah B'rachot

On Saturday evening, two *Havdalah b'rachot* are added to the Festival *Kiddush*.

Baruch Attah Adonai Eloheinu Melech ha-olam, Borei m'orei ha-esh (Blessed are You, O Lord our God, King of the universe, Who creates the lights of the fire)
Baruch Attah Adonai Eloheinu Melech ha-olam, Hamavdil bein kodesh l'chol ... Baruch Attah Adonai, Hamavdil bein kodesh l'kodesh (Blessed are You, O Lord our God, King of the universe, Who distinguishes between the sacred and the secular ... Blessed are You, O Lord, Who distinguishes between holiness [of the Sabbath] and holiness [of the Festival])

When a Festival falls on a Saturday night, the *b'rachah* over lights is recited as on a weekday Saturday night. However, the paragraph that follows is significantly different from the weekday version.

The Saturday night *Havdalah* (page 111) emphasizes the difference between *Shabbat* and weekdays, and concludes with the words *Hamavdil bein kodesh l'chol* (Who distinguishes between the holy and the **secular**). In the Festival *Kiddush*, however, a verse is added that refers to the difference between the [greater] holiness of the Sabbath and the [lesser] holiness of the Festival. This *b'rachah* concludes with the words *Hamavdil bein kodesh l'kodesh* (Who distinguishes between holiness [of the Sabbath] and **holiness** [of the Festival]).

Shehecheyanu

[On Sukkot only]
Baruch Attah Adonai Eloheinu Melech ha-olam, Asher kid'shanu b'mitzvotav, v'tzivanu leishev baSukkah (Blessed are You, O Lord our God, King of the universe, Who has sanctified us with His commandments, and has commanded us to dwell in the *Sukkah*)
[Omitted on last two nights of Pesach]
Baruch Attah Adonai Eloheinu Melech ha-olam, Shehecheyanu, v'kiy'manu, v'higianu la-z'man hazeh (Blessed are You, O Lord our God, King of the universe, Who has kept us alive, sustained us, and brought us to this season)

On Sukkot, the *b'rachah* on dwelling in the *Sukkah* is recited. It has the structure of a *Mitzvah* Form *b'rachah* (page 25).

On Festivals, the *b'rachah Shehecheyanu* (Who has kept us alive) is recited. This *b'rachah* is said, inter alia, on all seasonal events, such as eating a seasonal fruit for the first time that year.

For the Maven

Shehecheyanu is omitted on the last two days of Pesach because the last two days are not considered to be a separate Festival (or season), unlike *Sh'mini Atzeret* and *Simchat Torah.*

Shehecheyanu is said after *leishev baSukkah* on the first night of Sukkot because the *Shehecheyanu* also applies to saying *leishev baSukkah* for the first time that year. However, *leishev baSukkah* is said each time a meal is eaten in the *Sukkah*. On these subsequent occasions, no *Shehecheyanu* is said. For this reason, on the second night, *leishev baSukkah* follows *Shehecheyanu.*

More For the Maven

When a Festival occurs on Saturday night, the *Kiddush* consists of five components, (as shown on page 113). A mnemonic is used to help remember the order of the five components, as depicted in the table below:

B'rachah over wine	*Yayin* (wine)
Long Form *b'rachah* sanctifying the Festival	*Kiddush*
Two *Havdalah b'rachot*	*Ner* (candle) *Havdalah*
Shehecheyanu	*Z'man* (season)

The initial letters of *Yayin, Kiddush, Ner, Havdalah,* and *Z'man* yield the mnemonic *YaKN'HaZ.*

In some medieval illustrated manuscripts of *Haggadah shel Pesach,* the page on which the *Kiddush* appears has a picture of a hunter and a hare. The reason is that the mnemonic *YaKN'HaZ* is somewhat similar to the German phrase *Jagen den Hasen* (hunting the hare).

K'dushah

The essence of every *K'dushah* is two verses describing prophetic theophanies (visions of God), namely, those of Isaiah and Ezekiel. In Isaiah 6:3, angels call to one another and praise God beginning *Kadosh, Kadosh, Kadosh* (Holy, Holy, Holy). In Ezekiel 3:12, Ezekiel states that he heard a great voice saying *Baruch k'vod Adonai mi-m'komo* (Blessed be the glory of the Lord from His place). The remaining parts of the *K'dushah* are built around these two expressions of the holiness of God.

There are various forms of *K'dushah*. For example, *K'dushah d'Yotzer* is part of the Morning Service (page 95) and *K'dushah d'Sidra* (page 132) is in the weekday Morning Service, the Afternoon Service on *Shabbat*, and the Evening Service on Saturday night. However, the term "*K'dushah*" is most commonly associated with *K'dushah d'Amidah,* the material that replaces the third *b'rachah* when the *Amidah* is repeated by the Reader. Here, the congregation and Reader join in publicly proclaiming the holiness of God.

The three possible formats are shown in the next diagram (which reflects the *Ashkenazi* liturgy).

The Structure of the *K'dushah*

Here are the three forms of the *K'dushah* when the *Amidah* is repeated by the Reader:

Additional Service for *Shabbat* and Festivals	Morning Service for *Shabbat* and Festivals	All other Morning, Additional, and Afternoon Services
Na-aritz'cha v'nakdish'cha ... (We revere and sanctify You ...)	*N'kadesh et Shimcha ba-olam* ... (We sanctify Your Name in this world ...)	
Kadosh, Kadosh, Kadosh ... (Holy, Holy, Holy ...)		
K'vodo malei olam ... (His holiness fills the world ...)	*Az b'kol ra-ash gadol* ... (Then with a great rushing noise ...)	*L'umatam baruch yomeru* (They say to one another, Blessed)
Baruch k'vod Adonai mi-m'komo (Blessed be the glory of the Lord from His place)		
Mi-m'komo ... (From His place ...)	*Mi-m'komcha* ... (From Your place ...)	—
Sh'ma Yisra-el ... (Hear, O Israel ...)	—	
Hu Eloheinu (He is our God ...)		
Ani Adonai Eloheichem (I am the Lord your God)		
[Festivals only] *Adir Adirenu* ... (Mighty is our Mighty one ...)		
Uvdivrei kod-sh'cha katuv lemor (and in Your holy writings it is written)		*Uvdivrei kod-sh'cha katuv lemor* (and in Your holy writings it is written)
Yimloch Adonai l'olam ... (The Lord will live forever ...)		
L'dor vador ... *ha-El hakadosh* (From generation to generation ... the holy God)		

(In some liturgies, the *K'dushah* for Festivals is recited during the Additional Service on *Hoshana Rabbah*).

For the Maven

The *K'dushah* for *Musaf* contains two surprising elements, namely, the beginning of the first paragraph of the *Sh'ma*, that is, *Sh'ma Yisra-el, Adonai Eloheinu, Adonai Echad* (Hear, O Israel, the Lord is our God, the Lord is One), and the end of the last paragraph of the *Sh'ma*, namely, *Ani Adonai Eloheichem* (I am the Lord, your God). During the fifth century C.E., the Jews of Babylonia were forbidden to recite the *Sh'ma*. Government spies used to attend services to ensure that the decree was obeyed. However, the spies usually left before the end of the lengthy *Shabbat* service, so the Reader would then insert the *Sh'ma*, in abbreviated form, into the *K'dushah* for *Musaf*, where it has stayed ever since.

Introductory Sentence

The first part of the *K'dushah* is an introductory sentence that invites the congregation to recite the *K'dushah*.

Additional Service for *Shabbat* and Festivals	Morning Service for *Shabbat* and Festivals	All other Morning, Additional, and Afternoon Services
Na-aritz'cha v'nakdish'cha ... (We revere and sanctify You ...)	*N'kadesh et Shimcha ba-olam* ... (We sanctify Your Name in this world ...)	

In other liturgies, these introductory sentences can be vastly different. For example, the *K'dushah* for the Additional Service for *Shabbat* and Festivals in the *Sephardi* and Chassidic liturgies begins *Keter yitnu l'Cha* (A crown will be given to You) and the rest of the sentence bears little in common with its *Ashkenazi* counterpart.

For the Maven

These introductory sentences were originally recited by the Reader, inviting the congregation to join in the *K'dushah*. In many liturgies, however, these (and the other sentences of the *kedushah*) are now first recited by the congregation and then repeated by the Reader. In other liturgies, the *K'dushah* is recited responsively. But even here there can be major differences; parts said by the congregation in some liturgies may be said by the Reader in others.

Components of the *K'dushah*

Many of the components of the *K'dushah* are biblical verses or parts of verses, as shown in the diagram below:

Kadosh, Kadosh, Kadosh ... (Holy, Holy, Holy ...)	Isaiah 6:3
Baruch k'vod Adonai mi-m'komo (Blessed be the glory of the Lord from His place)	Ezekiel 3:12
Sh'ma Yisra-el ... (Hear, O Israel ...)	Deuteronomy 6:4
Li-h'yot lachem Leilohim (to be your God)	Numbers 15:41
Ani Adonai Eloheichem (I am the Lord your God)	Numbers 15:41
Adir Adirenu ... (Mighty is our Mighty one ...)	Psalm 8:10, Zechariah 14:9
Yimloch Adonai l'olam ... (The Lord will live forever ...)	Psalm 146:10

The other parts of the *K'dushah* can be viewed as the structure into which these verses are embedded.

This concludes our discussion of the *K'dushah*. We now consider the various forms of the *Kaddish*.

The Five Forms of the *Kaddish*

The name *Kaddish* literally means "sanctification." The theme of the *Kaddish* is effusive praise of God and the hope that He will speedily establish His kingdom on earth. The vast majority of the words of the *Kaddish* are in Aramaic, not Hebrew. Aramaic was the everyday language of the Jewish people from roughly 600 B.C.E. to 700 C.E. This is why both the Babylonian *Talmud* and the Jerusalem *Talmud* were written in Aramaic; in Talmudic times, Aramaic was the language that everyone spoke. In order to recite the *Kaddish*, there must be a *minyan* (quorum of ten). Thus, the *Kaddish* is an expression of communal, rather than individual, feelings. The most important part of the *Kaddish* is therefore the congregational response after the first paragraph.

Kaddish Shalem

The prayer *Kaddish Shalem* (full or complete *Kaddish*) is recited at the end of the last major component of every service. In almost all cases, this is the *Amidah* (but see For the Maven on the next page).

Paragraph 1	*Yitgadal v'yitkadash Sh'mei rabba* ... (May His great Name be magnified and sanctified ...)
Congregational response	*Y'hei Sh'mei rabba m'varach, l'alam ulal'mei al'maya* (May His great Name be blessed forever and ever)
Paragraph 2	*Yitbarach v'yishtabach* ... (Blessed and praised ...)
Paragraph 3	*Titkabel tz'lot'hon uva-ut'hon* ... (May the prayers and supplications be accepted ...)
Paragraph 4	*Y'hei sh'lamah rabba* ... (May there be abundant peace ...)
Paragraph 5	*Oseh shalom bimromav* ... (He Who makes peace in His celestial heights ...)

Kaddish Shalem consists of five paragraphs plus a congregational response. The first paragraph begins *Yitgadal v'yitkadash Sh'mei rabba* (May His great Name be magnified and sanctified). The theme of this paragraph is the same as that of the *Kaddish* as a whole, namely, praise of God and the hope of His speedily establishing His kingdom on earth. When the Reader reaches the end of this paragraph, the congregation responds *Y'hei Sh'mei rabba m'varach, l'alam ulal'mei al'maya* (May His great Name be blessed forever and ever). The Reader repeats this response and then continues with the second paragraph which begins *Yitbarach v'yishtabach* (Blessed and praised). The contents of this paragraph is all praises.

The wording of this second paragraph changes slightly between Rosh haShanah and Yom Kippur. Specifically, the phrase *l'ela min kol bir-chata* (beyond all blessings) is replaced by *l'ela u-l'ela mikol bir-chata* [in some traditions, *l'ela l'ela min kol bir-chata*] (utterly beyond all blessings).

The third paragraph, beginning *Titkabel tz'lot'hon uva-ut'hon* (May the prayers and supplications be accepted), is a plea that our prayers be accepted. Finally, both the fourth paragraph, *Y'hei sh'lamah rabba* (May there be abundant peace), and the fifth paragraph, *Oseh shalom bimromav* (He Who makes peace in His celestial heights), are similar prayers for peace. One difference is that the fifth paragraph is in Hebrew, whereas the fourth paragraph, like the rest of *Kaddish Shalem,* is in Aramaic.

For the Maven

It is not always true that *Kaddish Shalem* is recited after the *Amidah.* On *Chagim,* for example, when *Hallel* is said during *Shacharit* after the *Amidah, Kaddish Shalem* follows *Hallel,* not the *Amidah,* because *Hallel* is the last major component. Also, during *Shacharit l'Chol* (Morning Service for weekdays), *Kaddish Shalem* follows the prayer *Uva l'Tziyon go-el* (A redeemer shall come unto Zion); the *Amidah* occurs earlier in the service and is followed by *Tachanun* and *Chatzi Kaddish.* Also, during *Minchah l'Chol* (Afternoon Service for weekdays), the order of the prayers is the *Amidah,* then *Tachanun* (if said), and *Kaddish Shalem* after that.

The Forms of the *Kaddish*

There are five different forms of the *Kaddish*, namely, *Kaddish Shalem* (complete *Kaddish*), *Chatzi Kaddish* (half *Kaddish*), *Kaddish d'Rabbanan* (*Kaddish* of the rabbis), *Kaddish Yatom* (mourner's *Kaddish*), and *Kaddish l'It-chad'ta* (renewal *Kaddish*).

Form	Translation	When said
Kaddish Shalem	Complete *Kaddish*	At the end of the last major component of every service
Chatzi Kaddish	Half *Kaddish*	Delimits certain major components of the service
Kaddish d'Rabbanan	*Kaddish* of the rabbis	After studying a rabbinic text
Kaddish Yatom	Mourner's *Kaddish*	By mourners at the end of the service, and also after certain psalms
Kaddish l'It-chad'ta	Renewal *Kaddish*	At the graveside after a burial, and also at a *siyum* (a study session at which a tractate of the *Talmud* is completed)

However, all five forms have the same structure. To see this, we examine the differences between the structure of *Kaddish Shalem* that we have already described and the other four forms of the *Kaddish*.

Comparison of the Five Forms of the *Kaddish*

The diagram below shows how the other four forms of the *Kaddish* differ from *Kaddish Shalem*.

	Chatzi Kaddish (half *Kaddish*)	*Kaddish d'Rabbanan* (*Kaddish* of the rabbis)	*Kaddish Yatom* (mourner's *Kaddish*)	*Kaddish l'It-chad'ta* (renewal *Kaddish*)
Paragraph 1	Same as in *Kaddish Shalem*			Drastically changed from *Kaddish Shalem*
Congregational response	Same as in *Kaddish Shalem*			
Paragraph 2	Same as in *Kaddish Shalem*			
Paragraph 3	(Omitted)	Replaced by prayer for rabbinic scholars	(Omitted)	
Paragraph 4	(Omitted)	Same as in *Kaddish Shalem*		
Paragraph 5	(Omitted)	One word added, otherwise same as in *Kaddish Shalem*	Same as in *Kaddish Shalem*	

We now consider each of these in turn.

Chatzi Kaddish

As previously mentioned, *Kaddish Shalem* essentially delimits the end of the last major component in the service. *Chatzi Kaddish* delimits other major components of the service. During the Morning Service, *Chatzi Kaddish* is said before *K'riat Sh'ma* (or more precisely, *Ba-r'chu*), after the *Amidah* (or *Tachanun*, if applicable; see page 139) and after the *Torah* reading. During the Afternoon, Evening, and Additional Services, *Chatzi Kaddish* is said before the *Amidah*.

Paragraph 1	Same as in *Kaddish Shalem*
Congregational response	Same as in *Kaddish Shalem*
Paragraph 2	Same as in *Kaddish Shalem*
Paragraph 3	(Omitted)
Paragraph 4	(Omitted)
Paragraph 5	(Omitted)

The name *Chatzi Kaddish* (half *Kaddish*) is extremely appropriate because, as shown in the diagram, it consists of the first half of *Kaddish Shalem*.

Kaddish d'Rabbanan

Kaddish d'Rabbanan (*Kaddish* of the rabbis) is recited after studying a rabbinic text, that is, a talmudic or midrashic passage or the like. Unlike *Kaddish Yatom* (mourner's *Kaddish*), it can be recited by anyone, not just a mourner; the only restriction is that a *minyan* be present. The preliminary part of the Morning Service contains many rabbinic texts and these are followed by the recitation of *Kaddish d'Rabbanan*. In addition, two groups of rabbinic texts are read within the context of the *Shabbat* services. The last part of *Kabbalat Shabbat* (welcoming the Sabbath, that is, the portion of the Evening Service for *Shabbat* that precedes *Ba-r'chu*) consists of a chapter from the *Mishnah*. It begins *Bameh madlikin* (With what should we light [the Sabbath light]). It is followed by a paragraph from the *Talmud, Amar Rabi Elazar* (Rabbi Elazar said). After this, *Kaddish d'Rabbanan* is recited.

Similarly, toward the end of the Additional service for *Shabbat*, paragraphs are read from the *Talmud* and the *Mishnah*. The first paragraph begins *Pitum ha-k'toret* (The composition of the incense). Again, these rabbinic passages are followed by *Kaddish d'Rabbanan*.

Paragraph 1	Same as in *Kaddish Shalem*
Congregational response	Same as in *Kaddish Shalem*
Paragraph 2	Same as in *Kaddish Shalem*
Paragraph 3	Replaced by prayer for rabbinic scholars *Al Yisra-el v'al rabbanan* ... ([We pray] for Israel and for our teachers ...)
Paragraph 4	Same as in *Kaddish Shalem*
Paragraph 5	Word *b'rachamav* (in His compassion) added, otherwise same as in *Kaddish Shalem*

As shown in the table on page 127, *Kaddish d'Rabbanan* is identical to *Kaddish Shalem* except for the third paragraph, beginning *Al Yisra-el v'al rabbanan* ([We pray] for Israel and for our teachers) and the addition of the word *b'rachamav* (in His compassion) in the last paragraph.

Kaddish Yatom

Kaddish Yatom (mourner's *Kaddish*) is recited by mourners at the end of the service and also after certain psalms. Mourners recite this *Kaddish* during the eleven months after a parent's death and on the anniversary of their death (*Yahrzeit* in Yiddish). *Kaddish Yatom* is recited for thirty days in the case of a spouse, sibling, or child.

Paragraph 1	Same as in *Kaddish Shalem*
Congregational response	Same as in *Kaddish Shalem*
Paragraph 2	Same as in *Kaddish Shalem*
Paragraph 3	(Omitted)
Paragraph 4	Same as in *Kaddish Shalem*
Paragraph 5	Same as in *Kaddish Shalem*

The structure of *Kaddish Yatom,* as shown above, is identical to that of *Kaddish Shalem,* except that the third paragraph of *Kaddish Shalem, Titkabel tz'lot'hon uva-ut'hon* (May the prayers and supplications be accepted), is omitted in *Kaddish Yatom.* This is because the "prayers and supplications" of the third paragraph of *Kaddish Shalem* refer to the contents of the *Amidah* and this is inappropriate for *Kaddish Yatom.*

For the Maven

The reason that *Kaddish Yatom* is recited for eleven months rather than a full year after the death of a parent lies in the belief, which arose during the thirteenth century C.E. in Germany, that the recitation of the *Kaddish* saves the dead from the sufferings of *G'hinnom* (vaguely, hell). However, according to this belief, only the most wicked people spend twelve months in *G'hinnom.* Out of respect to one's own parents, *Kaddish Yatom* is therefore recited for only eleven months.

Kaddish l'It-chad'ta

Kaddish l'It-chad'ta (renewal *Kaddish*) is a version of *Kaddish Yatom* (mourner's *Kaddish*) that is recited at the graveside after a burial. For this reason it is sometimes referred to in English as the "Burial *Kaddish*." It is also recited at a *siyum* (a study session at which a tractate of the *Talmud* is completed).

Paragraph 1	Drastically changed from *Kaddish Shalem*
Congregational response	Same as in *Kaddish Shalem*
Paragraph 2	Same as in *Kaddish Shalem*
Paragraph 3	(Omitted)
Paragraph 4	Same as in *Kaddish Shalem*
Paragraph 5	Same as in *Kaddish Shalem*

The first paragraph begins *Yitgadal v'yitkadash Sh'mei rabba b'al'mah d'Hu atid l'it-chad'ta* (May His great Name be magnified and sanctified throughout the world which He will renew). It then speaks of reviving the dead and rebuilding Jerusalem. (For this reason, *Sephardi* Jews recite *Kaddish l'It-chad'ta* on Tish-ah b'Av.) Other than this first paragraph, the rest of *Kaddish l'It-chad'ta* is identical to *Kaddish Yatom*.

This concludes our discussion of the various forms of the *Kaddish* prayer. We now examine other components that are found in more than one part of the *Siddur*.

Uva l'Tziyon/V'Attah Kadosh

The prayer *Uva l'Tziyon* is recited during the weekday Morning Service, the Afternoon Service for *Shabbat* and Festivals, and (with the exception of the first two biblical verses) on *Motza-ei Shabbat* (the Evening Service on Saturday night), and during the Evening Service on Purim.

Uva l'Tziyon go-el ... me-attah v'ad olam (A redeemer will come unto Zion ... from now and forever)
V'Attah kadosh yoshev t'hilot Yisra-el ... (And You are holy, enthroned on the praises of Israel ...)
... Kadosh, Kadosh, Kadosh ... Baruch k'vod Adonai mi-m'komo ... Adonai yimloch l'olam va-ed ... (... Holy, Holy, Holy ... Blessed be the glory of the Lord from His place ... The Lord will reign for ever and ever ...)
... yagdil Torah v'yadir (... to make the Torah great and glorious)

Uva l'Tziyon is a collection of biblical passages so that by reading them all worshippers can participate in the study of *Torah*. *Uva l'Tziyon* is sometimes called *K'dushah d'Sidra* (the order of *K'dushah*) because it incorporates a *K'dushah* (page 119). One feature that is unique to this *K'dushah* is that each of the three passages in the third box is followed by a translation of that passage in Aramaic.

As previously mentioned, when this prayer is recited during the Evening Service (on Saturday night and on Purim), the first two verses are omitted; the prayer then begins *V'Attah kadosh* (And You are holy).

For the Maven

The first two verses of *Uva l'Tziyon go-el* are Isaiah 59:20–21. They are not recited at night because they refer to redemption; traditionally, redemption does not take place at night. They are also omitted on *Tish-a b'Av* and in a house of mourning.

Aleinu

The closing prayer, *Aleinu*, consists of two paragraphs, the first of which (in many editions of the *Siddur*) has a missing verse.

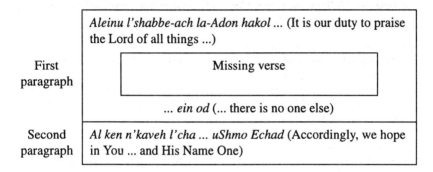

	Aleinu l'shabbe-ach la-Adon hakol ... (It is our duty to praise the Lord of all things ...)
First paragraph	Missing verse
	... *ein od* (... there is no one else)
Second paragraph	*Al ken n'kaveh l'cha* ... *uShmo Echad* (Accordingly, we hope in You ... and His Name One)

The first paragraph, beginning *Aleinu l'shabbe-ach la-Adon hakol* (It is our duty to praise the Lord of all things), praises God for having chosen the Jewish people who worship the One God rather than idols. In the second paragraph, beginning *Al ken n'kaveh l'cha* (Accordingly, we hope in You), we pray for the establishment of the Kingdom of God on earth and that all the inhabitants of the earth be united in worshipping the One God.

All but the final verse of *Aleinu*, beginning *V'ne-emar, v'hayah Adonai l'Melech al kol ha-aretz* (And it is said: The Lord will be King over all the earth) (Zech. 14:9) is taken from the *Malchuyot* section of the Rosh haShanah *Amidah* (see Chapter 18).

Missing Verse

The missing verse in the first paragraph was removed by Christian censors during the Middle Ages.

Missing verse
Shehem mishtachavim lahevel varik, umitpal'lim el el lo yoshia (For they bow down to vanity and emptiness, and pray to a god that cannot save)

Despite the fact that the verse is based on Isaiah 30:7 and 45:20 and, notwithstanding the fact that the verse in question (as well as *Aleinu* as a whole) was written before the Common Era, in 1400 a baptized Jew named Pesach Peter claimed that the verse slanders Christianity. He supported his contention by using *g'matria* (numerology), stating that the numerical value of *varik* (emptiness), that is, 316, is the same as that of *Yeshu*, the Hebrew name of Jesus.

Numerous attacks followed all over Europe and the censors forced the removal of the verse from most *Ashkenazi* editions of the *Siddur*. The verse has since been re-inserted in a number of recent *Siddurim*, especially in Israel. In some Diaspora editions (including the ArtScroll), the verse has been re-inserted, but in parentheses.

For the Maven

The word *rik* (emptiness) can also mean "spittle." As a result, the custom arose of spitting at that point of the service. This is the origin of the Yiddish expression *Er kummt tzum oysshpei-en* (he comes at the spitting), referring to someone who arrives at the service as late as the concluding *Aleinu* prayer.

More For the Maven

During the repetition of the *Malchuyot* portion of the *Amidah* on Rosh haShanah, the Ark is opened. The Reader starts to intone the first paragraph of *Aleinu* using a stirring melody (in the *Ashkenazi* liturgy). Suddenly the Ark is closed and immediately reopened. The reason for both the closing and the reopening is, once again, the censored verse. It is inappropriate for the Ark to be open when describing the actions of heathens, so the Ark was closed at that point. The custom of closing the Ark persisted even after the verse in question had been excised from the service. So when we reach the point in the service where the verse would be recited had it not been removed, we close the Ark. We then immediately reopen it; there is no need to wait until we have finished reciting that verse, because we don't recite it!

Tachanun

After the weekday *Amidah*, during the Morning and Afternoon Services, it is customary to recite a prayer known as *Tachanun* (supplication), a confession of sin and an entreaty for Divine aid. There are two versions of *Tachanun*. The short version is recited during the Afternoon Service and also during the Morning Service when the *Torah* is not read, that is, on Sunday, Tuesday, Wednesday, and Friday. The long version is said on Monday and Thursday mornings. We first examine the structure of the short version of *Tachanun*.

Short Version of *Tachanun*

On weekdays during the Afternoon Service and during the weekday Morning Service (except on Mondays and Thursdays), we say the short version of *Tachanun*.

Biblical verse
Vayomer David el Gad, tzar li m'od ... uvyad adam al epolah (David said to Gad, I am deeply troubled ... and do not let me fall into the hands of man)
Brief entreaty
Rachum v'chanun, chatati l'fanecha ... v'kabel tachanunai (O merciful and gracious God, I have sinned before You ... and accept my supplications)
Psalm 6:2–11
Adonai, al b'apcha tochicheni ... yevoshu raga (O Lord, do not punish me in Your anger ... be suddenly ashamed)
Four short prayers for protection
Shomer Yisra-el ... v'hoshi-enu (O Guardian of Israel ... and save us)
Prayer for forgiveness
Va-anachnu lo nedah mah na-aseh ... l'ma-an Sh'mecha (We do not know what to do ... for the sake of Your Name)

The short version starts with a biblical verse, namely, II Samuel 24:14, which begins *Vayomer David el Gad, tzar li m'od* (David said to Gad, I am deeply troubled). Then follows a brief entreaty, *Rachum v'chanun, chatati l'fanecha* (O merciful and gracious God, I have sinned before You). Next comes Psalm 6:2–11, beginning *Adonai, al b'apcha tochicheni* (O Lord, do not punish me in Your anger); in the *Sephardi* liturgy, Psalm 25 replaces Psalm 6. When *Tachanun* is recited in a room containing an Ark with a *Torah* scroll in it, this first part is recited with the forehead resting on the left arm (the right arm if *Tefillin* are worn on the left arm).

Next there are four short prayers for protection, beginning *Shomer Yisra-el* (Guardian of Israel), pleading that the Jewish People be saved from destruction. The short version of *Tachanun* is concluded with a prayer for forgiveness that begins *Va-anachnu lo nedah mah na-aseh* (We do not know what to do), which consists of biblical verses pleading for salvation and forgiveness from sin.

Long Version of *Tachanun*

On Monday and Thursday mornings, we recite the long version of *Tacha-nun*, which begins *V'Hu rachum, y'cha-per avon* (And He, being merciful, forgives iniquity). The long version of *Tachanun* is therefore sometimes referred to as "the long *V'Hu Rachum*" (even though there is no short *V'Hu Rachum*—the short version of the *Tachanun* does not contain these words).

Seven lengthy paragraphs of elegies and lamentations

V'Hu rachum, y'cha-per avon ... Adonai Echad (And He, being merciful, forgives iniquity ... the Lord is One)

> Biblical verse
>
> *Vayomer David el Gad, tzar li m'od ... uvyad adam al epo-lah* (David said to Gad, I am deeply troubled ... and do not let me fall into the hands of man)
>
> Brief entreaty
>
> *Rachum v'chanun, chatati l'fanecha ... v'kabel tachanunai* (O merciful and gracious God, I have sinned before You ... and accept my supplications)
>
> Psalm 6:2–11
>
> *Adonai, al b'apcha tochicheni ... yevoshu raga* (O Lord, do not punish me in Your anger ... be suddenly ashamed)

Responsive series of entreaties

Adonai Elohei Yisra-el ... hara l'amecha (Lord God of Israel ... the evil against Your people)

> Four short prayers for protection
>
> *Shomer Yisra-el ... v'hoshi-enu* (O Guardian of Israel ... and save us)
>
> Prayer for forgiveness
>
> *Va-anachnu lo nedah mah na-aseh ... l'ma-an Sh'mecha* (We do not know what to do ... for the sake of Your Name)

The five indented components are common to the short version of *Tacha-nun*. We next examine the two components unique to the long version of *Tachanun*.

Seven Lengthy Paragraphs of Elegies and Lamentations

> Seven lengthy paragraphs of elegies and lamentations
> *V'Hu rachum, y'cha-per avon ... Adonai Echad* (And He, being merciful, forgives iniquity ... the Lord is One)

The long version of *Tachanun* begins with seven extended paragraphs of elegies and lamentations listing the desperate straits of the Jewish people and pleading for an end to unwavering daily suffering. These paragraphs incorporate verses from the Bible, mainly from the Prophets and the Psalms.

These seven paragraphs are followed by the first three components of the short version of *Tachanun*, specifically, the biblical verse, brief entreaty, and Psalm 6:2–11 in the *Ashkenazi* liturgy (Psalm 25 in the *Sephardi* liturgy).

Responsive Series of Entreaties

> Responsive series of entreaties
> *Adonai Elohei Yisra-el ... hara l'amecha* (Lord God of Israel ... the evil against Your people)

Next come a series of entreaties, sometimes recited responsively, beginning *Adonai Elohei Yisra-el* (Lord God of Israel). The long version of *Tachanun* concludes with the remainder of the short version, as reflected in the diagram on the previous page.

For the Maven

In modern times, it has been suggested that the long *V'Hu Rachum* be dropped from the *Siddur*, on the grounds that the Jewish people are now no longer even remotely close to such dire circumstances. The unspeakable horrors of the Holocaust, however, tragically showed that this suggestion was premature. In *Siddur Sim Shalom,* however, the seven elegiac paragraphs have been somewhat shortened and Psalm 130 offered as an alternative to Psalm 6:2–11.

When *Tachanun* Is Not Said, and Why

Because of the intensely sorrowful nature of *Tachanun*, it is omitted from the service on *Shabbat* and Festivals; it is even omitted on Minor Festivals including *Chol haMo-ed, Rosh Chodesh,* Chanukah, *Tu b'Shvat,* Purim, *Shushan Purim, Purim Katan, Pesach Sheni, Yom ha-Atzma-ut, Lag ba-Omer, Yom Y'rushalayim,* and *Tu b'Av.* It is also omitted from the Afternoon Service preceding any of the above days. *Tachanun* is not recited during the entire month of *Nissan* (the month in which Pesach falls), the first eight days of the month of *Sivan* (Shavuot, the day on which the Ten Commandments were given, falls on the sixth and seventh of *Sivan*), the day before Rosh haShanah, and during the month of *Tishrei* from Yom Kippur until after Sukkot. *Tachanun* is also omitted in the presence of a newlywed during the first week after marriage, when a *Brit Milah* (ritual circumcision) is to take place later that day in the synagogue, or in the presence of one of the main participants (father, *Mohel,* or *Sandek*) in a *Brit Milah* to be held elsewhere.

Surprisingly enough, *Tachanun* is also not recited on Tish-ah b'Av. The Fast of Tish-ah b'Av is the saddest day of the Jewish calendar, the day on which both Temples were destroyed in Jerusalem and other national tragedies occurred. It would therefore seem highly appropriate to recite *Tachanun* on this day. However, there is a tradition that, in messianic times, Tish-ah b'Av will become a Festival. Because of this belief, that today's day of mourning will become tomorrow's day of rejoicing, *Tachanun* is not said on Tish-ah b'Av.

Perhaps even more surprising, *Tachanun* is not said in a house of mourning. There are two reasons for this. The first is that mourners do not need more grief. Second, it is consistently stated in *Tachanun* (particularly the long version) that the reason for our calamities is that we have sinned. This sentiment is totally inappropriate in a house of mourning.

Ashrei

The psalm conglomerate *Ashrei* is recited at least three times every day. Every Afternoon Service begins with *Ashrei* and it is recited twice during the Morning Service. During the Morning Service on both weekdays and *Shabbat,* the first time *Ashrei* is recited it is part of *P'sukei d'Zimrah* (Chapter 10). The second time it is recited toward the end of the Service. More specifically, on weekdays it is the first part of the concluding section of the Morning Service and on *Shabbat* and Festivals it is said before returning the *Torah* to the Ark.

Psalms 84:5, 144:15, 145, and 115:18
Ashrei yosh'vei veitecha ... me-attah v'ad olam, Halleluyah (Happy are they who dwell in Your House... from now and forever. Praise the Lord!)

As noted in the diagram, *Ashrei* consists of four components, namely, two single verses from *T'hillim* (the Book of Psalms), followed by the entire Psalm 145, and concluding with another single verse. This is shown in greater detail below.

Detailed Structure of *Ashrei*

Psalm 84:5
Ashrei yosh'vei veitecha od y'ha-l'luchah, Selah (Happy are they who dwell in Your House, they are forever praising You. *Selah*)
Psalm 144:15
Ashrei ha-am shekachah lo, ashrei ha-am she-Adonai Elohav (Happy is the people for whom this is so, happy is the people whose God is the Lord)
Psalm 145
Aromimchah Elohai haMelech ... Shem kodsho l'olam va-ed (I will exalt You, my God the King ... His holy Name forever and ever)
Psalm 115:18
Va-anachnu n'varech Yah, me-attah v'ad olam, Halleluyah (We will bless the Lord from now and forever. Praise the Lord!)

The structure of Psalm 145 is that of an acrostic with one missing verse. The twenty-one verses begin with successive letters of the Hebrew alphabet, from *aleph* (*Aromimchah Elohai haMelech ...*) to *tav* (*T'hilat Adonai ...*). However, there is no verse beginning with the letter *nun*.

Avinu Malkenu

Avinu Malkenu chatanu l'fanecha ... asei imanu tz'dakah vachesed v'hoshi-enu (Our Father, our King, we have sinned before You ... treat us with charity and kindness, and save us)

Avinu Malkenu is a series of supplications and entreaties. It is recited on Minor Fast Days as well as between Rosh haShanah and Yom Kippur. According to the *Talmud* (*Ta-anit* 25b), during a period of prolonged drought Rabbi Akiva said five brief supplications beginning *Avinu Malkenu* (Our Father, our King) and the rains came. Additional verses have been added over the years, and there are now over forty in the *Ashkenazi* liturgy and over fifty in the *Sephardi* liturgy [ArtScroll, pp. 121–124].

There are two types of supplication. First, there are requests for forgiveness of sin. Second, there are entreaties for nullification of harsh decrees, for health, for sustenance, and for life itself; in other words, for both personal and national needs.

The wording of certain verses changes slightly depending on whether they are recited on a Minor Fast Day or between Rosh haShanah and Yom Kippur. For example, on a Minor Fast Day we say *Avinu Malkenu, zochrenu l'chayim tovim* (Our Father, our King, remember us for a good life), whereas between Rosh haShanah and Yom Kippur we say *Avinu Malkenu, kotvenu b'Sefer Chayim Tovim* (Our Father, our King, inscribe us in the Book of Good Life).

Avinu Malkenu is not recited on *Shabbat* because of the plethora of requests it contains, many paralleling the petitions of the weekday *Amidah* (Chapter 6). There is one exception, however. When Yom Kippur falls on *Shabbat*, *Avinu Malkenu* is nevertheless said at the end of the *N'ilah* (concluding) Service.

Yigdal, Adon Olam

In many liturgies, the Friday Evening Service and *Shabbat* Additional Service are concluded with the singing of a hymn, either *Yigdal* or *Adon Olam*.

> *Yigdal Elohim chai ... baruch adei ad Shem t'hilato* (May the living God be exalted ... blessed be His praised Name forever)

Yigdal is a poetic version of the thirteen principles of faith as formulated by Rabbi Moses Maimonides, who is known as the *Rambam*, an acronym formed from the initial letters of his Hebrew name, *Rabi Moshe ben Maimon* (1135–1204). *Yigdal* was probably composed by Daniel ben Judah, who lived in Rome in the fourteenth century.

> *Adon olam Asher malach ... Adonai li, lo ira* (Master of the universe Who reigned ... the Lord is with me, I do not fear)

Adon Olam is probably the work of the Spanish poet Solomon ibn Gabirol (1021–1058). The major theme is the omnipotence of God.

For the Maven

Adon Olam has the distinction that it can be sung to virtually any tune. It fits both 3/4 (waltz) and 2/4 (march) time. At the *Chavurah* I attend, the children compete with one another at the end of *Shabbat Musaf* to select the tune of a well-known song for *Adon Olam*. To date, no matter what they have picked, they have managed to fit the words to the music.

Chanukah and Purim

There are similarities in the liturgies for the two Minor Festivals of Purim and Chanukah, both of which are rabbinic and not biblical festivals. For example, in Chapter 6 it was pointed out that closely related material is inserted into the second to last *b'rachah* of the *Amidah* on both Purim and Chanukah (the same material is inserted into Grace after Meals). Part of the diagram on page 62 is reproduced here:

[On Chanukah and Purim add] *Al hanisim ... bayamim hahem ba-z'man hazeh* (For the miracles ... in those days at this season)	
[On Chanukah add] *Bimei Matityahu ... l'Shimcha hagadol* (In the days of Mattathias ... to Your great Name)	[On Purim add] *Bimei Mord'chai ... v'et banav al ha-etz* (In the days of Mordechai ... and his sons on the gallows)

The primary way that each of the two Festivals is observed in the synagogue is totally different. On Chanukah, lights are kindled before the start of the Evening Service (on Saturday evening, the lights are kindled after *Shabbat* is out, that is, after the *Amidah*). On Purim, *M'gillat Ester* (The Scroll of Esther) is read at both the Evening Service and the Morning Service. Nevertheless, there are some similarities in the structure of the liturgy for these two otherwise dissimilar rituals. This is shown on the next page.

For the Maven

Of course, there are also major differences between the liturgies for Purim and Chanukah. For example, as explained in Chapter 9, *Hallel* is said on Chanukah but not on Purim.

Structure of Liturgy for Chanukah and Purim

Chanukah	Purim
Mitzvah Form *b'rachah* before	
kindling the Chanukah lights	reading *M'gillat Ester*
B'rachah recalling the miracles that occurred at that time	
[On Purim but on only the first night of Chanukah] *Shehecheyanu* (pages 117–118)	
The Chanukah lights are kindled	*M'gillat Ester* is read
Prayer while kindling the lights	*B'rachah* after reading the *M'gillah*
Hymn after kindling the lights	Hymn after reading the *M'gillah*

We now examine these various components in more detail.

B'rachot before Kindling Chanukah Lights and Reading the *M'gillah*

Chanukah	Purim
Baruch Attah Adonai Eloheinu Melech ha-olam, Asher kid'shanu b'mitzvotav v'tzivanu (Blessed are you, O Lord Our God, King of the Universe, Who has sanctified us with His commandments, and has commanded us)	
l'hadlik ner shel Chanukah (to kindle the Chanukah lights)	*al mikra M'gillah* (concerning the reading of the *M'gillah*)
Baruch Attah Adonai ... She-asa nisim la-avoteinu bayamim hahem ba-z'man hazeh (Blessed are You, O Lord our God ... Who performed miracles for our fathers in those days at this season)	
[On Purim, but on only the first night of Chanukah] *Shehecheyanu* (pages 117–118)	

The first *b'rachah*, before kindling the Chanukah lights or reading the *M'gillah*, has the structure of a *Mitzvah* Form *b'rachah*. The second *b'rachah* acknowledges the miracles that were performed at those times, that is, the miracles of Chanukah and of Purim as spelled out in the respective paragraphs added to the *Amidah* (page 62). The third *b'rachah*, *Shehecheyanu*, is said both evening and morning before reading the *M'gillah*, but on only the first night of Chanukah.

Structure of Remainder of Chanukah Liturgy

Chanukah
[While kindling the lights from left to right] *Ha-nerot halalu ... v'al y'shu-ate-cha* (These lights ... and for Your salvations)
[Hymn after kindling the lights] *Ma-oz Tzur y'shu-ati ...* (Stronghold, Rock of my salvation ...)

The prayer *Ha-nerot halalu* (These lights) explains why we kindle the lights, that is, on account of the miracles performed at that time. It stresses that we may make no use of the Chanukah lights; we may only look at them.

Ma-oz Tzur (Stronghold, Rock) is a hymn with five stanzas. The initial letters of each stanza spell the name Mordechai, who presumably was the author. The hymn describes the travails of the Jewish people in Egypt, Babylon, and Shushan, each of which ended in salvation. The fifth stanza refers to the events of Chanukah. (A sixth stanza was added later.)

Structure of Remainder of Purim Liturgy

Purim
[B'rachah after reading the M'gillah] *Baruch Attah Adonai ... ha-El Hamoshia* (Blessed are You, O Lord ... the God Who saves)
[Hymn after reading the *M'gillah:* Evening Service] *Asher heni atzah goyim ... al ha-etz talita* (He Who frustrated the plan of the nations ... you hanged on the gallows)
[Hymn after reading the *M'gillah:* Morning Service] *Shoshanat Ya-akov ... zachur latov* (The rose of Jacob ... be remembered for good)

After reading the *M'gillah,* a *b'rachah* is recited that thanks God for exacting vengeance and punishing our oppressors. It ends with the words *ha-El Hamoshia* (the God Who saves).

In the Evening Service, the hymn *Asher heni atzah goyim* (He Who frustrated the plan of the nations) is recited. It retells the Purim story in twenty stanzas. The first word of each stanza begins with successive letters of the Hebrew alphabet, starting with *aleph* and ending with *reish. Shoshanat Ya-akov* (The rose of Jacob) is the corresponding hymn for the Morning Service (and also the Evening Service in some liturgies).

10
The Structure of Components from the Psalms

T'hillim (the Psalter, or Book of Psalms) consists of 150 psalms, divided into five books. Psalms are found throughout the *Siddur*. For example, we have seen in Chapter 9 that Psalm 6:2–11 is an integral part of *Tachanun*. Also, *Ashrei* (see Chapter 9) consists of Psalm 145 plus three individual verses from other psalms. In this chapter, we consider other ways that psalms form part of the service and examine the corresponding structures.

Psalm of the Day

Each day we recite, as part of the Morning Service, the psalm that the Levites recited in the Temple on that day.

Sunday	Psalm 24	*L'David mizmor. Ladonai ha-aretz u-m'lo-ah* ... (A psalm of David. The earth is the Lord's, and its entire contents ...)
Monday	Psalm 48	*Shir mizmor livnei Korach. Gadol Adonai, u-m'hulal m'od* ... (A song, a psalm of the sons of Korach. Great is the Lord, and much praised ...)
Tuesday	Psalm 82	*Mizmor l'Assaf. Elohim nitzav ba-adat El* ... (A psalm of Assaf. God stands in the assembly of God ...)
Wednesday	Psalm 94; 95:1–3	*El n'kamot Adonai* ... (God of retribution, Lord ...)
Thursday	Psalm 81	*La-m'natze-ach al hagittit l'Assaf. Harninu Leilohim uzenu* ... (For the choirmaster, on the *gittit* [a musical instrument]; a psalm of Assaf. Sing aloud to the God of our might ...)
Friday	Psalm 93	*Adonai malach, ge-ut lavesh* ... (The Lord has reigned, He has robed Himself in majesty ...)
Shabbat	Psalm 92	*Mizmor shir l'Yom haShabbat. Tov l'hodot Ladonai* ... (A psalm, a song for the Sabbath day. It is good to praise the Lord ...)

Psalms for Special Days

At specific times of the year, such as *Rosh Chodesh* (the New Month Festival, marked by the appearance of the new moon) or during the month of *Elul* (or more precisely, from *Rosh Chodesh Elul* until *Sh'mini Atzeret*), special psalms are recited.

On *Rosh Chodesh*	Psalm 104	*Ba-r'chi nafshi et Adonai* ... (Bless the Lord, O my soul ...)
From *Rosh Chodesh Elul* to *Sh'mini Atzeret*	Psalm 27	*L'David. Adonai ori v'yishi* ... (A psalm of David. The Lord is my light and my salvation ...)
Between Rosh haShanah and Yom Kippur	Psalm 130	*Shir haMa-alot. Mima-amakim k'ratichah Adonai* ... (A song of the *Ma-alot.* From the depths I called you, O Lord ...)
On Chanukah	Psalm 30	*Mizmor shir chanukat haBayit l'David* ... (A psalm, a song for the dedication of the Temple, by David ...)
In a house of mourning	Psalm 49	*La-M'natze-ach livnei Korach mizmor* ... (For the conductor. A psalm by the sons of Korach ...)

In addition, there are specific psalms for the three *Chagim*, such as Psalm 136 for (the last day of) *Pesach*. These Festival psalms are omitted here, as they do not appear in most standard *Siddurim*; the interested reader should consult a *Machzor* for the relevant *Chag*.

For the Maven

The maven will no doubt have noticed the deliberate error on this page. The Hebrew word for a Festival prayer book is *Machazor*. In everyday speech, this has become shortened to *Machzor*.

Hallel

Hallel (praise) consists of six psalms, namely, Psalms 113–118. *Hallel* is recited on the *Chagim*, that is, on Pesach, Shavuot, and Sukkot, and also on *Rosh Chodesh*, Chanukah, and, in many liturgies, on *Yom ha-Atzma-ut* as well. To be more precise, on the last six days of Pesach and on *Rosh Chodesh* an abridged version of *Hallel*, *Hallel b'dilug* (sometimes called "half Hallel") is recited; the first eleven verses of Psalm 115 and the first eleven verses of Psalm 116 are omitted.

The structure of *Hallel* is shown on the next page. The two items that are omitted on the last six days of Pesach and on *Rosh Chodesh* are shown indented.

For the Maven

Hallel is not recited on Rosh haShanah or Yom Kippur because the sentiment of joy is inappropriate for those solemn days. It is not said on Purim because, unlike on Chanukah, the deliverance was only partial; the people remained in exile in the kingdom of Ahasueras.

A number of reasons have been put forward why only "half *Hallel*" is recited on the last six days of Pesach. One explanation is that the drowning of the Egyptian army at the Red Sea (on the Seventh Day of the first Pesach) prevents the last six days from being an occasion for complete rejoicing.

With regard to *Rosh Chodesh*, the custom of reciting *Hallel* on this Minor Festival arose in Babylon as late as Talmudic times [Hertz, p. 756]; it is therefore not surprising that the complete *Hallel* is not said.

More For the Maven

There are two exceptions to the rule that the abridged *Hallel* is said on *Rosh Chodesh*, namely, the month of Tishrei and the month of Tevet. First, *Rosh Chodesh Tishrei* is Rosh haShanah, so *Hallel* is not said. Second, *Rosh Chodesh Tevet* always occurs during Chanukah, so the full *Hallel* is recited.

B'rachah before reciting *Hallel*
Baruch Attah Adonai ... v'tzivanu likro et haHallel (Blessed are You, O Lord ... and Who has commanded us to read the *Hallel*)

Psalm 113
Halleluyah ha-l'lu avdei Adonai ... em habanim s'mechah, Halleluyah (Praise the Lord! Give praise, you servants of the Lord ... a happy mother of children. Praise the Lord!)

Psalm 114
B'tzet Yisra-el miMitzraim ... chalamish l'mai-y'no maiyim (When Israel went out of Egypt ... the flint into a flowing fountain)

Psalm 115:1–11
Lo lanu Adonai, lo lanu ... Ezram uMaginam Hu (Not for our sake, O Lord, not for our sake ... He is their Help and their Shield)

Psalm 115:12–18
Adonai z'charanu y'varech ... me-attah v'ad olam, Halleluyah (The Lord Who has remembered us will bless ... from now and forever. Praise the Lord!)

Psalm 116:1–11
Ahavti ki yishma Adonai et koli tachanunai ... kol ha-adam kozev (I love Him, for the Lord hears my voice and my supplications ... all men are liars)

Psalm 116:12–19
Mah ashiv Ladonai ... b'tochechi Y'rushalayim, Halleluyah (What can I render to the Lord ... in the midst of Jerusalem. Praise the Lord!)

Psalm 117
Ha-l'lu et Adonai, kol goyim ... v'emet Adonai l'olam, Halleluyah (Praise the Lord, all nations ... the truth of the Lord is eternal. Praise the Lord!)

Psalm 118
Hodu Ladonai ki tov ... ki l'olam chasdo (Give thanks to the Lord, for He is good ... His mercy endures forever)

B'rachah after reciting *Hallel*
Y'ha-l'luchah Adonai Eloheinu ... Melech M'hulal b'tishbachot (All [Your works] praise You ... King Who is lauded with praises)

We now examine each of these components.

B'rachah before Reciting *Hallel*

Baruch Attah Adonai ... v'tzivanu likro et haHallel (Blessed are You, O Lord ... and Who has commanded us to read the *Hallel*)

This has the structure of a *Mitzvah* Form *b'rachah* (page 25).

On Sukkot (except on *Shabbat*), this *b'rachah* is preceded by the *b'rachah* on taking the *lulav* (page 26), and followed by *Shehecheyanu* (pages 117–118) on the first day that this is done.

For the Maven

Some authorities have suggested that the *b'rachah* to be said before reciting the full *Hallel* should be **ligmor** *et haHallel* (to **complete** the *Hallel*), whereas the *b'rachah* on the top of this page, **likro** *et haHallel* (to **read** the *Hallel*), should be said before the abridged *Hallel*.

Psalm 113

Halleluyah ha-l'lu avdei Adonai ... em habanim s'mechah, Halleluyah
(Praise the Lord! Give praise, you servants of the Lord ... a happy mother of
children. Praise the Lord!)

Psalm 113 calls for the Lord to be praised at all times. The power of the
Lord to elevate the poor and give children to a barren woman are mentioned.

Psalm 114

B'tzet Yisra-el miMitzraim ... chalamish l'mai-y'no maiyim (When Israel
went out of Egypt ... the flint into a flowing fountain)

Hallel is frequently referred to as *Hallel haMitzri* (the Egyptian *Hallel*)
because this psalm refers to the Exodus from Egypt. Psalm 114 describes, in
poetic terms, the dividing of the Red Sea and the Jordan river, and the earth-
quake that accompanied the giving of the *Torah*.

Psalm 115

[Omitted on the last six days of Pesach and on *Rosh Chodesh*]
Psalm 115:1–11

Lo lanu Adonai, lo lanu ... Ezram uMaginam Hu (Not for
our sake, O Lord, not for our sake ... He is their Help and
their Shield)

Psalm 115:12–18

Adonai z'charanu y'varech ... me-attah v'ad olam, Halleluyah (The Lord
Who has remembered us will bless ... from now and forever. Praise the Lord!)

The major theme of the first half of Psalm 115 is a plea to God to save His
people from degradation. Verses 12 through 18 constitute a statement that the
Lord will indeed bless His people.

Psalm 116

[Omitted on the last six days of Pesach and on *Rosh Chodesh*]
Psalm 116:1–11

Ahavti ki yishma Adonai et koli tachanunai ... kol ha-adam kozev (I love Him, for the Lord hears my voice and my supplications ... all men are liars)

Psalm 116:12–19

Mah ashiv Ladonai ... b'tochechi Y'rushalayim, Halleluyah (What can I render to the Lord ... in the midst of Jerusalem. Praise the Lord!)

The first eleven verses of Psalm 116 describe how the Lord saved the psalmist when he was in grave danger. The second half (verses 12 through 19) is a prayer of thanksgiving for this deliverance.

Psalm 117

Ha-l'lu et Adonai, kol goyim ... v'emet Adonai l'olam, Halleluyah (Praise the Lord, all nations ... the truth of the Lord is eternal. Praise the Lord!)

Psalm 117 is the shortest chapter in the Bible, consisting of just two verses. The psalm calls on all nations to praise the Lord because His truth is everlasting.

Psalm 118

There are various traditions associated with the way Psalm 118 is recited in the synagogue, almost all involving repetition and antiphony. For example, in the *Ashkenazi* liturgy, Psalm 118 is broken into five parts.

Congregation responds to each verse with the first verse	**Psalm 118:1–4** *Hodu Ladonai ki Tov ... ki l'olam chasdo* (Give thanks to the Lord, for He is Good ... His mercy endures forever)
No repetition	**Psalm 118:5–20** *Min ha-metzar karati Yah ... tzadikim yavo-u vo* (In my distress I called on the Lord ... the righteous shall enter through it)
Each verse is recited twice	**Psalm 118:21–24** *Od'chah ki anitani ... nagilah v'nis-m'chah vo* (I thank You because You have answered me ... let us rejoice and be happy on it)
Recited responsively	**Psalm 118:25** *Ana Adonai hoshiah na ... Ana Adonai hatzlicha na* (Please, O Lord, save now... Please, O Lord, cause us to succeed now)
Each verse is recited twice	**Psalm 118:26–29** *Baruch haba b'Shem Adonai ... ki l'olam chasdo* (Blessed be he who comes in the Name of the Lord ... His mercy endures forever)

A characteristic of ancient Jewish poetry is synonymous parallelism. That is, the idea expressed in a verse is repeated, in a slightly different way, in the second half of that verse or in a following verse. Verses 5 through 20 of this psalm exhibit synonymous parallelism, but the first four and last nine verses do not; each of these verses expresses a new idea. For this reason, verses 1 through 4 and verses 21 through 29 of Psalm 118 are repeated.

B'rachah after Reciting *Hallel*

Y'ha-l'luchah Adonai Eloheinu ... Melech M'hulal b'tishbachot (All [Your works] praise You ... King Who is lauded with praises)

Hallel both begins and ends with a *b'rachah*. The closing *b'rachah* expresses the overall theme of the *Hallel*, namely, that God should be praised.

P'sukei d'Zimrah and its Psalms

During the Morning Service, *P'sukei d'Zimrah* (verses of praise) are recited. This large component of the first part of the service includes a number of psalms, as shown on this page. Some of the material is said every day, some only on weekdays, and some only on *Shabbat* and Festivals. The precise psalms that are included depend on the specific liturgy.

Introductory Psalm to *P'sukei d'Zimrah*, Psalm 30 *Mizmor shir chanukat haBayit l'David ... l'olam odeka* (A psalm, a song for the inauguration of the Temple, by David ... I will forever thank You)
Kaddish Yatom (page 130)
B'rachah before reciting *P'sukei d'Zimrah* *Baruch She-amar ... Melech M'hulal b'tishbachot* (Blessed be He Who spoke ... King Who is lauded with praises)
Lengthy succession of biblical verses, mainly from the Psalms *Hodu Ladonai, kiru viShmo ... uShmo Echad* (Give thanks to the Lord, declare His Name ... and His Name One)
[On *Shabbat* and Festivals] *Nishmat* *Nishmat kol chai ... avd'cha m'shichecha* (The soul of every living creature ... Your servant, Your annointed one)
B'rachah after reciting *P'sukei d'Zimrah* *Yishtabach Shimcha la-ad, Malkenu ... Melech El Chei ha-olamim* (Praised be Your Name forever, our King ... King, God, Life of the universe)

The overall structure of *P'sukei d'Zimrah* is that of a Series Form *b'rachah* with two component *b'rachot:* the *B'rachah* before reciting *P'sukei d'Zimrah* and the *B'rachah* after reciting *P'sukei d'Zimrah*. The body of *P'sukei d'Zimrah* is sandwiched between these two *b'rachot*.

Now we examine these components in detail.

Introductory Psalm to *P'sukei d'Zimrah*

> Psalm 30
>
> *Mizmor shir chanukat haBayit l'David ... l'olam odeka* (A psalm, a song for the inauguration of the Temple, by David ... I will forever thank You)

This psalm is not part of *P'sukei d'Zimrah*. In fact, it became part of the liturgy as late as the seventeenth century [ArtScroll, p. 55]. Psalm 30 was added because its content is a fitting prelude to *P'sukei d'Zimrah*, the verses of praise. The psalmist describes how the Lord saved him from his travails and concludes that it is appropriate to thank God continually.

B'rachah before Reciting *P'sukei d'Zimrah*

> *Baruch She-amar ... Melech M'hulal b'tishbachot* (Blessed be He Who spoke ... King Who is lauded with praises)

The structure of this *b'rachah,* which begins *Baruch She-amar* (Blessed be He Who spoke), is that of the first *b'rachah* in a Series Form *b'rachah*. It is preceded by a series of phrases in which different aspects of God are blessed. *Yishtabach,* the *b'rachah* said after reciting *P'sukei d'Zimrah,* and the second and final *b'rachah* in the Series Form of two *b'rachot,* is also preceded by a similar series of phrases.

Lengthy Succession of Biblical Verses, Mainly from the Psalms

These biblical verses constitute the main body of *P'sukei d'Zimrah*. They fall into ten groups, as shown in the diagram.

I Chronicles 16:8–36
Hodu Ladonai, kiru viShmo ... (Give thanks to the Lord, declare His Name ...)

Eighteen excerpts from the Psalms
Ro-m'mu Ladonai Eloheinu ... (Exalt the Lord, our God ...)

[Almost every weekday, including *Hoshana Rabbah*] Psalm 100: *Mizmor l'todah* ... (A psalm for the thank-offering ...)	[*Shabbat* and Festivals only, also *Hoshana Rabbah*] Nine psalms (*Ashkenazi* liturgy) Fourteen psalms (*Sephardi* liturgy)

Verses primarily from the Bible
Y'hi ch'vod Adonai l'olam ... (May the glory of the Lord be forever ...)

Ashrei (Page 140)
Ashrei yosh'vei veitecha ... (Happy are they who dwell in Your House ...)

Five *Halleluyah* Psalms
Halleluyah, ha-l'li nafshi et Adonai ... (Praise the Lord! Praise the Lord, O my soul ...)

Three doxologies from the Psalms
Baruch Adonai l'olam ... (Blessed be the Lord forever ...)

Three biblical passages
Va-y'varech David ... (David blessed ...)

Three biblical verses
Ki Ladonai ha-m'luchah ... (For sovereignty is the Lord's ...)

We now examine the nine new groups of biblical verses. We have previously considered *Ashrei* (page 140).

I Chronicles 16:8–36

Hodu Ladonai, kiru viShmo ... v'hallel Ladonai (Give thanks to the Lord, declare His Name ... and praise the Lord)

These twenty-nine verses from I Chronicles 16 praise God in different ways, the overall theme of *P'sukei d'Zimrah*.

Eighteen Excerpts from the Psalms

Psalms 99:5, 99:9, 78:38, 40:12, 25:6, 68:35–36, 94:1–2, 3:9, 46:8, 84:13, 20:10, 28:9, 33:20–22, 85:8, 44:27, 81:11, 144:15, and 13:6
Ro-m'mu Ladonai Eloheinu ... ki gamal alai (Exalt the Lord, our God ... because He has dealt kindly with me)

Much of *P'sukei d'Zimrah* consists of verses from the psalms, starting with this section of eighteen excerpts from *T'hillim* (Book of Psalms). As a consequence of their common theme, these twenty-three verses are sometimes referred to as *P'sukei d'Rachmei* (verses of mercy).

Psalm 100

[Almost every weekday, including *Hoshana Rabbah*]

Mizmor l'todah ... dor vador emunato (A psalm for the thank-offering ... His faithfulness endures forever)

Psalm 100 was recited in the Temple on those days when individual thank-offerings were given. Because only communal offerings were presented on *Shabbat* and Festivals, Psalm 100 is omitted on those days. An individual thank-offering was not offered on *Erev Pesach* (the day before Pesach) or during Pesach because the thank-offering contained *chametz* (leaven). Also, a thank-offering could not be offered on *Erev Yom Kippur,* because it could not be eaten that night. Accordingly, Psalm 100 is not recited on *Erev Pesach, Chol haMo-ed Pesach* (Intermediate Days of Pesach), or *Erev Yom Kippur.*

Nine Psalms (*Ashkenazi* Liturgy)/ Fourteen Psalms (*Sephardi* Liturgy)

> [*Shabbat* and Festivals only, also *Hoshana Rabbah*]
>
> Nine psalms (*Ashkenazi* liturgy)
>
> Psalms 19, 34, 90, 91, 135, 136, 33, 92, and 93
>
> Fourteen psalms (*Sephardi* liturgy)
>
> Psalms 103, 19, 33, 90, 91, 98, 121–124, 135, 136, 92, and 93

On *Shabbat* and Festivals, additional psalms were added to *P'sukei d'Zimrah* because there is more time for prayers on those days. Ideas that are common to the selected psalms include *Shabbat* as a day of rest, *Shabbat* as a foretaste of the world to come, and remembrance of the Exodus from Egypt.

Verses Primarily from the Bible

> Psalms 104:31, 113:2–4, 135:13, 103:19; I Chronicles 16:31; Psalms 10:16, 93:1; Exodus 15:18; Psalms 10:16, 33:10; Proverbs 19:21; Psalms 33:11, 33:9, 132:13, 135:4, 94:14, 78:38, 20:10
>
> *Y'hi ch'vod Adonai l'olam ... haMelech ya-anenu v'yom korenu*
> (May the glory of the Lord be forever ... the King will answer us when we call on Him)

This section is titled "Verses Primarily from the Bible" rather than "Biblical Verses" because one of the verses is not in the Bible. Specifically, the verse *Adonai melech, Adonai malach, Adonai yimloch l'olam va-ed* (The Lord reigns, the Lord has reigned, the Lord will reign forever and ever) is not to be found anywhere in the Bible. However, the three component clauses of that verse each come from a biblical verse, namely, part of Psalm 10:16, part of Psalm 93:1, and Exodus 15:18.

Five *Halleluyah* Psalms

> *Halleluyah, ha-l'li nafshi et Adonai ... kol ha-n'shamah t'hallel Yah, Halle-*
> *luyah* (Praise the Lord! Praise the Lord, O my soul ... let every soul praise
> the Lord. Praise the Lord!)

The last five psalms (Psalms 146–150) of *T'hillim* (Book of Psalms) are
called the *Halleluyah* Psalms because they begin and end with the word *Halle-*
luyah (Praise the Lord!). Completion of *T'hillim* is traditionally considered a
praiseworthy act; reading the last five Psalms is a symbolic completion of the
whole book.

Three Doxologies from the Psalms

> Psalms 89:53, 135:21, 72:18–19
>
> *Baruch Adonai l'olam ... Amen v'Amen* (Blessed be the Lord forever ...
> Amen and Amen)

As mentioned at the beginning of this chapter, *T'hillim* (the Psalter) is
divided into five books. Each of the first four books is terminated by a doxology, or expression of praise to God. Two of the four doxologies, namely,
Psalm 89:53, which terminates Book III, and Psalm 72:18–19, at the end of
Book II, appear at this point in *P'sukei d'Zimrah*. Between them appears the
doxology at the end of Psalm 135.

For the Maven

The fifth and last book of *T'hillim* is not terminated with a doxology. However, the
last psalm in Book V, Psalm 150, is considered by some to be a doxology for the whole
Psalter. From this viewpoint there are then four consecutive doxologies in *P'sukei*
d'Zimrah, namely, Psalm 150 followed by the three doxologies on this page.

More For the Maven

The doxology from Psalm 135 also occurs earlier in *P'sukei d'Zimrah*, at least on
Shabbat and Festivals. The reason is that Psalm 135 is one of the additional nine
psalms in the *Ashkenazi* liturgy (and one of the fourteen in the *Sephardi* liturgy) that
are said on *Shabbat* and on Festivals.

Three Biblical Passages

> I Chronicles 29:10–13, Nehemiah 9:6–11, Exodus 14:30–15:18
>
> *Va-y'varech David ... Adonai yimloch l'olam va-ed* (David blessed ... The Lord will reign forever and ever)

Three biblical passages follow the three doxologies. The first passage is the prayer of David when he inaugurated the building of the Temple (I Chron. 29:10–13). The second is a passage that briefly reviews Israel's past, including the covenant with Abraham and especially the crossing of the Red Sea (Neh. 9:6–11).

This leads to the third passage, *Shirat haYam* (The Song of the Sea). This is Exodus 14:30–15:18, the Song of Moses after the deliverance at the Red Sea.

Three Biblical Verses

Now come three biblical verses that deal with divine kingship.

> Psalm 22:29, Obadiah 1:21, Zechariah 14:9
>
> *Ki Ladonai ha-m'luchah ... uShmo Echad* (For sovereignty is the Lord's ... and His Name One)

This concludes our examination of the ten groups of biblical verses. We now consider the next major portion of *P'sukei d'Zimra, Nishmat*.

Nishmat

Nishmat is recited only on *Shabbat* and Festivals.

> [*Shabbat* and Festivals]
> *Nishmat kol chai* ... (The soul of every living creature ...)
>
> *Ha-El b'ta-atzumot uzecha ... haMelech Hayoshev al kisei ram v'nisa* (You are God in Your tremendous power ... the King Who sits on a high and lofty throne)

Nishmat (the soul [of]) is a poetic outpouring of praise and gratitude for God's mercy. It includes excerpts from Isaiah and *T'hillim*, as well as material based on biblical verses. *Nishmat* concludes with the verse *ha-El b'ta-atzumot uzecha ... al kisei ram v'nisa* (You are God in Your tremendous power ... on a high and lofty throne). The preliminary Morning Service (as opposed to the Morning Service proper) is deemed to end here. Thus, if different individuals lead the *Shabbat* service, the Reader for the Morning Service takes over at the end of *Nishmat*.

On Festivals, however, the Morning Service starts with the last verse of *Nishmat*. More specifically, on *Chagim*, the Reader starts with the first words of the last verse of *Nishmat*, *ha-El b'ta-atzumot uzecha* (You are God in Your tremendous power); whereas on Rosh haShanah and Yom Kippur, the Reader for the Morning Service starts mid-verse, with the word *haMelech* (The King). These different starting places can be explained in terms of the corresponding *Shabbat* and Festival themes. The Exodus from Egypt is central to the three *Chagim*, so a phrase expressing the power of God is an apposite place to begin. Divine kingship is a major theme of Rosh haShanah and Yom Kippur; it therefore is appropriate to start with *haMelech* (The King). With regard to *Shabbat*, a major theme of *Shabbat* is the Creation, which accords with *Shochen ad* (He Who abides forever), the opening words of the next prayer.

For the Maven

There is a slight change of wording on Rosh haShanah and Yom Kippur. During the rest of the year, we say *haMelech Hayoshev al kisei* (the King Who sits on His throne). On Rosh haShanah and Yom Kippur the definite article *ha* is deleted; the verse reads *haMelech yoshev al kisei* (the King is sitting [at this moment] on His throne). This variant highlights the belief that God judges His people between Rosh haShanah and Yom Kippur.

More For the Maven

A strange myth arose in medieval France and Germany. It was claimed that *Nishmat* was written by the Apostle Peter as a vehicle for renouncing his new faith. The great French commentator Rashi (Rabbi Shlomo Yitzchaki, 1040–1105) was the first of many who denounced this preposterous belief [Hertz, p. 416].

Beginning of the Morning Service Proper

> *Shochen ad ... uvkerev k'doshim titkadash* (He Who abides forever ... in the midst of the holy You are sanctified)

The prayer begins *Shochen ad* (He Who abides forever), an allusion to Isaiah 57:15, and continues with Psalm 33:1, *Ran'nu tzadikim Badonai* (Rejoice in the Lord, O righteous ones).

Then follow four stiches of praise, beginning *B'fi y'sharim tit-halal* (By the mouth of the righteous You are praised). The first letters of the second word of each stich, namely, *Y'sharim, TZadikim, CHasidim,* and *K'doshim,* spell *YiTZCHaK* (Isaac).

In the *Sephardi* liturgy, the third letters of the third word of each stich, namely, *titRomam, titBarach, titKadash,* and *titHalal,* spell *RiVKaH* (Rebecca, the wife of Isaac). The four words appear in a different order in the *Ashkenazi Siddur.* However, in the *Ashkenazi* liturgy for Rosh haShanah and Yom Kippur, the third words of each stich are arranged as in the *Sephardi* liturgy.

B'rachah after Reciting *P'sukei d'Zimrah*

> *Yishtabach Shimcha la-ad, Malkenu ... Melech El Chei ha-olamim* (Praised be Your Name forever, our King ... King, God, Life of the universe)

As previously pointed out, the structure of *P'sukei d'Zimrah* is that of a Series Form *b'rachah* consisting of two *b'rachot.* The first *b'rachah* is *Baruch She-amar* (Blessed be He who spoke), the *b'rachah* before reciting *P'sukei d'Zimrah* (page 158); the second *b'rachah* is *Yishtabach* (Praised), the *b'rachah* after reciting *P'sukei d'Zimrah.* The body of *P'sukei d'Zimrah* is sandwiched between these two *b'rachot.*

The structure of *Yishtabach* is similar to that of *Baruch She-amar;* the *b'rachah* itself is preceded by a series of phrases that praise different aspects of God. In the case of *Yishtabach,* there are fifteen such phrases.

For the Maven

Paralleling the fifteen phrases of praise before the *b'rachah* itself, there are fifteen words after the phrase *Baruch Attah Adonai.* Fifteen is also the number of the *Shir haMa-alot* psalms, the subject of the next section.

Other *Shabbat* Psalms

Numerous additional psalms are recited on *Shabbat*. In this chapter we have already examined the psalms added to the weekday *P'sukei d'Zimrah*. The six psalms of *Kabbalat Shabbat* (preliminary Friday evening service) are described in Chapter 13. In this chapter we now consider *Ba-r'chi Nafshi* and the *Shir haMa-alot* psalms recited after the Shabbat Afternoon Service and then the psalms of *Motza-ei Shabbat* (Saturday evening).

Ba-r'chi Nafshi and the *Shir haMa-alot* Psalms

At the end of the Afternoon Service for *Shabbat* between Sukkot and Pesach, sixteen psalms are recited.

Psalm 104
Ba-r'chi nafshi et Adonai ... *Ba-r'chi nafshi et Adonai, Halleluyah* (Bless the Lord, O my soul ... Bless the Lord, O my soul. Praise the Lord!)
Psalms 120–134
Shir haMa-alot. El Adonai, b'tzara-at li ... *y'varech'cha Adonai miTziyon, Oseh shamayim va-aretz* (A song of the *Ma-alot*. In my distress I cried to the Lord ... May the Lord, the Maker of heaven and earth, bless you from Zion)

Psalm 104, beginning with the words *Ba-r'chi nafshi et Adonai* (Bless the Lord, O my soul), parallels the Creation story in Genesis. As has been stated before, the Creation is a major theme of *Shabbat* and Psalm 104 is therefore appropriate in this context.

Next come the fifteen psalms that begin with the words *Shir haMa-alot*. As with so much else regarding the wording of the psalms, there is no agreement as to the meaning of this phrase. Scholars have suggested a wide variety of meanings, including "a song of ascents" and "a pilgrim song." The safest way out is simply to leave it untranslated!

For the Maven

Nit-pickers will surely want to know that only fourteen of the fifteen psalms begin with the words *Shir haMa-alot* ... ("A song of the *Ma-alot* ..."). Psalm 121 starts *Shir laMa-alot* ... ("A song to the *Ma-alot* ...").

More For the Maven

With regard to the meaning of *Shir haMa-alot*, the translation "a song of the ascents" relates to the return from Babylon after the exile. It fits Psalm 126 perfectly, but the First Temple is still standing in Psalms 122 and 134. The translation "a pilgrim psalm," that is, a psalm sung by the pilgrims as they went up to Jerusalem to celebrate the three *Chagim*, is ideal for Psalm 122, but not the others. Some scholars connect *Ma-alot* with "steps," specifically the fifteen steps in the Second Temple leading down from the Court of the Israelites described in the *Mishnah* in connection with the Sukkot celebrations. However, the *Mishnah* does not state that the psalms were recited on these steps [Hertz, p. 589].

Psalms before the Saturday Evening Service

On *Motza-ei Shabbat* (Saturday evening; literally, the going out of the *Sabbath*), two psalms are recited before the Evening Service.

Psalm 144
L'David Baruch Adonai Tzuri ... ashrei ha-am she-Adonai Elohav (A psalm of David. Blessed is the Lord, my Rock ... happy is the people whose God is the Lord)
Psalm 67
La-m'natze-ach bin-ginot ... kol asfei aretz (To the choirmaster. On *n'ginot* [probably stringed instruments] ... all the ends of the earth)

Psalm 144, with its opening theme of fighting, reminds us of the coming weekday struggle. The psalm concludes with a request for agricultural prosperity and a peaceful life.

Psalm 67 begins with a paraphrase of the Priestly blessing (page 88), followed by a call to praise the Lord. Psalm 67, too, concludes with a vision of agricultural plenty. (In some liturgies, Psalm 29 is recited between Psalm 144 and Psalm 67.)

Psalm at the End of the Saturday Evening Service

Psalm 91
Yoshev b'seter Elyon ... v'arehu bishu-ati (He who dwells in the refuge of the Most High ... and I will show him My salvation

Psalm 91 is a prayer for protection from the dangers of the world, an appropriate petition for the start of the working week. It is preceded by a single verse from the Psalms (see page 221).

For the Maven

The last verse of Psalm 91 is repeated when the psalm is read in the synagogue. The reason is that Psalm 91 has 124 words. Traditionally, there are 248 organs and limbs of the body. If the whole psalm were repeated, this would symbolically represent a request for protection of every part of our body. Instead of repeating the entire psalm, the last verse is repeated, a symbolic representation of the symbolic protection!

11
The Structure of
K'riat haTorah

The major *Torah* reading of the week is on *Shabbat*, at the end of the Morning Service. The *Torah* is also read during the Afternoon Service on *Shabbat* and on Monday and Thursday mornings. On the latter three occasions the reading is shorter; only the first part of the *Torah* reading for the following *Shabbat* is read.

In addition, the *Torah* is read on the Festivals (Rosh haShanah, Yom Kippur, Sukkot, Pesach, Shavuot); the Minor Festivals (*Chol haMo-ed, Rosh Chodesh*, Chanukah, Purim); Tish-ah b'Av; and the Minor Fast Days (*Tzom G'dalyah, Assarah b'Tevet, Tzom Ester*, and *Shiv-ah Assar b'Tammuz*). In some liturgies, the *Torah* is also read on *Yom ha-Atzma-ut*.

The structure of the associated services reflects the fact that some prayers are said only on *Shabbat* morning, some only on weekdays, and some only on Festivals that fall on weekdays. The table on the next three pages gives an overview of the structure.

	Shabbat Morning; Festivals falling on *Shabbat*	Festivals falling on weekdays	*Shabbat* Afternoon; Monday; Thursday; Minor Festivals; Fast Days
Before opening the Ark	*Ein kamocha ...* (There is none like You ...) *Av harachamim heitivah virtzon'chah et Tziyon ...* (Merciful Father, may it be Your will to do good for Zion ...)		[Most Mondays and Thursdays] *El erech apayim ...* (O God Who is slow to anger ...)
On opening the Ark	*Va-y'hi binso-a ha-aron ...*(And when the Ark started to move forward ...)		
In front of the Ark	—	*Adonai Adonai ...* (The Lord, the Lord ...) *Ribono shel olam ...* (Master of the universe ...) *Yi-h'yu l'ratzon ...* (May [the words] find favor ...) *Va-ani t'filati ...* (As for me, may my prayer ... ")*	—
	B'rich Sh'mei d'Marei al'ma ... (Blessed be the Name of the Master of the universe ...)		
On taking the scroll	*Sh'ma Yisra-el ...* (Hear O Israel ...) *Echad Eloheinu ...* (Our God is one ...)		—
	Ga-d'lu Ladonai iti ... (Magnify the Lord with me ...)		
	L'cha Adonai ha-g'dulah ... (Yours, O Lord, is the greatness ...)		
Procession I	*Al hakol ...* (Above all ...)		—
	Av harachamim Hu y'rachem ... (May the Father of mercy have compassion ...)		
On unrolling the scroll	*V'ya-azor v'yagen ...* (May He help and shield ...)		*V'tigaleh v'tera-eh malchuto ...* (May His kingship be revealed and be seen ...)

	Shabbat Morning; Festivals falling on *Shabbat*	Festivals falling on weekdays	*Shabbat* Afternoon; Monday; Thursday; Minor Festivals; Fast Days
Prescribed readings	At least seven *Aliyot*	Five or six *Aliyot*	Three or four *Aliyot*
After the prescribed readings	[Except *Shabbat* Afternoon] *Chatzi Kaddish* (page 128)		
Additional reading	*Maftir*		—
On raising the scroll	*V'zot haTorah* ... (This is the Torah ...)		
Reading from the Prophets	*Haftarah*		[Fast Days only] *Haftarah*
Prayers before returning the scroll	*Y'kum purkan* ... (May salvation arise ...)	[*Chagim* only] *Yah Eli* ... (O Lord, my God ...)	[Most Mondays and Thursdays] *Y'hi ratzon milifnei* ... (May it be the will ...)
	[*Shabbat* preceding new month] *Birkat haChodesh* (Blessing of the new month)	—	—
	[Yom Kippur and last day of each *Chag*] *Yizkor* (Memorial Service)		
	[Usually] *Av harachamim Shochen m'romim* ... (May the Father of Mercies Who dwells on high ...)	—	
	Ashrei (page 140)		
On taking the scroll	*Y'ha-l'lu et Shem Adonai* ... (Praise the Name of the Lord ...)		

	Shabbat Morning; Festivals falling on *Shabbat*	Festivals falling on weekdays	*Shabbat* Afternoon; Monday; Thursday; Minor Festivals; Fast Days
Procession II	*Mizmor l'David* ... (A psalm of David ...)	*L'David mizmor* ... (A psalm of David ...)	
In front of the Ark	*U-v'nucho yomar* ... (And when it rested ...)		

Each of these components is now examined.

Before Opening the Ark

Shabbat Morning; Festivals falling on *Shabbat*	Festivals falling on week-days	*Shabbat* Afternoon; Monday; Thursday; Minor Festivals; Fast Days
Ein kamocha ... et ammo vashalom (There is none like You ... His people with peace)		[Most Mondays and Thursdays]
Av harachamim heitivah virtzon'chah et Tziyon ... Adon olamim (Merciful Father, may it be Your will to do good for Zion ... eternal Master)		*El erech apayim ... k'rov rachamecha El* (O God Who is slow to anger ... in accordance with Your abundant mercies, O God)

In the Morning Service on *Shabbat* and Festivals, two prayers are recited before opening the Ark. *Ein kamocha* (There is none like You) expresses the uniqueness of the Lord. It begins with two verses from *T'hillim* (Ps. 86:8, 145:13); the middle is the composite biblical verse *Adonai melech* (The Lord reigns) discussed on page 161. It ends with another verse from *T'hillim*, Psalm 29:11. *Av harachamim* (Merciful Father) is a short prayer for rebuilding Jerusalem. It incorporates Psalm 51:20.

On Mondays and Thursdays (except *Chol haMo-ed, Rosh Chodesh,* Purim, *Shushan Purim,* Chanukah, Tish-ah b'Av, the day before Pesach, and the day before Yom Kippur), a prayer for forgiveness beginning *El Erech apayim* (O God Who is slow to anger) is said. There are two similar versions of the prayer. Most liturgies include the one or the other; some include both.

No fewer than three of the prayers associated with the reading of the *Torah* begin with the words *Av harachamim*. To reduce confusion, the succeeding words of each prayer are also given in the relevant diagrams.

For the Maven

M'vinim refer to each of the many prayers that begin with the words *Av harachamim* simply as *Av harachamim*. The fact that they know from the context precisely which prayer is meant is proof positive that they are *m'vinim!*

On Opening the Ark

Shabbat Morning; Festivals falling on *Shabbat*	Festivals falling on week-days	*Shabbat* Afternoon; Monday; Thursday; Minor Festivals; Fast Days
Va-y'hi binso-a ha-aron ... l'ammo Yisra-el bi-k'dushato (And when the Ark started to move forward ... to His people Israel in His holiness)		

The prayer that is said when the Ark is opened begins with Numbers 10:35, which states what Moses used to say when the Ark started to move forward. The final sentence blesses God for having given the *Torah* to His people.

In Front of the Ark

On Festivals that fall on weekdays (and in some liturgies, also on *Hoshana Rabbah,* the last of the Intermediate Days of Sukkot), four prayers are said.

Shabbat Morning; Festivals falling on *Shabbat*	Festivals falling on week-days	*Shabbat* Afternoon; Monday; Thursday; Minor Festivals; Fast Days
—	*Adonai Adonai ... v'nakei* (The Lord, the Lord ... and acquitting)	—
	Ribono shel olam ... chesed y'sov'venu, Amen (Master of the universe ... may kindness surround him, Amen)	
	Yi-h'yu l'ratzon ... Tzuri v'Go-ali (May [the words] find favor ... my Rock and my Redeemer)	
	Va-ani t'filati ... be-emet yishecha (As for me, may my prayer ... in the truth of Your salvation)	

The first prayer, *Adonai Adonai* (The Lord, the Lord), is a recitation of the Thirteen Attributes of Divine Mercy as they appear in Exodus 34:6–7. The passage is said three times.

Next comes the prayer *Ribono shel olam* (Master of the universe). This personal prayer comes in two forms. One version is said on the three *Chagim* (Pesach, Shavuot, and Sukkot), and the other on *Yamim Nora-im* (Rosh haShanah and Yom Kippur). Both versions are written in the first person and begin by asking for one's deepest requests for good to be fulfilled. The version for the *Chagim* accentuates obeying the *Mitzvot*; the version for *Yamim Nora-im* stresses forgiveness from sin and a resulting long life.

This is followed by Psalm 19:15, beginning *Yi-h'yu l'ratzon* (May [the words] find favor). The section concludes with another individual verse from *T'hillim*, Psalm 69:14, beginning *Va-ani t'filati* (As for me, may my prayer). This verse is also said three times.

The reason that this material is not recited when a Festival coincides with *Shabbat* is that personal supplications are not made on the Sabbath.

For the Maven

The custom of reciting the Thirteen Attributes of Divine Mercy is relatively recent, dating from 1805 [Hertz, p. 477].

B'rich Sh'mei

Shabbat Morning; Festivals falling on *Shabbat*	Festivals falling on week-days	*Shabbat* Afternoon; Monday; Thursday; Minor Festivals; Fast Days
B'rich Sh'mei d'Marei al'ma ... l'tav u-l'chayin ulishlam (Blessed be the Name of the Master of the universe ... for good, and for life, and for peace)		

This prayer (in Aramaic, not Hebrew) is taken from the *Zohar*, a primary work of Jewish mysticism. It is stated in the *Zohar* (*Parshat Vayakhel*) that when the congregation prepares to read from the *Torah*, the gates of mercy are opened and God's love is awakened. At this point, the prayer beginning *B'rich Sh'mei d'Marei al'ma* (Blessed be the Name of the Master of the universe) should be recited [Birnbaum, pp. 119–120].

On Taking the Scroll

The Reader now takes the *Torah*.

Shabbat Morning; Festivals falling on *Shabbat*	Festivals falling on week-days	*Shabbat* Afternoon; Monday; Thursday; Minor Festivals; Fast Days
Sh'ma Yisra-el ... Adonai Echad (Hear O Israel ... the Lord is One)		—
Echad Eloheinu ... kadosh [v'nora] Sh'mo (Our God is one ... holy [and awesome] is His Name)		
Ga-d'lu Ladonai iti ... Sh'mo yachdav (Magnify the Lord with me ... His Name together)		

In the Morning Service on *Shabbat* and Festivals (and, in some liturgies, also on *Hoshana Rabbah,* the last of the Intermediate Days of Sukkot), the Reader faces the congregation and says the first verse of the *Sh'ma* (Chapter 8), followed by a sentence affirming the unity of God. The additional word *v'nora* (and awesome) is added on *Yamim Nora-im* (and on *Hoshana Rabbah*).

Then, on all occasions when the *Torah* is read, the Reader faces the Ark, bows, and says *Ga-d'lu Ladonai iti* (Magnify the Lord with me), exalting the Lord.

Procession I

A procession is now formed, led by the *Torah* bearer (or bearers, on those occasions when more than one scroll is read—see page 184).

Shabbat Morning; Festivals falling on *Shabbat*	Festivals falling on week-days	*Shabbat* Afternoon; Monday; Thursday; Minor Festivals; Fast Days
L'cha Adonai ha-g'dulah ... ki kadosh Adonai Eloheinu (Yours, O Lord, is the greatness ... because the Lord our God is holy)		
Al hakol ... ki pi Adonai diber (Above all ... for the mouth of the Lord has spoken)		—
Av harachamim Hu y'rachem ... y'shu-ah v'rachamim (May the Father of mercy have compassion ... salvation and mercy)		

The congregation sings *L'cha Adonai ha-g'dulah* (Yours, O Lord, is the greatness). This prayer consists of three biblical verses that again extol the greatness of the Lord: I Chronicles 29:11, Psalm 99:5, and Psalm 99:9.

On *Shabbat* and Festivals (and in some liturgies, on *Hoshana Rabbah*), the paragraph *Al hakol* (Above all) is said; it glorifies the majesty of the Lord.

Finally, on all occasions that the *Torah* is read, a prayer for mercy and salvation follows, beginning *Av harachamim Hu y'rachem* (May the Father of mercy have compassion).

On Unrolling the Scroll

The Reader unrolls the *Sefer Torah* (scroll) and recites an introductory formula at the end of which the first person is called to the reading of the *Torah*.

Shabbat Morning; Festivals falling on *Shabbat*	Festivals falling on weekdays	*Shabbat* Afternoon; Monday; Thursday; Minor Festivals; Fast Days
V'ya-azor v'yagen ... l'ammo Yisra-el bi-k'dushato (May He help and shield ... to His people Israel in His holiness)		*V'tigaleh v'tera-eh malchuto ... l'ammo Yisra-el bi-k'dushato* (May His kingship be revealed and be seen ... to His people Israel in His holiness)
V'atem hadvekim Badonai Eloheichem chayim kulchem hayom (And you who cling to the Lord your God are all alive today)		

There are two different introductory formulae. In the Morning Service on *Shabbat* and Festivals, *V'ya-azor v'yagen* (May He help and shield) is used; whereas on the other occasions when the *Torah* is read, the formula is *V'tigaleh v'tera-eh malchuto* (May His kingship be revealed and be seen).

In both instances, the congregational response is the same, namely, *V'atem hadvekim Badonai Eloheichem, chayim kulchem hayom* (And you who cling to the Lord your God are all alive today) (Deut. 4:4).

Prescribed Readings

An *Aliyah* is the honor of being called up to read from the *Torah*. The following is the specified number of *Aliyot*:

Shabbat Morning and Festivals falling on *Shabbat*	seven (more are permitted)
Yom Kippur	six
Rosh haShanah; *Chagim*	five
Chol haMo-ed (Intermediate Days of *Chagim*); *Rosh Chodesh*	four
Shabbat Afternoon; Monday; Thursday; Fast Days; Purim; Chanukah	three

Originally, each person called up read the *Torah* for himself; if one could not read the *Torah*, one was not called up. This practice led to difficulties. The handwritten scroll contains only consonants; there are no vowels or punctuation marks. In addition, the text is chanted in accordance with the *t'amei hamikra* (cantillation marks—*trop* in Yiddish), which appear in only printed editions of the *Torah*, not on the scroll itself. Thus, reading from a scroll is a relatively limited skill in most communities. A trained Reader, the *Ba-al K'riah*, was therefore appointed to read from the *Sefer Torah* on behalf of those who did not possess this skill.

Nowadays the custom has arisen that the *Ba-al K'riah* reads on behalf of everyone who is called up for an *Aliyah*, even those who can read from the *Torah*. This is to avoid embarrassing those who do not possess this particular skill.

For the Maven

There must be at least three *Aliyot*. Each *Aliyah* must consist of at least three verses, at least one of which must be a previously unread verse. A minimum of ten verses must be read in all. However, there is one exception to this—on Purim only nine verses are read.

Structure of Order of *Aliyot*

The first person called up should be a *Kohen* (a descendant of the Temple Priests), the second a *Levi* (a descendant of the Levites), and the others *Yisra-el* (neither a *Kohen* nor a *Levi*). But what if no *Kohen* and/or *Levi* is present? The answer is given in the following table:

	First *Aliyah*	Second *Aliyah*	Remaining *Aliyot*
Kohen and *Levi* present	*Kohen*	*Levi*	*Yisra-el*
Kohen present, but no *Levi*	*Kohen*	Same *Kohen*	*Yisra-el*
Levi present, but no *Kohen*	*Levi*	*Yisra-el*	*Yisra-el*
Neither *Kohen* or *Levi* present	*Yisra-el*	*Yisra-el*	*Yisra-el*

The structure of each *Aliyah* is given below.

Structure of Each *Aliyah*

The person called to the *Torah* recites a sequence of *b'rachot*.

Person called to the *Torah*	*Ba-r'chu et Adonai Ha-m'vorach* (Bless the Lord Who is to be blessed)
Congregation, repeated by person called to the *Torah*	*Baruch Adonai Ha-m'vorach l'olam va-ed* (Blessed be the Lord Who is to be blessed forever and ever)
Person called to the *Torah* (*b'rachah* before the reading)	*Baruch Attah Adonai ... Asher bachar banu mikol ha-amim ... Baruch Attah Adonai, Noten haTorah* (Blessed are You, O Lord ... Who has chosen us from all the peoples ... Blessed are You, O Lord, Giver of the *Torah)*

The *Torah* portion is read

Person called to the *Torah* (*b'rachah* after the reading)	*Baruch Attah Adonai ... Asher natan lanu Torat emet ... Baruch Attah Adonai, Noten haTorah* (Blessed are You, O Lord ... Who has given us the *Torah* of truth ... Blessed are You, O Lord, Giver of the *Torah)*

The person called to the *Torah* begins by declaring *Ba-r'chu et Adonai Ha-m'vorach* (Bless the Lord Who is to be blessed). The congregation responds *Baruch Adonai Ha-m'vorach l'olam va-ed* (Blessed be the Lord Who is to be blessed forever and ever). The person called to the *Torah* repeats this response, then says the Long Form *b'rachah* before the *Aliyah*, namely, *Baruch Attah Adonai ... Asher bachar banu mikol ha-amim ... Baruch Attah Adonai, Noten haTorah* (Blessed are You, O Lord ... Who has chosen us from all the peoples ... Blessed are You, O Lord, Giver of the *Torah*).

The *Torah* portion is now read, after which the person called to the *Torah* says the Long Form *b'rachah* after the *Aliyah*, namely, *Baruch Attah Adonai ... Asher natan lanu Torat emet ... Baruch Attah Adonai, Noten haTorah* (Blessed are You, O Lord ... Who gave us the *Torah* of truth ... Blessed are You, O Lord, Giver of the *Torah*).

Additional *B'rachot*

There are two occasions when additional *b'rachot* are recited. First, if a person has been in peril, then the following *b'rachah* (*Birkat haGomel*) and response are recited.

One who has been through a dangerous experience adds	*Baruch Attah Adonai ... She-g'malani kol tov* (Blessed are You, O Lord ... Who has bestowed all goodness on me)
The congregation responds	*Mi-She-g'molcha ... kol tov, Selah* (May He Who has bestowed ... all goodness. *Selah*)

Originally, there were four hazardous experiences for which this *b'rachah* was required to be said, if possible within three days of the incident, namely, completing a sea voyage, completing a hazardous land journey, release from imprisonment, and recovery from a serious illness. This has been extended to all other life-threatening situations.

The father of a *Bar Mitzvah* adds	*Baruch She-p'tarani me-onsho shel zeh* (Blessed be He Who has relieved me of the responsibility for this child)

At the age of thirteen, a boy becomes a *Bar Mitzvah,* that is, responsible for his own religious behavior. After a *Bar Mitzvah* has completed his first *Aliyah,* his father says *Baruch She-p'tarani me-onsho shel zeh* (Blessed be He Who has relieved me of the responsibility for this child).

Misheberach

After completing the *b'rachot,* the person who has been called to the *Torah* is blessed. Because the prayer begins with the word *Misheberach* (May He who blessed), the prayer is referred to as a *Misheberach.*

Shabbat Morning; Festivals falling on *Shabbat*	Festivals falling on week-days	*Shabbat* Afternoon; Monday; Thursday; Minor Festivals; Fast Days
Misheberach avoteinu Avraham, Yitzchak, v'Ya-akov ... v'nomar Amen (May He who blessed our fathers Abraham, Isaac, and Jacob ... and let us say, *Amen*)		

An additional *Misheberach* is said on a variety of special occasions, such as the naming of a baby girl, the celebration of a *Bar Mitzvah* or an *ufruf* (the *Aliyah* on the *Shabbat* prior to being married), or on behalf of a sick person.

In addition, in some liturgies the prayer beginning *El malei rachamim* (O God who is full of compassion) is said on the day of or preceding a *Yahrzeit* (anniversary of a death).

After Prescribed Readings

After the prescribed readings, except during the Afternoon Service for *Shabbat, Chatzi Kaddish* is said at this point.

Shabbat Morning; Festivals falling on *Shabbat*	Festivals falling on weekdays	*Shabbat* Afternoon; Monday; Thursday; Minor Festivals; Fast Days
	[Except *Shabbat* Afternoon] *Chatzi Kaddish* (page 128)	

As explained in Chapter 9, the *Chatzi Kaddish* delimits certain major components of the service, in this case, the *Torah* reading. It is true that, as will shortly be discussed, in many services there is a further *Torah* reading (the *Maftir*) followed by a reading from the Prophets (*Haftarah*). However, these elements were added later and are not part of the prescribed *Torah* reading.

For the Maven

The reason why the *Chatzi Kaddish* is not said after the reading on *Minchah l'Shabbat* is because *Chatzi Kaddish* follows immediately afterwards, just before the *Minchah Amidah*.

More For the Maven

On Fast Days, the third person called to the *Torah* is also the *Maftir*. The *Chatzi Kaddish* is said **after** the *Maftir* reading because the third person is part of the prescribed requirement of a minimum of three *Aliyot*.

Additional Reading

In the Morning Service on *Shabbat* and Festivals, there is an additional *Torah* reading, the *Maftir*.

Shabbat Morning; Festivals falling on *Shabbat*	Festivals falling on week-days	*Shabbat* Afternoon; Monday; Thursday; Minor Festivals; Fast Days
Maftir (additional reading)		—

During the time of King Antiochus (around 165 B.C.E.), the Jews in Israel were prohibited from reading the *Torah* during public worship. They substituted a reading from the Prophets that was related content-wise to the forbidden *Torah* reading.

After the successful Maccabee revolt (celebrated in the festival of Chanukah) the ban was lifted but the custom of reading from the Prophets remained. In order to prevent the congregation from thinking that the reading from the Prophets was of equal importance to the *Torah* reading, it was decided that the person who read from the Prophets should first read from the *Torah*. This additional *Torah* reading was termed the *Maftir* (literally, completion).

On *Shabbat* morning this additional reading is at the end of the statutory reading; it is usually a repetition of the last few verses. However, a second *Torah* is read on Festivals. These special *Maftir* readings are from *Parshat Pinchas* (Num. 25:10–29:40); they describe the Temple sacrifices for that occasion (see page 73).

A separate *Maftir* from a second *Torah* is also read on *Arba Parshiot*, the four special *Shabbatot* before Pesach—*Parshat Sh'kalim, Parshat Zachor, Parshat Parah*, and *Parshat haChodesh*), on *Rosh Chodesh Tevet* (which coincides with Chanukah), on *Rosh Chodesh* when it falls on *Shabbat*, and on *Shabbat* Chanukah.

For the Maven

There are four occasions when three *Sifrei Torah* are read. The first occasion occurs every year on *Simchat Torah;* the last section of Deuteronomy is read from the first scroll, the first section of Genesis from the second scroll, and the *Maftir* from the third scroll as described at the end of this chapter. The second occasion occurs if *Shabbat* Chanukah coincides with *Rosh Chodesh Tevet*. The usual *Shabbat parashah* is then read from the first scroll, the *Rosh Chodesh Maftir* from the second scroll, and the Chanukah *Maftir* from the third scroll. The third occasion is if *Parshat Sh'kalim* coincides with *Rosh Chodesh Adar*. The usual *Shabbat parashah* is then read from the first scroll, the *Rosh Chodesh Maftir* from the second scroll, and the *Parshat Sh'kalim Maftir* from the third scroll. The fourth occasion is if *Parshat haChodesh* coincides with *Rosh Chodesh Nissan*. The usual *Shabbat parashah* is then read from the first scroll, the *Rosh Chodesh Maftir* from the second scroll, and the *Parshat haChodesh Maftir* from the third scroll.

On Raising the Scroll

In the *Ashkenazi* liturgy, after the *Sefer Torah* has been read it is raised and displayed to the congregation; in the *Sephardi* liturgy, it is raised and displayed before it is read.

Shabbat Morning; Festivals falling on *Shabbat*	Festivals falling on week-days	*Shabbat* Afternoon; Monday; Thursday; Minor Festivals; Fast Days
V'zot haTorah ... b'yad Moshe (This is the *Torah* ... by the hand of Moses)		

The congregation recites *V'zot haTorah* (This is the *Torah*). This sentence consists of parts of Deuteronomy 4:44 and Numbers 9:23. In some liturgies, additional biblical verses are recited at this point.

Reading from the Prophets

On *Shabbat*, Festivals, and Fast Days there is also a reading from the Prophets, as described on page 184. This reading, termed the *Haftarah* (completion), relates to the contents of the *Torah* reading for that day.

On Tish-ah b'Av and Yom Kippur, a *Haftarah* is read at both the Morning Service and Afternoon Service; on the Minor Fasts, it is read at the Afternoon Service only.

B'rachah before *Haftarah*	*Baruch Attah Adonai ... uvinvi-ei ha-emet vatzedek* (Blessed are You, O Lord ... and the true and righteous prophets)

The *Haftarah* is read

First *b'rachah* after *Haftarah*	*Baruch Attah Adonai ... ha-El ha-ne-eman b'chol d'varav* (Blessed are You, O Lord ... the faithful God in all His words)
Second *b'rachah* after *Haftarah*	*Rachem al Tziyon ... M'same-ach Tziyon b'vanehah* (Have mercy on Zion ... Who makes Zion rejoice through her children)
Third *b'rachah* after *Haftarah*	*Sa-m'chenu ... Magen David* (Gladden us ... the Shield of David)
[Not on Fast Days] Fourth *b'rachah* after *Haftarah*	*Al haTorah ...* (For the *Torah* reading ...)

One *b'rachah* is said before reading the *Haftarah*. After the reading, there are four *b'rachah* components (three on Fast Days), comprising a Series Form *b'rachah*. The wording of the fourth component, *Al haTorah* (For the *Torah* reading), varies according to the specific occasion, namely, *Shabbat* or Festival.

Prayers before Returning Scroll to the Ark

Before returning the Scroll to the Ark, three different sets of prayers are said, one set on *Shabbat*, the second on Festivals, and the third on Mondays and Thursdays.

Shabbat Morning; Festivals falling on *Shabbat*	Festivals falling on weekdays	*Shabbat* Afternoon; Monday; Thursday; Minor Festivals; Fast Days
Y'kum purkan ... (May salvation arise ...)	[*Chagim* only] *Yah Eli* ... (O Lord, my God ...)	[Most Mondays and Thursdays] *Y'hi ratzon milifnei* ... (May it be the will ...)
[*Shabbat* preceding new month] *Birkat haChodesh* (Blessing of the new month)	—	—
[Yom Kippur and last day of each *Chag*] *Yizkor* (Memorial Service)		
[Usually] *Av harachamim Shochen m'romim* ... (May the Father of Mercies Who dwells on high ...)	—	
Ashrei (page 140)		

We consider each of these three sets of prayers in turn, starting with those said on *Shabbat* morning.

Prayers before Returning Scroll to the Ark: *Shabbat* Morning

First we consider the five components that are recited on *Shabbat* morning.

Shabbat Morning; Festivals falling on *Shabbat*	Festivals falling on week-days	*Shabbat* Afternoon; Monday; Thursday; Minor Festivals; Fast Days
Prayers for scholars, the congregation, the government, and the State of Israel		
[On *Shabbat* preceding new month] *Birkat haChodesh* (Blessing of the new month)		
[On Yom Kippur, the last day of Pesach and Shavuot, and *Sh'mini Atzeret*] *Yizkor* (Memorial Service)		
[On most *Shabbatot*] *Av harachamim Shochen m'romim* (May the Father of Mercies Who dwells on high)		
Ashrei (page 140)		

We now examine the first four of these five components of the *Shabbat* morning service; *Ashrei* is described on page 140.

Prayers for Scholars, Congregation, Government, and Israel

Shabbat Morning; Festivals falling on *Shabbat*	Festivals falling on week-days	*Shabbat* Afternoon; Monday; Thursday; Minor Festivals; Fast Days
Y'kum purkan min sh'maya ... l'marranan v'rabbanan ... kol z'man v'idan, v'nomar Amen (May salvation arise from heaven ... to our scholars and sages ... at every season and time, and let us say, Amen)		
Y'kum purkan min sh'maya ... l'chol k'hala kadisha ha-dein ... kol z'man v'idan, v'nomar Amen (May salvation arise from heaven ... to this entire congregation ... at every season and time, and let us say, Amen)		
Misheberach avoteinu Avraham, Yitzchak, v'Ya-akov ... im kol Yisra-el acheihem, v'nomar Amen (May He Who blessed our fathers, Abraham, Isaac, and Jacob ... with all Israel, their brethren, and let us say, Amen)		
Hanoten t'shu-ah la-m'lachim ... v'chen y'hi rat-zon, v'nomar Amen (May He Who grants salvation to kings ... and may this be His will, and let us say, Amen)		
Avinu shebashamayim, Tzur Yisra-el v'Go-alo ... umalchuto bachol mashala, Amen, Selah (Our Father in heaven, Rock and Redeemer of Israel ... and His majesty rules over all, Amen, *Selah*)		

On *Shabbat* morning, prayers for scholars, the congregation, and the State of Israel are added at this point in the service. The first two prayers are very similar. They are both written in Aramaic, the language of the Jews of Babylonia until approximately the eighth century C.E. The first part and the last part of both prayers are identical. The middle part of the first *Y'kum Purkan* states that this is a prayer *l'marranan v'rabbanan* (for our scholars and sages), whereas the second is *l'chol k'hala kadisha ha-dein* (for to this entire congregation).

Next comes a prayer in Hebrew for the congregation, *Misheberach avoteinu Avraham, Yitzchak, v'Ya-akov* (May He Who blessed our fathers, Abraham, Isaac, and Jacob).

This is followed by *Hanoten t'shu-ah la-m'lachim* (May He Who grants salvation to kings), a prayer for the welfare of the government. The body of the prayer changes with the country. For example, British Jews pray for "Our Sovereign Lady Queen Elizabeth; Elizabeth, the Queen Mother; Philip, Duke of Edinburgh; Charles, Prince of Wales; and all the Royal Family." Whereas American Jews pray for "The President and the Vice-President and all the officers of this country."

Finally, in some liturgies, a prayer is said for the welfare of the State of Israel. It begins *Avinu shebashamayim, Tzur Yisra-el v'Go-alo* (Our Father in heaven, Rock and Redeemer of Israel).

Birkat haChodesh

On the *Shabbat* morning preceding a new month, additional prayers are added to proclaim the date of the new moon and bless the new month. In Temple times, the new month was proclaimed by the *Bet Din* (rabbinical court) in Jerusalem, on the basis of eye-witness sightings of the new moon. The decision was then signaled to the whole of Israel by means of bonfires lit on mountain tops.

Around 400 C.E., the Patriarch Hillel II drew up rules for the calendar; on the basis of these computations, an announcement was made in synagogues on the *Shabbat* morning before each new month. Later, instead of just an announcement, it became the custom to bless the new month.

Shabbat Morning; Festivals falling on *Shabbat*	Festivals falling on weekdays	*Shabbat* Afternoon; Monday; Thursday; Minor Festivals; Fast Days
Y'hi ratzon mi-l'fanecha ... mishalot libenu l'tovah, Amen, Selah (May it be Your will ... the wishes of our heart for goodness, Amen. *Selah*)		
Announcement of the *Molad* (exact time of the new moon in Jerusalem)		
Mi she-asa nissim ... chaverim kol Yisra-el, v'nomar Amen (May He Who has performed miracles ... all Israel as brethren, and let us say, Amen)		
Proclamation of the new moon *Rosh Chodesh ... v'al kol Yisra-el l'tovah* (The new month of ... and on all Israel for goodness)		
Y'cha-d'shehu ... lishu-a u-l'nechamah, v'nomar Amen (May He renew ... for salvation and consolation, and let us say, Amen)		

Birkat haChodesh (blessing of the new month) begins with *Y'hi ratzon mi-l'fanecha* (May it be Your will), a prayer that the new month may bring peace and happiness. This prayer is essentially a version of the daily prayer of Rav, a Babylonian scholar, with the addition of a phrase referring to the new moon. This prayer was added to the *Siddur* in the eighteenth century [Hertz, p. 509], making it one of the newest items in the *Siddur*.

Next, in many liturgies the congregation is informed of the *Molad*, the exact time of the new moon in Jerusalem, to the nearest *chelek* (3-1/3 seconds). This is followed by *Mi she-asa nissim* (May He Who has performed miracles), a prayer for national salvation and ingathering of the exiles.

Now, the day or days of *Rosh Chodesh* (New Month Festival) are announced. Months alternate between twenty-nine and thirty days; when a month has 30 days, the last day of that month and the first day of the next month are both *Rosh Chodesh,* otherwise just the first day of the next month is *Rosh Chodesh.*

Finally, we pray that the new month will bring life, peace, joy, and salvation, beginning with the words *Y'cha-d'shehu haKadosh baruch Hu* (May the Holy One, blessed be He, renew).

For the Maven

The Jewish calendar is a soli-lunar calendar, that is, it is based on the position of both the sun and the moon. Each of the Festivals must occur at a specific season; for example, Pesach must always occur in the Spring. To keep each Festival at the correct time of the year, an additional month is added in years 3, 6, 8, 11, 14, 17, and 19 of the 19-year cycle. Thus, in place of the month of Adar, in a leap year we have the month of First Adar followed by Second Adar (or *v'Adar*).

A further complication is that certain Festivals cannot fall on specific days. For instance, Yom Kippur cannot fall on Friday (because it is forbidden to prepare for *Shabbat* on Yom Kippur) or on Sunday (because it is forbidden to prepare for Yom Kippur on *Shabbat*). To ensure the necessary flexibility, two months (Kislev and Tevet) can be either 29 or 30 days long. There are thus three exceptions to the rule that the months are alternately 29 and 30 days long, namely, the variable length of *Kislev,* the variable length of Tevet, and the fact that, in a leap year, the 29-day month of Adar is replaced by the 30-day month of First Adar followed by the 29-day month of Second Adar.

Which is the leap month, First Adar or Second Adar? We are told in the *Talmud* (*Bavli P'sachim* 64b) that what is usually done in Adar of a regular year must be done during First Adar of a leap year. Thus, Second Adar would appear to be the leap month. Nevertheless, in leap years the various special days such as Purim and *Arba Parshiot* (the four special *Shabbatot* before Pesach) fall in Second Adar. A boy born in Adar of a regular year celebrates his Bar Mitzvah in Second Adar. Some authorities hold that a *Yahrzeit* (the anniversary of a death) in Adar of a regular year is observed in Second Adar of a leap year; most authorities state that it should be observed in First Adar. Accordingly, I do not have the faintest idea which of the two is the leap month.

The Structure of *Yizkor*

Yizkor, the Memorial Service, is recited on Yom Kippur, the last day of Pesach, the last day of Shavuot, and on *Sh'mini Atzeret*.

On Pesach and Shavuot, except on last day, and on Sukkot, except on *Sh'mini Atzeret*	On Yom Kippur, the last day of Pesach and Shavuot, and *Sh'mini Atzeret*	On Rosh haShanah
	Biblical Verses *Adonai mah Adam ... el Elohim Asher n'tanah* (O Lord, what is man ... to God Who gave it)	
	Psalm 91 *Yoshev b'seter Elyon ... v'arehu bishu-ati* (He who dwells in the refuge of the Most High ... and I will show him My salvation)	
	Prayers for individual deceased relatives *Yizkor Elohim ...* (May God remember ...)	
	Prayer for martyrs, prayer for fallen members of the Israel Defense Force *El malei rachamim ...* (O God, full of mercy ...)	

Yizkor begins with a series of biblical verses, *Adonai mah adam* (O Lord, what is man), followed by Psalm 91, *Yoshev b'seter Elyon* (He who dwells in the refuge of the Most High).

Personalized memorial prayers for deceased relatives follow, each beginning with the words *Yizkor Elohim* (May God remember).

The memorial service concludes with a series of prayers expressing communal mourning, all beginning *El malei rachamim* (O God, full of mercy). Such prayers are usually offered for Jewish martyrs, including the six million who were killed during the Holocaust and for the members of the Israel Defense Force who were killed in the defense of Israel. The precise wording of each prayer varies from liturgy to liturgy.

For the Maven

A superstition associated with *Yizkor* is that if someone whose parents are alive stays in the synagogue when *Yizkor* is recited, a parent will die in the coming year. In some liturgies, particularly the Lithuanian, the entire congregation remains in the synagogue for *Yizkor*.

Prayer for Martyrs

On most *Shabbatot*, a prayer for Jewish martyrs is added at this point.

Shabbat Morning; Festivals falling on *Shabbat*	Festivals falling on week-days	*Shabbat* Afternoon; Monday; Thursday; Minor Festivals; Fast Days
Av harachamim Shochen m'romim ... al ken yarim rosh (May the Father of Mercies Who dwells on high ... consequently he will raise his head in triumph)		

The prayer *Av harachamim Shochen m'romim* (May the Father of Mercies Who dwells on high) was probably composed during the Crusades, when major pogroms took place. The prayer asks God to avenge the blood of the martyrs.

It is omitted when *Rosh Chodesh* or Chanukah falls on *Shabbat*, on Festivals, and on distinguished *Shabbatot* such as *Arba Parshiot* (the four special *Shabbatot* before Pesach). In some liturgies, it is omitted on all occasions when *Tachanun* would be omitted on a weekday (page 139), such as the entire month of *Nissan*.

Prayers before Returning Scroll to the Ark: Festivals

On Festivals, the following prayers are recited:

On Pesach and Shavuot, except on last day, and on Sukkot, except on *Sh'mini Atzeret*	On Yom Kippur, the last day of Pesach and Shavuot, and *Sh'mini Atzeret*	On Rosh haShanah
[Omitted on *Shabbat*] *Yah Eli ... b'ashrei yosh'vei veitecha* (O Lord, my God ... happy are they who dwell in Your House)	*Yizkor* (Memorial Service)	—
Ashrei (page 140)		

The prayer *Yah Eli* ... (O Lord, my God ...) is an expression of joy in recalling the Temple sacrifices and the hope that we may be able to recite *Ashrei* (page 140) in the rebuilt Temple; *Yah Eli* is immediately followed by *Ashrei*. Because of its cheerful nature, it is inappropriate for us to recite *Yah Eli* just before *Yizkor*, the Memorial Service, which is said on the last day of Pesach and Shavuot, and on *Sh'mini Atzeret,* occasions when *Yah Eli* would otherwise be said. *Yizkor* is described on page 193.

Prayers before Returning Scroll to the Ark: Mondays and Thursdays

On Monday and Thursday mornings when *Tachanun* is said (see Chapter 9), the Reader adds the following:

Shabbat Morning; Festivals falling on *Shabbat*	Festivals falling on week-days	*Shabbat* Afternoon; Monday; Thursday; Minor Festivals; Fast Days
		[On Mondays and Thursdays when *Tachanun* is said] *Y'hi ratzon milifnei Avinu shebashamayim ... hashta ba-agala uvizman kariv, v'nomar Amen* (May it be the will of our Father in heaven ... now, speedily, and soon, and let us say, Amen)

This prayer consists of five paragraphs, the first four of which begin with the words *Y'hi ratzon milifnei Avinu shebashamayim* (May it be the will of our Father in heaven). We ask for the Temple to be rebuilt, for protection of all Jewish communities, scholars, and travelers, and for redemption.

On Taking the Scroll

Shabbat Morning; Festivals falling on *Shabbat*	Festivals falling on week-days	*Shabbat* Afternoon; Monday; Thursday; Minor Festivals; Fast Days
Y'ha-l'lu et Shem Adonai ki nisgav Sh'mo l'vado (Praise the Name of the Lord, for His Name alone is exalted)		
Hodo al eretz v'shamayim ... am k'rovo Halleluyah (His glory is above the heaven and the earth ... the people close to Him. Praise the Lord!)		

On taking the *Sefer Torah,* the Reader says the first part of Psalm 148:13, *Y'ha-l'lu et Shem Adonai ki nisgav Sh'mo l'vado* (Praise the Name of the Lord, for His Name alone is exalted).

The congregation responds with the rest of the verse, together with the next verse, *Hodo al eretz v'shamayim ... am k'rovo Halleluyah.* (His glory is above the heaven and the earth ... the people close to Him. Praise the Lord!)

Procession II

Shabbat Morning; Festivals falling on *Shabbat*	Festivals falling on week-days	*Shabbat* Afternoon; Monday; Thursday; Minor Festivals; Fast Days
Mizmor l'David ... et ammo vashalom (A psalm of David ... His people with peace)	*L'David mizmor ... Hu Melech haKavod, Selah* (A psalm of David ... He is the King of Glory. *Selah*)	

A procession is formed to return the scroll to the Ark. On *Shabbat* morning, the congregation recites Psalm 29, *Mizmor l'David* (A psalm of David). At all other times, Psalm 24 is said instead, *L'David mizmor* (A psalm of David).

In Front of the Ark

After returning the *Torah* to the Ark, the following is said:

Shabbat Morning; Festivals falling on *Shabbat*	Festivals falling on week-days	*Shabbat* Afternoon; Monday; Thursday; Minor Festivals; Fast Days
U-v'nucho yomar ... chadesh yamenu k'kedem (And when it rested ... renew our days as of old)		

As described on page 174, the prayer on opening the Ark begins with Numbers 10:35, which states what Moses would say when the Ark started to move forward. Similarly, when the *Sefer Torah* is replaced in the Ark, the prayer begins with the following verse, Numbers 10:36, which states what was said when the Ark was lowered after it had been carried to a new place.

The rest of the prayer consists of seven other biblical verses: Psalm 132:8–10; Proverbs 4:2, 3:18, and 3:17; and Lamentations 5:21.

This concludes the description of the basic structure of *K'riat haTorah.* This structure is somewhat modified on *Simchat Torah,* as described in the next section.

For the Maven

In a *Torah* scroll, the two verses Numbers 10:35–36 are preceded and followed by an inverted letter *nun.* The meaning of these Masoretic marks has been hotly debated in the rabbinic literature. Rabbi Yehuda haNasi even went so far as to suggest that these two verses constitute a complete book of the Bible.

Torah Reading on *Simchat Torah*

Hakafot

On *Simchat Torah* the *Torah* is read at the end of both the Evening and Morning Services. On these two occasions, the structure of *K'riat haTorah,* as previously described in this chapter, is somewhat changed.

Biblical verses added to *Ein kamocha* (There is none like You) and *Av harachamim* (Merciful Father)

Attah horeta lada-at ... Adon Olamim (You have learned to know ... eternal Lord)

Va-y'hi binso-a ha-aron ... l'ammo Yisra-el bi-k'dushato (And when the Ark started to move forward ... to His people Israel in His holiness)

Seven Processions

Ana Adonai hoshiah na ... anenu v'yom korenu (We beseech You, O Lord, save us ... answer us on the day we call)

Elohei haruchot ... anenu v'yom korenu (God of all souls ... answer us on the day we call)

Sisu v'simchu ... ki hi lanu oz v'orah (Rejoice and be glad ... because it is our strength and light)

Sh'ma Yisra-el ... Adonai Echad (Hear O Israel ... the Lord is One)

First, the two paragraphs of biblical verses, namely, *Ein kamocha* (There is none like You) and *Av harachamim* (Merciful Father), are augmented by the addition of further verses. The first verse (Deut. 4:35) begins *Attah horeta lada-at* (You have learned to know). In some liturgies these verses are said responsively, in others individuals are called to the *Bimah* to chant each verse, which is then repeated by the congregation.

Next, *Va-y'hi binso-a ha-aron* (And when the Ark started to move forward) is said as usual. Now, all the scrolls are taken from the Ark and carried around the synagogue seven times in procession.

The first *Hakafah* (circuit) is preceded by the sentence *Ana Adonai hoshiah na ... anenu v'yom korenu* (We beseech You, O Lord, save us ... answer us on the day we call). For each *Hakafah,* three stiches are recited responsively. The initial letters of each stich form an alphabetic acrostic, beginning *Elohei haruchot* (God of all souls). The seventh *Hakafah* has six stiches, the last three all starting with the letter *tav.*

The hymn *Sisu v'simchu* (Rejoice and be glad) is chanted either during the *Hakafot* or after the *Torah* reading.

All but three scrolls are returned to the Ark (one scroll in the Evening Service) and the service proceeds as usual with *Sh'ma Yisra-el* (Hear, O Israel), as shown in the diagram.

Torah **Reading**

	Evening Service	Morning Service
First Scroll:	Three *Aliyot* (Deut. 33:1–33:17)	Five *Aliyot* (Deut. 33:1–33:26), repeated as necessary
	—	*Me-r'shut ha-El* ... (With the permission of God ...)
		One *Aliyah* (Deut. 33:27–34:12)
		Chazak (Be strong)
Second Scroll:	—	*Me-r'shut M'romam* ... (With the permission of the Elevated ...)
		One *Aliyah* (Gen. 1–2:3)
	Chatzi Kaddish (page 128)	
Third Scroll:	—	*Maftir* (Num. 29:35–30:1)
		Haftarah (Joshua 1)

During the Evening Service on *Simchat Torah,* we read from one scroll. In most liturgies, three *Aliyot* are read from Deuteronomy 33:1–33:17.

During the Morning Service, the five *Aliyot* of Deuteronomy 33:1–33:26 are read repeatedly from the first scroll until everyone in the congregation has had an *Aliyah*. Traditionally, the individual who is given the final *Aliyah* is called up together with all the boys under thirteen years of age. After that *Aliyah*, the blessing of Joseph, beginning *Hamalach hago-el* (The redeeming angel) (Gen. 48:15–16), is said for the boys.

Next, a lengthy formula beginning *Me-r'shut ha-El* (With the permission of God) is recited in calling up the *Chatan Torah* (Bridegroom of the *Torah*), the person honored with reading the last section of the last book of the *Torah*

(Deut. 33:27–34:12). As with the other four books of the *Torah*, the congregation rises just before the last sentence is read. When the Book of Deuteronomy has been completed, the congregation, followed by the Reader, says *Chazak, chazak, v'nitchazek* (Be strong, be strong, and let us be strengthened).

Now a similar lengthy formula beginning *Me-r'shut M'romam* (With the permission of the Elevated) is recited to call up the *Chatan B'reshit* (Bridegroom of Genesis), the person honored with reading the first section of the *Torah* (Gen. 1:1–2:3) from the second scroll. Thus, after concluding the *Torah* we immediately start again by reading from the beginning. During the reading from Genesis, the congregation says the repeated phrase beginning *Va-y'hi erev va-y'hi voker* (And it was morning and it was evening) each time before the Reader chants it. The final paragraph, beginning *Va-y'chulu hashamayim v'ha-aretz v'chol tz'va-am* (Thus the heavens and the earth and all their host were finished) (Gen. 2:1–3), is also first recited by the congregation and then chanted by the Reader.

The final *Aliyah* is the *Maftir*, which describes the relevant Temple sacrifices (Num. 29:35–30:1). This is read from the third scroll. The *Haftarah* is the first chapter of Joshua, the Book of the *Tanach* that immediately follows Deuteronomy.

For the Maven

The last section of Deuteronomy describes the death of Moses. The *Haftarah* explains how the work of Moses was continued by Joshua. Thus, the choice of *Haftarah* also expresses the *Simchat Torah* theme of continuity and lack of ending.

12
The Structure of the Afternoon Service

The structure of *Minchah* (Afternoon Service), like that of every other service, consists of three parts, namely, the section before the *Amidah*, the *Amidah* itself, and the section after the *Amidah*.

Shabbat; Chagim falling on *Shabbat*	*Chagim* falling on weekdays	Weekdays; Minor Festivals; Fast Days
Section before the *Amidah*		
Amidah section		
Section after the *Amidah*		

This is shown in more detail on the next page.

Shabbat; Chagim falling on Shabbat	Chagim falling on weekdays	Weekdays; Minor Festivals; Fast Days
Ashrei (page 140)		
Uva l'Tziyon Go-el (page 132)		—
Chatzi Kaddish (page 128)		
[Omitted on Chagim] Va-ani t'filati ... (As for me, my prayer ...)	—	—
Torah reading (Chapter 11)		[On Fast Days] Torah reading (Chapter 11)
Amidah (Chapter 5, 6, or 7)		
—	—	[Between Rosh haShanah and Yom Kippur and on Minor Fasts, except on Friday afternoon] Avinu Malkenu (page 141)
[Usually] Tzidka-t'cha ... (Your righteousness ...)		[Usually] Tachanun (page 135)
Kaddish Shalem (page 124)		
[Between Sukkot and Pesach] Ba-r'chi Nafshi (page 167) Kaddish Yatom (page 130)		
[Between Pesach and Rosh haShanah; omitted on Shavuot] Pirkei Avot (Chapters of the Fathers) Kaddish d'Rabbanan (page 129)		
Aleinu (page 133)		
Kaddish Yatom (page 130)		

Almost all the components shown in the diagram have been previously discussed. The three new items are now described. All are from the Afternoon Service for *Shabbat*; however, none of them are said when a Festival falls on *Shabbat*.

Va-Ani T'filati

Shabbat; Chagim falling on Shabbat	Chagim falling on week-days	Weekdays; Minor Festivals; Fast Days
[Omitted on *Chagim*] *Va-ani t'filati ... aneni be-emet yishecha* (As for me, my prayer ... answer me in the truth of Your salvation)		

This is a single verse from *T'hillim*, specifically, Psalm 69:14. The verse, *Va-ani t'filati ... aneni be-emet yishecha* (As for me, my prayer ... answer me in the truth of Your salvation), is recited before the *Torah* reading of the After-noon Service for *Shabbat*. It is omitted on Festivals.

Tzidka-t'cha

Shabbat; Chagim falling on Shabbat	Chagim falling on week-days	Weekdays; Minor Festivals; Fast Days
[Usually] *Tzidka-t'cha tzedek l'olam ... toshia, Adonai* (Your righteousness is an ever-lasting righteousness ... You save, Lord)		

This prayer consists of three verses from *T'hillim* (Ps. 119:142, 71:19, 36:7), all of which start with the word *Tzidka-t'cha* (Your righteousness). It is omitted on those occasions when *Tachanun* is omitted on weekdays (page 139) and hence on Festivals.

Pirkei Avot

Shabbat; Chagim falling on *Shabbat*	*Chagim* falling on weekdays	Weekdays; Minor Festivals; Fast Days
[Between Pesach and Rosh haShanah; omitted on Shavuot] *Pirkei Avot* (Chapters of the Fathers) *Kaddish d'Rabbanan* (page 129)		

On *Shabbat*, additional components are added after *Kaddish Shalem*. Specifically, between Sukkot and the *Shabbat* before Pesach we say *Ba-r'chi Nafshi* (the sixteen psalms discussed on page 167), followed by *Kaddish Yatom* (mourner's *Kaddish*) (page 130). On *Shabbat* between Pesach and *Rosh ha-Shanah*, one chapter of *Pirkei Avot* (Chapters of the Fathers) is read. *Pirkei Avot* is one of the sixty-three chapters of the *Mishnah*, so it is followed by *Kaddish d'Rabbanan* (page 129), which is recited after studying a rabbinic text.

This concludes the description of the structure of the Afternoon Service.

For the Maven

On *Shabbat haGadol* (the *Shabbat* before Pesach), it is customary in many liturgies to study part of the *Haggadah shel Pesach* in place of *Ba-r'chi Nafshi*.

13

The Structure of *Kabbalat Shabbat*

The first part of the Evening Service for *Shabbat* is called *Kabbalat Shabbat* (welcoming the Sabbath). This part of the service was introduced by the Kabbalists of Safed (in Northern Israel) in the sixteenth century. As early as Talmudic times, the Sabbath has been personified as a bride; the Kabbalists now wished to express this concept through prayer.

Shabbat	If a Festival or *Chol haMo-ed* falls on Friday or *Shabbat*
Six Psalms *L'chu n'ra-n'nah Ladonai* ... (Come, let us sing to the Lord ...)	—
Ana b'ko-ach ... (We beseech You, with the strength ...)	
L'chah dodi ... (Come, my beloved ...)	
Psalms 92, 93 *Mizmor shir l'Yom haShabbat* ... (A psalm, a song for the Sabbath day ...)	
Kaddish Yatom (page 130)	
Bameh madlikin ... (With what should we light [the Sabbath light] ...)	—
Kaddish d'Rabbanan (page 129)	

These components are now examined.

Six Psalms

Kabbalat Shabbat begins with six psalms, as shown in the diagram.

Shabbat	If a Festival or *Chol haMo-ed* falls on Friday or *Shabbat*
Psalms 95–99, 29 *L'chu n'ra-n'nah Ladonai ... Adonai y'varech et ammo vashalom* (Come, let us sing to the Lord ... The Lord will bless His people with peace)	

These six psalms were recited by the Kabbalists of the sixteenth century "to greet the *Shabbat* bride" as they walked into the fields outside Safed. The theme common to these psalms is that the Lord is the Creator of the world and Master of the universe. Six psalms were chosen to symbolize the Creation of the world in six days, followed by *Shabbat*.

In some liturgies, *Kabbalat Shabbat* commences with the recitation of *Shir haShirim* (The Song of Songs) and/or the hymn *Y'did Nefesh* (Beloved of the soul).

For the Maven

In some synagogues, the Reader leads this part of the service from the *Bimah* (the desk from which the *Torah* is read in the middle of the synagogue), rather than from the *Amud* (the Reader's desk at the front of the synagogue), in order to point out that the 400-year-old *Kabbalat Shabbat* is a "new" addition to the service.

Ana b'Ko-ach

Shabbat	If a Festival or *Chol haMo-ed* falls on Friday or *Shabbat*
Ana b'ko-ach ... l'olam va-ed (We beseech You, with the strength ... forever)	

This prayer has been ascribed to Nechunya ben Hakana, a mystic who lived in the second century C.E. It consists of forty-two words, the initial letters of which spell "the secret forty-two-letter Name of God" [ArtScroll, p. 315]. (This sequence of forty-two letters was probably an acronym formed from the initial letters of forty-two words that describe God; it is hard to conceive of a Hebrew word that is forty-two letters long.)

L'chah Dodi

Shabbat	If a Festival or *Chol haMo-ed* falls on Friday or *Shabbat*
L'chah dodi likrat kalah ... Bo-i Chalah, Bo-i Chalah (Come, my beloved, to greet the bride ... Come O Bride, Come O Bride!)	

L'chah Dodi was written by the sixteenth century Kabbalist Shlomo Halevi Alkabetz; the initial letters of the first eight stanzas spell the name of the author. Elements are taken from many books of the Bible, especially Isaiah. The image of the Sabbath as bride reaches poetic heights in *L'chah Dodi*.

When reaching the last words of the last stanza, *Bo-i Chalah, Bo-i Chalah* (Come O Bride, Come O Bride!), it is customary to turn toward the door (or, in some liturgies, toward the setting sun) and bow.

For the Maven

A vast array of tunes have been composed for *L'chah Dodi*. In some liturgies it is customary to use a different tune for the last four stanzas (and, in at least one congregation, for every stanza!).

Psalms 92 and 93

Shabbat	If a Festival or *Chol haMo-ed* falls on Friday or *Shabbat*
Psalms 92, 93 *Mizmor shir l'Yom haShabbat ... Adonai, l'orech yamim* (A psalm, a song for the Sabbath day ... the Lord, forever)	

Shabbat proper begins with the recitation of Psalm 92. Public mourning is not permitted on the Sabbath. Accordingly, mourners enter the synagogue at this point and are greeted with the traditional formula of consolation, *haMakom y'nachem etchem b'toch sh'ar avelei Tziyon Virushalayim* (May the Almighty comfort you among the other mourners for Zion and Jerusalem).

Psalm 92 begins with a statement that it is specifically intended for *Shabbat*. Indeed, it was the psalm recited on the Sabbath in the Temple by the Levites (see page 148). Notwithstanding this, there is no direct reference to the Sabbath in the psalm; it speaks of the rewards of righteousness.

Psalm 93 describes the majesty of God and His power over nature.

Bameh Madlikin

Shabbat	If a Festival or *Chol haMo-ed* falls on Friday or *Shabbat*
Bameh madlikin ... v'tom'nin et hachamin (With what should we light [the Sabbath light] ... and store hot food)	
Tanya, amar Rabi Chananya ... hilch'ta rab'ta l'Shab'ta (It has been taught, Rabbi Chananya said ... a major law concerning the Sabbath)	
Amar Rabi Elazar ... Adonai y'varech et ammo vashalom (Rabbi Elazar said ... the Lord will bless His people with peace)	

At this point in the service three rabbinic passages (two in some traditions) are read. First there is a passage from the *Mishnah* (*Shabbat, Perek* 2) that begins *Bameh madlikin* (With what should we light [the Sabbath light]). This passage describes the laws concerning how light may be provided in the home on *Shabbat*.

In some liturgies, this is followed by *Tanya, amar Rabi Chananya* (It has been taught, Rabbi Chananya said). This passage is from the *Talmud* (*Shabbat* 12a).

Finally, another passage from the *Talmud* (*B'rachot* 64a) stresses peace. *Amar Rabi Elazar* (Rabbi Elazar said) uses a play on words. It quotes Isaiah 54:13, part of which states *v'rav shalom banayich* (and great shall be the peace of your children). The *Talmud* says, *al tikra banayich, ela bonayich* (do not read the word as *banayich* [your children], but rather as *bonayich* [your builders]), that is, students of *Torah* are the true builders of abundant peace.

This is followed, as are all rabbinic teachings, by *Kaddish d'Rabbanan* (page 129), the last element of *Kabbalat Shabbat*.

14
The Structure of the Evening Service

The overall structure of the Evening Service (*Arvit* or *Ma-ariv*) is shown in the diagram on the next page.

In Chapter 12, the structure of the Afternoon Service is displayed in a three-column format, with column headings *Shabbat*; *Chagim*; and weekdays. Superficially, it might appear that the material for *Shabbat* and for *Chagim* could be combined. However, there are so many additional components in the Afternoon Service for *Shabbat* that a separate column is needed to display the structure.

In the case of the Evening Service, the services for *Shabbat* and *Chagim* are largely similar in structure. However, the Evening Service for Saturday night (*Motza-ei Shabbat*) has many more components than the weekday Evening Service, because of the additional prayers associated with the transition from the Sabbath to the working week. That is why the three columns for this chapter are headed *Shabbat* and *Chagim*; Weekdays; and *Motza-ei Shabbat* (Saturday evening).

The diagram shows the overall structure of the Evening Service

Shabbat and Chagim	Weekdays; Minor Festivals; Fast Days	Motza-ei Shabbat (Saturday evening)
[On Chanukah] Kindle lights (page 144)		Psalms 144 and 67 (page 168)
[On *Shabbat*] *Kabbalat Shabbat* (Chapter 13)	*V'Hu rachum* ... (And He, being merciful ...)	
K'riat Sh'ma (Chapter 8)		
Biblical verses	—	
Chatzi Kaddish (page 128)		
Amidah (Chapter 5, 6, or 7)		
Section after *Amidah*	—	[Except if a Festival occurs in the coming week] Section after *Amidah*
Kaddish Shalem (page 124)		
Kiddush (Chapter 9)	[On Tish-ah b'Av] *M'gillat Eichah* (Book of Lamentations) *Kinnot* (dirges)	[On Chanukah] Kindle lights (page 144)
—	[On Purim] *M'gillat Ester* (page 144)	—
[Between Pesach and Shavuot] Count the *Omer* (page 26)		
—		*P'sukei B'rachah* (Verses of blessing)
Aleinu (page 133)		
Kaddish Yatom (page 130)		
[From *Rosh Chodesh Elul* to *Sh'mini Atzeret*] Psalm 27: *L'David Adonai Ori* (page 149) *Kaddish Yatom* (page 130)		
Yigdal or *Adon olam* (page 142)	—	

Evening Service for
Shabbat and *Chagim*

More details of the Evening Service for *Shabbat* and *Chagim* are now shown. In particular, the diagram on this page shows the differences between the Evening Service for *Shabbat* (and *Chagim* falling on *Shabbat*) and the Evening Service for *Chagim* falling on weekdays.

Shabbat; *Chagim* falling on *Shabbat*	*Chagim* falling on weekdays
Kabbalat Shabbat (Chapter 13)	
K'riat Sh'ma (Chapter 8)	
Biblical verses	
Chatzi Kaddish (page 128)	
Amidah (Chapter 5 or 7)	
Va-y'chulu hashamayim v'ha-aretz v'chol tz'va-am ... (Thus the heavens and the earth and all their host were finished ...)	—
[Except first night of Pesach] *B'rachah Me-ein Sheva*	
Kaddish Shalem (page 124)	
[Between Pesach and Shavuot] The *Omer* is counted (page 26)	
[Omit on the first two nights of Pesach] *Shabbat* or Festival *Kiddush* (page 113)	[Omit on the first two nights of Pesach] Festival *Kiddush* (page 113)
Aleinu (page 133)	
Kaddish Yatom (page 130)	
[From *Rosh Chodesh Elul* to *Sh'mini Atzeret*] Psalm 27: *L'David Adonai Ori* (page 149) *Kaddish Yatom* (page 130)	
Yigdal or *Adon Olam* (page 142)	

We now describe the structure of the three elements not covered earlier in this book.

Biblical Verses

Before the *Chatzi Kaddish* preceding the *Amidah*, biblical verses that relate to *Shabbat* and/or the appropriate *Chag* are said (the material for Rosh haShanah and Yom Kippur is included here for completeness and for the sake of comparison).

Shabbat; *Chagim* falling on *Shabbat*	*Chagim* falling on weekdays
[On *Shabbat*]	
V'sha-m'ru Vnei Yisra-el et haShabbat ... uvayom ha-sh'vi-i shavat vayinafash (The Children of Israel shall keep the Sabbath ... and on the seventh day He ceased from work and rested)	
[On *Chagim*]	
Va-y'daber Moshe et mo-adei Adonai el Bnei Yisra-el (Moses announced the Festivals of the Lord to the Children of Israel)	
[On Rosh haShanah]	
Tiku vachodesh shofar ... mishpat Leilohei Ya-akov (Sound the *shofar* on the new moon ... an ordinance for the God of Jacob)	
[On Yom Kippur]	
Ki vayom hazeh ... lifnei Adonai titharu (For on this day ... you will be clean before the Lord)	

On *Shabbat*, Exodus 31:16–17, beginning *V'sha-m'ru Vnei Yisra-el et haShabbat* (The Children of Israel shall keep the Sabbath), is said. These two verses state a reason for keeping *Shabbat*, namely, because God refrained from creation after the sixth day and rested on the seventh day.

The verse for *Chagim* is Leviticus 23:44, beginning *Va-y'daber Moshe et mo-adei Adonai* (Moses announced the Festivals of the Lord).

Psalm 81:4–5, *Tiku vachodesh shofar* (Sound the *shofar* on the new moon), is recited on Rosh haShanah. These verses refer to the sounding of the *shofar*.

Finally, the verse for Yom Kippur is Leviticus 16:30, beginning *Ki vayom hazeh* (For on this day).

Va-y'chulu

Shabbat; Chagim falling on Shabbat
Va-y'chulu hashamayim v'ha-aretz v'chol tz'va-am ... asher bara Elohim la-asot (Thus the heavens and the earth and all their host were finished ... which God had created)

After the *Amidah*, three verses from the *Torah* are recited, Genesis 2:1–3, beginning *Va-y'chulu hashamayim v'ha-aretz v'chol tz'va-am* (Thus the heavens and the earth and all their host were finished). These verses paraphrase the reason for observing *Shabbat* stated on the previous page.

For the Maven

The *Amidah* is not repeated during *Arvit*. *Va-y'chulu* is part of the *Shabbat Amidah*, so it is reasonable to inquire why this paragraph is repeated. The reason is that the various *Amidot* for Festivals do not contain this passage and it has to be recited when a Festival falls on *Shabbat*. As a result, *Va-y'chulu* has become the rule for every *Shabbat*.

B'rachah Me-ein Sheva

Shabbat; *Chagim* falling on *Shabbat*
Baruch Attah Adonai ... Koneh shamayim va-aretz (Blessed be You, O Lord ... Master of heaven and earth)
Magen avot ... zecher l'ma-asei v'reshit (Shield of our fathers ... in remembrance of the work of the Creation)
Eloheinu Velohei avoteinu ... Baruch Attah Adonai, M'kadesh haShabbat (Our God and God of our fathers ... blessed are You, O Lord, Who sanctifies the Sabbath)

Except if first night Pesach falls on *Shabbat*, three paragraphs are said every *Shabbat* after *Va-y'chulu*. Their structure is that of a Long Form *b'rachah*, interposed by the second paragraph, *Magen avot* (Shield of our fathers).

The first paragraph begins with the same sentence as the first *b'rachah* of the *Amidah* (*Avot*), but ends with the words *Koneh shamayim va-aretz* (Master of heaven and earth).

Next comes *Magen avot* (Shield of our fathers). This paragraph essentially summarizes the seven *b'rachot* of the *Shabbat Amidah*. For this reason, it is called *B'rachah Me-ein Sheva* (The seven appropriate blessings).

Finally, *Eloheinu Velohei avoteinu* (Our God and God of our fathers), the *Shabbat* prayer common to the fourth *b'rachah* of every *Shabbat Amidah* (see pages 30–33), is repeated here.

For the Maven

This material was originally added for late-comers. As explained on page 106, in Talmudic times, many Babylonian rulers would not allow Jewish worship inside their towns. Synagogues were therefore located in open fields outside the town. At night, it was dangerous to walk unescorted in such areas. Accordingly, the service was extended to give late-comers time to complete their prayers and then walk back to the town in the company of the rest of the congregation.

However, *B'rachah Me-ein Sheva* is not said if first night Pesach falls on *Shabbat*. This is because *Leil Pesach* is described in Exodus 12:42 as *Leil Shimurim*, a night of protection.

Evening Service for Weekdays

As explained at the beginning of this chapter, the Evening Service for weekdays is drastically different from the service on *Motza-ei Shabbat* (Saturday evening).

Weekdays; Minor Festivals; Fast Days	*Motza-ei Shabbat* (Saturday evening)
[On Chanukah] Kindle lights (page 144)	Psalms 144 and 67 (page 168)
V'Hu rachum ... (And He, being merciful ...)	
K'riat Sh'ma (Chapter 8)	
Chatzi Kaddish (page 128)	
Weekday *Amidah* (Chapter 5 or 7)	
—	[Omit on Purim, Tish-ah b'Av, or if a Festival falls in the coming week] *Chatzi Kaddish* (page 128) *Vihi no-am* ... (May the pleasantness ...) *Yoshev b'seter Elyon* ... (He who dwells in the refuge of the Most High ...) *V'Attah Kadosh* (page 132)
Kaddish Shalem (page 124)	
—	[On Chanukah] Kindle lights (page 144)
[Between Pesach and Shavuot] Count the *Omer* (page 26)	
[On Tish-ah b'Av] *M'gillat Eichah* (Book of Lamentations) *Kinnot* (dirges)	
[On Purim] *M'gillat Ester* (page 144)	
—	[On Purim] *Vihi no-am* ... (May the pleasantness ...)

Weekdays; Minor Festivals; Fast Days	Motza-ei Shabbat (Saturday evening)
[On Purim and Tish-ah b'Av] *V'Attah Kadosh* (page 132) *Kaddish Shalem* without the paragraph *Titkabel* ... (May [...] be accepted ...) (page 124)	
—	[Omit on Purim and Tish-ah b'Av] *P'sukei B'rachah* (Verses of blessing)
	Havdalah (pages 107–108)
Aleinu (page 133)	
Kaddish Yatom (page 130)	
[Between Rosh haShanah and Sh'mini Atzeret] Psalm 27: *L'David Adonai Ori* (page 149) *Kaddish Yatom* (page 130)	
[In a house of mourning add] Psalm 49: *La-m'natze-ach livnei Korach mizmor* (page 149) *Kaddish Yatom* (page 130)	

Material not covered elsewhere in this book is now described.

V'Hu Rachum

Weekdays; Minor Festivals; Fast Days	Motza-ei Shabbat (Saturday evening)
V'Hu rachum ... haMelech ya-anenu v'yom korenu (And He, being merciful ... the King will answer us when we call on Him)	

If the Evening Service is not recited directly after the Afternoon Service then, in some liturgies, the Evening Service starts with Psalm 134 and *Kaddish Yatom* (page 130).

The Evening Service proper commences with two verses from *T'hillim* beginning *V'Hu rachum* (And He, being merciful) (Psalms 78:38 and 20:10). These verses ask for mercy, perhaps a natural reaction to the very human fears associated with the darkness of night.

Section after *Amidah*, Saturday Evening

On *Motza-ei Shabbat* (except on Purim or Tish-ah b'Av, or if a Festival occurs in the coming week), three paragraphs are added.

Weekdays; Minor Festivals; Fast Days	*Motza-ei Shabbat* (Saturday evening)
	Psalm 90:17 *Vihi no-am ... uma-asei yadeinu kon'nehu* (May the pleasantness ... may He establish the work of our hands)
	Psalm 91 (page 168) *Yoshev b'seter Elyon ... v'arehu bishu-ati* (He who dwells in the refuge of the Most High ... and I will show him My salvation)
	V'Attah Kadosh (page 132)

Vihi no-am (May the pleasantness) is Psalm 90:17. In this verse we ask for blessings on the work of our hands in the coming week.

This is followed by Psalm 91, *Yoshev b'seter Elyon* (He who dwells in the refuge of the Most High). This psalm is a prayer for protection from the dangers of life, again a fitting theme for the start of the new week.

V'Attah Kadosh (And you, Holy One) is all but the first two verses of *Uva l'Tziyon go-el* (A redeemer shall come to Zion), as described on page 132.

P'sukei B'rachah

In most liturgies, a number of scriptural passages are recited toward the end of the Evening Service on Saturday night. These are termed *P'sukei B'rachah* (verses of blessing). They are omitted on Tish-ah b'Av and Purim.

Weekdays; Minor Festivals; Fast Days	*Motza-ei Shabbat* (Saturday evening)
	V'yiten l'cha ha-Elohim ... shalom al Yisra-el (May God grant you ... may there be peace upon Israel)

These passages cover a wide variety of sentiments, including divine blessing, redemption, salvation, consolation, and peace. The second to last passage begins with an extract from the *Talmud* (*M'gillah* 31a), *Amar Rabi Yochanan* (Rabbi Yochanan said). This is a plea for humility.

P'sukei B'rachah ends with Psalm 128, one of the *Shir haMa-alot* (page 167). It concludes with the words *shalom al Yisra-el* (may there be peace upon Israel), an appropriate sentiment for the end of *Shabbat* and the start of the work week.

15
The Structure of the Preliminary Morning Service

Congregational prayer is preceded by a series of prayers recited individually. For completeness, these are shown in the diagram on the next page. In some liturgies, all but the first three are recited in the home before leaving for the synagogue.

The order of these prayers can vary greatly depending on the specific liturgy. Even within a given religious tradition, the order can vary from *Siddur* to *Siddur*.

[Verses on entering the synagogue] *Ma tovu ohalecha Ya-akov* ... (How goodly are your tents, O Jacob ...)

[Prayers on putting on the *tallit*] *Ba-r'chi nafshi et Adonai* ... (Bless the Lord, O my soul ...)

[Prayers on putting on the *t'fillin*] *Hi-n'ni m'chaven* ... (Behold, I intend ...)

Adon olam Asher malach ... (Master of the universe Who reigned ...)

Yigdal Elohim chai ... (May the living God be exalted ...)

[*B'rachah* on washing the hands] ... *al n'tilat yadayim* (... concerning the lifting up of hands)

[*B'rachah* for creating Humankind] ... *Rofei chol basar umafli la-asot* (... Who heals all creatures and does wonders)

[B'rachot before studying the *Torah*] ... *v'tzivanu la-asok b'divrei Torah* ... *Noten haTorah* (... and has commanded us to occupy ourselves in the words of the *Torah* ... Giver of the *Torah*)

[Passage from the *Torah*] (Num. 6:24–26) *Y'varech'cha Adonai v'yishm'recha* ... (May the Lord bless you and protect you ...)

[Passage from the *Mishnah*] (*Peah* 1:1) *Elu d'varim she-ein lahem shiur* ... (These are items for which no limit is prescribed ...)

[Passage from the *Talmud*] (*Shabbat* 127a) *Elu d'varim she-adam ochel peroteihem* ... (These are items for which a person enjoys the fruits ...)

[Blessing for restoring the soul] *Elohai, n'shamah shenatata bi* ... (My God, the soul that You placed in me ...)

Structure of *Birchot haShachar*

Now we consider the Preliminary Morning Service itself. It is referred to as *Birchot haShachar* (blessings of the morning).

List of fifteen *b'rachot*
Baruch Attah Adonai ... Hama-avir Shenah me-einai ... Gomel chasadim tovim l'ammo Yisra-el (Blessed are You, O Lord ... Who removes sleep from my eyes ... Who bestows loving kindness on His people Israel)
Y'hi ratzon mi-l'fanecha ... (May it be Your will ...)
[Omitted on *Shabbat* and Festivals] *Eloheinu Velohei avoteinu, zochreinu b'zichron tov ...* (Our God and God of our fathers, remember us for a good memory ...)
Akedah (The binding of Isaac) (Gen. 22:1–19) *Va-y'hi achar ha-d'varim ha-eleh ...* (And it happened after these things ...)
[Omitted on *Shabbat* and Festivals] *Ribono shel olam ...* (Master of the universe ...)
L'olam y'hei adam y'rei shamayim ... (May people always be God-fearing ...)
Ribon kol ha-olamim ... (Master of all the worlds ...)
Aval anachnu am'cha ... (But we are Your people ...)
L'fichaf anachnu chayavim ... (Therefore, we are obligated ...)
First verse of the *Sh'ma* (Deut. 6:4)
Attah Hu ad shelo ... (It was You before ...)
Attah Hu Adonai Eloheinu ... (It is You Who are the Lord our God ...)
Various prayers interspersed with sections from the *Torah* and *Talmud* that relate to the sacrifices and incense in the Temple
Obligatory Talmudic passages
Y'hi ratzon mi-l'fanecha ... (May it be Your will ...)
Kaddish d'Rabbanan (page 129)

We now examine each of these items in turn.

List of Fifteen *B'rachot*

The Preliminary Morning Service begins with a list of fifteen *b'rachot*, traditionally said upon arising. Each is a complete *b'rachah* in itself; this is not a Series Form *b'rachah*.

Baruch Attah Adonai Eloheinu Melech ha-olam, Asher natan l'sechvi vinah l'havchin bein yom uvein leilah (Blessed are You, O Lord our God, King of the universe, Who has given the rooster the understanding to distinguish between day and night)
[Thirteen other *b'rachot*]
Baruch Attah Adonai Eloheinu Melech ha-olam, Hanoten laya-ef ko-ach (Blessed are You, O Lord our God, King of the universe, Who gives strength to the weary)

The contents and order of the *b'rachot* vary with the specific liturgy. For example, in the *Ashkenazi* liturgy, the fourth *b'rachah* is *Sheloh asani ishah* (Who has not made me a woman). In the fourteenth century, an alternative for women was introduced, *She-assah li kirtzono* (Who has made me according to His will).

In the Conservative liturgy, this concept is expressed in the second *b'rachah, She-assah li b'tzalmo* (Who has made me in His image). Furthermore, the fifteen Conservative *b'rachot* do not contain the negative phrase *Shelo asani* (Who has not made me); instead, they substitute the positive form, *She-assah li* (Who has made me).

Hama-avir Shenah

> *Baruch Attah Adonai, Eloheinu Melech ha-olam, Hama-avir shenah me-einai ... Baruch Attah Adonai, Gomel chasadim tovim l'ammo Yisra-el* (Blessed are You, O Lord our God, King of the universe, Who removes sleep from my eyes ... Blessed are You, O Lord, Who bestows loving kindness on His people Israel)

In many *Siddurim*, this part of the service is printed in two paragraphs. The first paragraph, which consists of just one sentence, appears to be a simple *b'rachah* that begins *Baruch Attah Adonai, Eloheinu Melech ha-olam, Hama-avir shenah me-einai* (Blessed are You, O Lord our God, King of the universe, Who removes sleep from my eyes). This is followed by a second paragraph beginning with *Y'hi ratzon mi-l'fanecha* (May it be Your will) and ending with *Baruch Attah Adonai, Gomel chasadim tovim l'ammo Yisra-el* (Blessed are You, O Lord, Who bestows loving kindness on His people Israel). This is a prayer asking that we not succumb to evil.

In fact, notwithstanding the disparate nature of the two parts, the structure of these two paragraphs constitutes the first element in a Series Form *b'rachah* with two component *b'rachot*. The second *b'rachah*, *Attah Hu ad shelo* (It was You before), is found in the middle of the Preliminary Morning Service (page 230); many passages are interspersed between the first and the second *b'rachot* in the series.

Y'hi Ratzon Mi-l'fanecha

> *Y'hi ratzon mi-l'fanecha ... uvein she-eino ven b'rit* (May it be Your will ... or if he is not a member of the covenant)

This is the first of two prayers beginning *Y'hi ratzon mi-l'fanecha* (May it be Your will) in *Birchot haShachar*. It asks for protection in our everyday dealings. (The second *Y'hi ratzon mi-l'fanecha* is the second to last item in *Birchot haShachar*. It is discussed on page 231.)

Zochrenu b'Zichron Tov

[Omitted on *Shabbat* and Festivals] *Eloheinu Velohei avoteinu, zochrenu b'zichron tov l'fanecha ... kakatuv b'Toratecha* (Our God and God of our fathers, remember us for a good memory before You ... as it is written in Your *Torah*)
Akedah (The binding of Isaac) (Gen. 22:1–19) *Va-y'hi achar ha-d'varim ha-eleh ... vayeshev Avraham biVer Shava* (And it happened after these things ... and Abraham dwelt in Beersheba)
[Omitted on *Shabbat* and Festivals] *Ribono shel olam ... v'ha-aretz ezkor* (Master of the universe ... and I will remember the land)

The story of the *Akedah* (binding), the putative sacrifice of Isaac (Gen. 22:1–19), appears in full at this point of the service. It is preceded and followed by passages that refer to the *Akedah*. These two passages are omitted on *Shabbat* and Festivals because of their supplicatory nature.

In more detail, the *Akedah* is preceded by the paragraph *Eloheinu Velohei avoteinu, zochrenu b'zichron tov l'fanecha* (Our God and God of our fathers, remember us for a good memory before You).

Next comes the story of the *Akedah* itself, beginning *Va-y'hi achar ha-d'varim ha-eleh* (And it happened after these things). It describes the supreme trial of Abraham. He was told to sacrifice his son Isaac but this was averted at the last second.

This is followed by the prayer *Ribono shel olam* (Master of the universe). Here, we entreat God to be compassionate with us.

For the Maven

Although they are not recited on *Shabbat* or Festivals, *Zochrenu b'zichron tov* is taken from the *Zichronot* section of the *Musaf Amidah* for Rosh haShanah (Chapter 18) and *Ribono shel olam* from the *Amidah* for Yom Kippur.

L'Olam Y'hei Adam

L'olam y'hei adam y'rei shamayim b'seter uvagalu-i ... vayashkem v'yomar: (May people always be God-fearing in private and in public ... and rise early and say:)
Ribon kol ha-olamim ... ki hakol havel (Master of all the worlds ... because everything is vanity)
Aval anachnu am'cha ... Yisra-el Vishurun (But we are Your people ... Israel and Jeshurun)
L'fichaf anachnu chayavim ... v'om'rim pa-amayim b'chol yom: (Therefore, we are obligated ... and say twice every day:)
Sh'ma Yisra-el, Adonai Eloheinu, Adonai Echad (Hear, O Israel, the Lord is our God, the Lord is One)

During the reign of King Yezdejerd II in the fifth century C.E., the Jews of Babylonia faced a religious crisis because it was forbidden to recite the *Sh'ma.* The Rabbis decreed that at least the first verse of the *Sh'ma* should be recited at home before coming to the synagogue. That is why the first paragraph begins *L'olam y'hei adam y'rei shamayim b'seter* (May people always be God-fearing **in private**).

The next paragraph, beginning *Ribon kol ha-olamim* (Master of all the worlds), is taken from the Yom Kippur service. It is an admission of the powerlessness and weakness of mankind.

Aval anachnu am'cha (But we are Your people) stresses the covenant and the ties with Abraham, Isaac, and Jacob. *L'fichaf anachnu chayavim* (Therefore, we are obligated) carries these ideas further. As a consequence of God's relationship with our fathers, it is our duty to give thanks and to recite the *Sh'ma* twice a day. This is followed by the first verse of the *Sh'ma.*

For the Maven

Although we are obligated to recite the entire *Sh'ma* twice a day, in case of an emergency just the first verse will suffice. That is why only the first verse appears here and in the *K'dushah* of the *Shabbat* and Festival *Amidah* (see "For the Maven" page 121).

Attah Hu ad Shelo

Attah Hu ad shelo nivra ha-olam ... Baruch Attah Adonai, M'kadesh et Shimcha barabim (It was You before the Creation of the world ... Blessed are You, O Lord, Who sanctifies Your Name in the presence of all mankind)

Attah Hu ad shelo (It was You before) begins by expressing the constancy of God. The prayer then calls for the Name of God to be sanctified.

From the viewpoint of structure, this is the second component *b'rachah* in the series of two *b'rachot* that began with *Hama-avir shenah* (Who removes sleep) (page 227).

Attah Hu Adonai Eloheinu

Attah Hu Adonai Eloheinu ... amar Adonai (It is You Who are the Lord our God ... said the Lord)

This prayer stresses that God is restricted neither in time nor in space. It concludes with a plea for the end of the dispersion.

Korbanot

Various prayers interspersed with sections from the *Torah* and *Talmud* that relate to the sacrifices and incense in the Temple

The theme of the conclusion of the previous paragraph is redemption. This leads on to *Korbanot* (sacrifices), a lengthy sequence of items dealing with the sacrifices offered in the Temple. The connection between redemption and sacrifice is the belief that forgiveness from sin can be achieved by recitation of the order of sacrifices and that this activity is equivalent to offering the sacrifices themselves. (The sacrificial rites terminated with the destruction of the Second Temple in 70 C.E.)

This portion of the Preliminary Morning Service consists of excerpts from the *Torah* and *Talmud*, interspersed with prayers. The passages include descriptions of the following: the laver that the Priests used to pour water on their hands and feet before performing their duties (Exod. 30:17–21), removal of the ashes from the previous day's sacrifices (Lev. 6:1–6), the *tamid* (continual or daily) offering (Num. 28:1–8; Lev. 1:11), the incense (Exod. 30:34–36; Exod. 30:7–8; *Talmud*

K'reitot 6a; *Y'rushalmi Yoma* 4:5; *Talmud Yoma* 33a), and, on *Shabbat* and/or *Rosh Chodesh,* the *musaf* (additional) offerings for those days (Num. 28:9–10; 28:11–15).

Obligatory Talmudic Passages

Eizehu m'koman shel z'vachim ... v'eino ne-echal ela tzali (What is the location of the sacrifices? ... and it may not be eaten unless it is roasted)
Rabi Yishma-el omer: Bishlosh esrai midot ... ad sheyavo hakatuv hashlishi v'yachria beineihem (Rabbi Ishmael says: By means of thirteen rules ... until a third passage comes to reconcile them)

It is stated in the *Talmud* (*Kiddushin* 30a) that the *Tanach* (Bible) and *Talmud* must be studied every day. Following on the *Torah* passages on the sacrifices, a passage from the *Mishnah* (*Z'vachim* 5) dealing with the same topic was chosen, namely, *Eizehu m'koman shel z'vachim* (What was the location of the sacrifices?). This passage deals with all the different sacrifices that were offered in the Temple.

In the *Talmud,* the term *Mishnah* (literally, second) refers to a listing of laws, whereas *G'mara* (literally, completion) deals with the application and interpretation of those laws. The *Baraita* (literally, outside of the *Mishnah*) of Rabbi Ishmael is the introduction to *Sifra* (a commentary on Leviticus). *Rabi Yishma-el omer: Bishlosh esrai midot* (Rabbi Ishmael says: By means of thirteen rules) is the obligatory *G'mara* passage, corresponding to the *Mishnah* passage *Eizehu m'koman.* It is a description of the thirteen rules used in scriptural interpretation.

Y'hi Ratzon Mi-l'fanecha

Y'hi ratzon mi-l'fanecha ... uchshanim kadmoniot (May it be Your will ... as in former years)

The second *Y'hi ratzon mi-l'fanecha* in the Preliminary Morning Service is a prayer for the restoration of the Temple. It consists of two verses, namely, *Mishnah Avot* 5:23 and *Malachi* 3:4.

The Preliminary Morning Service concludes with *Kaddish d'Rabbanan,* recited after a rabbinic teaching (page 129).

16
The Structure of the Morning Service

There are two different basic structures for the Morning Service. On *Shabbat*, Festivals, *Chol haMo-ed*, and *Rosh Chodesh*, the Morning Service is followed by the Additional Service. On all other occasions, there is no Additional Service.

When there is an Additional Service, a major consequence is that the material that otherwise would conclude the Morning Service is postponed until the end of the Additional Service (in the *Ashkenazi* liturgy).

Like that of all other services, *Shacharit* (the Morning Service) consists of three sections. These are the section before the *Amidah*; the *Amidah* itself; and the section after the *Amidah*.

Shabbat; Chagim; Chol haMo-ed; Rosh Chodesh	Weekdays, including Purim, Chanukah, and Fast Days
Section before the *Amidah*	
Amidah section	
Section after the *Amidah*	

This is shown in more detail on the next page

233

Shabbat; Chagim; Chol haMo-ed; Rosh Chodesh	Weekdays, including Purim, Chanukah, and Fast Days
Preliminary Morning Service (Chapter 15)	
P'sukei d'Zimrah (page 157)	
[Between Rosh haShanah and Yom Kippur] Psalm 130: *Shir haMa-alot* (page 149)	
Chatzi Kaddish (page 128)	
K'riat Sh'ma (Chapter 8)	
Amidah (Chapter 5, 6, or 7)	
[On *Chagim, Chol haMo-ed, Rosh Chodesh,* and Chanukah] *Hallel* (page 150)	
—	[On Minor Fast Days] *S'lichot* (Penitential prayers)
	[Between Rosh haShanah and Yom Kippur, and on Minor Fast Days add] *Avinu Malkenu* (page 141)
	[Usually] *Tachanun* (page 135)
Kaddish Shalem (page 124)	*Chatzi Kaddish* (page 128)
[On *Shabbat, Chagim, Chol haMo-ed, Rosh Chodesh,* Chanukah, Purim, Mondays, Thursdays, and Fast Days] *Torah* Reading (Chapter 11)	
—	[On Purim] *M'gillat Ester* (page 144)
	[On Tish-ah b'Av] *Kinnot* (dirges)
	Ashrei (page 140)
	[Usually] Psalm 20: *La-m'natze-ach mizmor l'David* ... (For the choirmaster. A psalm of David ...)
	Uva l'Tziyon (page 132)
	Kaddish Shalem (page 124)
	Concluding material

Psalm 20 and the concluding material are now discussed.

Psalm 20

Shabbat; Chagim; Chol haMo-ed; Rosh Chodesh	Weekdays, including Purim, Chanukah, and Fast Days
	[Usually] Psalm 20 *La-m'natze-ach mizmor l'David ... haMelech ya-anenu v'yom korenu* (For the choirmaster. A psalm of David ... the King will answer on the day we call)

Because of its somber content, Psalm 20 is omitted on *Chol haMo-ed, Rosh Chodesh,* Chanukah, Purim, *Shushan Purim, Purim Katan,* Tish-ah b'Av, the day before Pesach, the day before Yom Kippur, and in a house of mourning. The psalm assures us that God will answer us in time of trouble.

Concluding Material

Shabbat; Chagim; Chol haMo-ed; Rosh Chodesh	Weekdays, including Purim, Chanukah, and Fast Days
	Aleinu (page 133)
	Kaddish Yatom (page 130)
	Shir haYom (Psalm of the Day) (page 148)
	Kaddish Yatom (page 130)
	[From *Rosh Chodesh Elul* to the day before Rosh haShanah] The *Shofar* is sounded
	[From *Rosh Chodesh Elul* to *Sh'mini Atzeret*] Psalm 27: *L'David Adonai Ori* (page 149) *Kaddish Yatom* (page 130)
	[On Chanukah] Psalm 30: *Mizmor Shir Chanukat haBayit* (page 149) *Kaddish Yatom* (page 130)
	[In a house of mourning] Psalm 49: *La-m'natze-ach Livnei Korach Mizmor* (page 149) *Kaddish Yatom* (page 130)

As explained at the beginning of this chapter, there is no concluding material on those days when the Morning Service is followed by the Additional Service; the concluding material is then shifted to the end of the Additional Service.

17
The Structure of the Additional Service

In the Temple in Jerusalem, the *musaf* (additional) sacrifice was offered on *Shabbat*, Festivals, *Chol haMo-ed*, and *Rosh Chodesh*. After the destruction of the Second Temple, synagogue services took the place of the sacrificial Temple rites. In particular, the *Musaf* (Additional) Service was introduced on those days when the *musaf* sacrifice had been offered.

The bulk of the Additional Service is the *Amidah*. The theme of the fourth *b'rachah, K'dushat haYom* (holiness of the day), is invariably the Temple and the sacrifices that were offered there.

The structure of the Additional Service is shown on the next page.

Shabbat; Chagim	Rosh Chodesh; Chol haMo-ed
Chatzi Kaddish (page 128)	
Amidah (Chapter 5 or 7)	
[On Sukkot] Hoshanot	
Kaddish Shalem (page 124)	
Ein Keloheinu ... (There is none like our God ...)	—
Pitum ha-k'toret ... (The incense mixture ...)	
Kaddish d'Rabbanan (page 000)	
Aleinu (page 133)	
Kaddish Yatom (page 130)	
Shir haKavod (Hymn of Glory)	—
Kaddish Yatom (page 130)	
Shir haYom (Psalm of the Day) (page 148)	
Kaddish Yatom (page 130)	
[From *Rosh Chodesh Elul* to *Sh'mini Atzeret*] Psalm 27: *L'David Adonai Ori* (page 149) Kaddish Yatom (page 130)	
[On *Rosh Chodesh*] Psalm 104: *Ba-r'chi Nafshi* (page 149) Kaddish Yatom (page 130)	
[On Chanukah] Psalm 30: *Mizmor Shir Chanukat haBayit* (page 149) Kaddish Yatom (page 130)	
Yigdal or *Adon olam* (page 142)	—

(In some rituals, on *Hoshana Rabbah* the Additional Service is that for *Chagim*.)

The various new items are now described.

Hoshanot

First 6 days of Sukkot (excluding *Shabbat*)	*Shabbat Chol haMo-ed Sukkot*	*Hoshana Rabbah*
Hoshana l'ma-ancha Eloheinu Hoshana ... (Please save, for Your sake, Our God, please save ...)		
Weekday *Hoshana* 1, 2, 3, 4, 5, or 6	*Hoshana* for *Shabbat*	Weekday *Hoshanot* 1, 2, 3, and 4
Ani vaho, hoshiah na (I implore, please save)		
Weekday *Hoshana* 7	—	Weekday *Hoshana* 7
Ani vaho, hoshiah na (I implore, save now)		*Ani vaho, hoshiah na* (I implore, save now)
—		Lengthy additional prayers
Hoshiah et amecha ... (Save Your people ...)		
	—	Closing prayer

On Sukkot, *Hoshanot* is recited after the repetition of the *Amidah*. The term *Hoshanot* is the plural of *hoshana* [or *hoshia na*] (please save), a phrase that is repeatedly used here.

This part of the service is structured around eight sets of hymns referred to as *Hoshanot*, seven of which are recited on weekdays and one is recited on *Shabbat*. The phrase "*hoshana*" is generally added to each stich of the hymns, at the beginning, the end, or both, depending on the specific liturgy.

On weekdays on Sukkot, after the Reader's repetition of the *Musaf Amidah*, the Ark is opened and a *Torah* scroll taken to the *Bimah*, where it is held for the remainder of the ceremony. The four introductory stiches beginning *Hoshana, l'ma-ancha Eloheinu* (Please save, for Your sake, Our God) are recited responsively. Then a procession is formed, lead by the Reader, consisting of worshippers holding the *lulav* and *etrog*. One of the six weekday *Hoshanot* is recited (see page 242 for details). Next, the seventh weekday *Hoshana* is recited. The scroll is then returned to the Ark.

On *Shabbat*, the Ark is opened but no *Torah* is taken out and there is no procession with *lulav* and *etrog*. The *Hoshana* for *Shabbat* is recited.

Finally, on *Hoshana Rabbah* (The Great *Hoshana*, the last day of *Chol haMo-ed Sukkot*), all the scrolls are taken from the Ark to the *Bimah*. Weekday *Hoshanot* 1, 2, 3, and 4 (a total of seven acrostic hymns) are recited, with an additional verse added to the end of each hymn. The *Bimah* is circled seven times. Then, as on other weekdays, the seventh *Hoshana* is recited. Finally, there is lengthy additional material added for *Hoshana Rabbah*.

We now examine each of these components.

Acrostic Hymn Sets

	Weekday *Hoshanot*
1.	*L'ma-an amitach* ... (For the sake of Your truth ...)
2.	*Even sh'tiyah* ... (Foundation stone ...)
3.	*Om ani chomah* ... (Nation [that says] "I am a wall" ...)
4.	*Adon Hamoshia* ... (The Lord Who saves ...) *Adam uvhemah* ... (Man and animals ...) *Adamah me-erer* ... (Accursed ground ...) *L'ma-an Eitan* ... (For the sake of the strong one ...)
5.	*E-eroch shu-i* ... (I shall arrange my prayer ...)
6.	*El l'mosha-ot* ... (God Who saves ...)
7.	*K'hoshata elim* ... (As You saved the terebinths ...)

	Shabbat *Hoshanot*
8.	*Om n'tzurah k'vavat* ... (Nation protected like the apple of one's eye ...) *K'hoshata Adam* ... (As You saved Adam ...)

The first weekday *Hoshana* begins *L'ma-an amitach* (For the sake of Your truth). It is a list of twenty-two attributes of God. Each stich consists of the word *L'ma-an* (For the sake of) followed by an attribute starting with the next letter of the Hebrew alphabet.

Even sh'tiyah (Foundation stone) is a list of twenty-two phrases appertaining to the Temple or to Jerusalem. The acrostic pattern is found in the first letter of each phrase. This acrostic pattern is common to all but two of the other hymns.

The third weekday *Hoshana*, beginning *Om ani chomah* (Nation [that says] "I am a wall"), is a list of twenty-two qualities of the Jewish nation.

The fourth weekday *Hoshana* consists of four acrostic hymns. Both *Adon Hamoshia* (The Lord Who saves) and *Adam uvhemah* (Man and animals) are lists of requests for agricultural plenty, whereas *Adamah me-erer* (Accursed ground) is a list of twenty-two destructive forces. The hymn beginning *L'ma-an Eitan* (For the sake of the strong one) is a list of twenty-two allusions to specific individuals through actions that they performed, all involving fire. As with the very first hymn, each stich consists of the word *L'ma-an* (For the sake of) followed by a phrase starting with the next letter of the alphabet.

The theme of the next weekday *Hoshana*, *E-eroch shu-i* (I shall arrange my prayer), is repentance and that of *El l'mosha-ot* (God Who saves) is salvation.

Salvation is also the theme of the seventh weekday *Hoshana*; it begins *K'hoshata elim* (As You saved the terebinths). The underlying structure of this *Hoshana* is again an acrostic pattern. There are twenty-two stiches each beginning with a successive letter of the alphabet. The phrase *K'hoshata* (As You saved) prefaces each pair of stiches and the phrase *Ken hoshana* (Therefore please save) follows each pair.

The final *Hoshana* is recited only on *Shabbat*. It consists of two acrostic hymns, each describing twenty-two aspects of *Shabbat*. Each stich of the first *Shabbat* hymn, beginning *Om n'tzurah k'vavat* (Nation protected like the apple of one's eye), begins with the next letter of the alphabet. The structure of the second hymn, *K'hoshata Adam* (As You saved Adam), is identical to that of *K'hoshata elim* (As You saved the terebinths), described in the previous paragraph.

For the Maven

In the preface to his admirable *Siddur*, Philip Birnbaum states that the *Hoshanot*, incorporating "many intricate acrostics and a variety of Hebrew synonyms," are essentially untranslatable and "can be appreciated only in the Hebrew" [Birnbaum, pp. xvii–xviii]. After rereading my efforts at translating just the initial phrase of each *Hoshana*, I am fully inclined to agree with him!

Order of *Hoshanot*

The first day of Sukkot can fall on a Monday, Tuesday, Thursday, or *Shabbat*. The *Hoshana* (acrostic hymn set) for a specific day of Sukkot depends on the day of the week and on which day Sukkot begins that year, as reflected in the table below. (The numbers correspond to the acrostic hymn sets listed on page 000.)

First Day of Sukkot falls on	Day of Week											
	Mon.	Tue.	Wed.	Thu.	Fri.	*Shab-bat*	Sun.	Mon.	Tue.	Wed.	Thu.	Fri.
Monday	1, 7	2, 7	5, 7	3, 7	6, 7	8	1–4, 7					
Tuesday		1, 7	2, 7	5, 7	6, 7	8	4, 7	1–4, 7				
Thursday				1, 7	2, 7	8	5, 7	6, 7	4, 7	1–4, 7		
Shabbat						8	1, 7	5, 7	2, 7	6, 7	4, 7	1–4, 7

Ani Vaho

First 6 days of Sukkot (excluding *Shabbat*)	*Shabbat Chol haMo-ed Sukkot*	*Hoshana Rabbah*
Ani vaho, hoshiah na (Please, O Lord, save now)		

The phrase *Ani vaho* is hard to understand. The numerical value of *Ani vaho* is seventy-eight, the same as *Ana Adonai* (Please, O Lord). It has been suggested that the phrase *Ani vaho* was substituted to reduce repeated invocation of the Name of God.

Hoshiah et Amecha

First 6 days of Sukkot (excluding *Shabbat*)	*Shabbat Chol haMo-ed Sukkot*	*Hoshana Rabbah*
Hoshiah et amecha ... ki Adonai Hu ha-Elohim, ein od (Save Your people ... that the Lord is God, there is no other)		

The paragraph *Hoshiah et amecha* (Save Your people) consists of three biblical verses, namely, Psalm 28:9 and I Kings 8:59–60.

This concludes the discussion of *Hoshanot*. We return to the description of the Additional Service.

Ein Keloheinu

Shabbat; Chagim	Rosh Chodesh; Chol haMo-ed
Ein Keloheinu ... et k'toret hasamim (There is none like our God ... the incense of spices)	

The initial letters of the first twelve stiches of the hymn *Ein Keloheinu* (There is none like our God) spell the word *Amen* (Amen) four times. The last stanza refers to the incense that used to be burned in the Temple, which leads to the next section.

Talmudic Passages

Shabbat; Chagim	Rosh Chodesh; Chol haMo-ed
Pitum ha-k'toret ... mi-p'nei hakavod (The incense mixture ... out of respect)	
Hashir sheha-L'vi-im hayu om'rim ... l'chayei ha-olamim (The psalm that the Levites used to say ... for the eternal life)	
Tana d'vei Eliyahu ... elah halachot (The teaching of the school of Elijah ... but laws)	
Amar Rabi Elazar ... Adonai y'varech et ammo vashalom (Rabbi Elazar said ... the Lord will bless His people with peace) (page 211)	

Four Talmudic passages are read. The first is *Pitum ha-k'toret* (The incense mixture) (*K'reitot* 6a), which describes how the various spices were to be combined in the incense that was burned in the Temple.

Hashir sheha-L'vi-im hayu om'rim (The psalm that the Levites used to say) lists the psalm for each day of the week (see page 148). The passage is from the *Mishnah* (*Tamid* 7:4).

The last two passages are both from the *Talmud* and both are plays on words. The first is *Tana d'vei Eliyahu* (The teaching of the school of Elijah) (*M'gillah* 28b). This is followed by *Amar Rabi Elazar* (Rabbi Elazar said) (*B'rachot* 64a). This latter paragraph is said both on Friday evening (see pages 210–211) and here.

Hymn of Glory

Shabbat; Chagim	Rosh Chodesh; Chol haMo-ed
Shir haKavod (Hymn of Glory) *Anim z'mirot ... yashmia kol t'hilato* (Pleasant hymns ... declare all His praise)	

This beautiful poem, beginning *Anim z'mirot* (Pleasant hymns) was probably written by Rabbi Judah of Regensburg, who died in 1217. In some liturgies it is recited on *Shabbat* and Festivals, in others just on Festivals, and some recite it only on Rosh haShanah and Yom Kippur.

18
The Structure of the *Amidah* for the Additional Service on Rosh haShanah

This book is about the *Siddur* and many *Siddurim* do not include the prayers for *Yamim Nora-im* (Days of Awe—Rosh haShanah and Yom Kippur). Notwithstanding this, the structure of the *Amidah* for the Additional Service on Rosh ha-Shanah is so interesting that it has been included as a final chapter of this book.

The diagram shows the overall structure of the Rosh haShanah *Amidah* for the Additional Service. There are three *b'rachot* in the second section of this *Amidah*. Thus the *Amidah* for the Additional Service on Rosh haShanah is a Series Form *b'rachah* with nine *b'rachot*.

First section	First three *B'rachot*	Praises
	Introduction	*Attah v'chartanu* ... (You have chosen us ...)
Second section	Three Intermediate *B'rachot*	*Malchuyot* (Kingship) *Zichronot* (Remembrances) *Shofarot* (*Shofar* Blasts)
Third section	Last three *b'rachot*	Thanksgiving

In this chapter we examine the second section in some detail.

Attah V'chartanu

Attah v'chartanu ... aleinu karata (You have chosen us ... proclaimed to us)
[Modified on *Shabbat*] *Vatiten lanu ... zecher litziat Mitzraim* (You have given us ... in remembrance of the Exodus from Egypt)
Umi-p'nei chata-einu ... mipi ch'vodecha ka-amur (But because of our sins ... from the mouth of Your glory, as it is said)

[On *Shabbat*] *Uvyom haShabbat ... v'niskah* (And on the Sabbath day ... and its libation)

Uvachodesh ha-sh'vi-i ... isheh Ladonai (And in the seventh month ... a burnt offering to the Lord)

[On Shabbat] *Yis-m'chu v'malchu-t'cha ... zecher l'ma-asei v'reshit* (They shall rejoice in Your kingdom ... a remembrance of the Creation)

The first part of the second section of the Rosh haShanah *Amidah* begins *Attah v'chartanu* (You have chosen us). This part of the *Amidah* is frequently referred to as *K'dushat haYom* (holiness of the day) because it describes the reasons why Rosh haShanah is sanctified. It is similar in structure and content to the *K'dushat haYom* section of the *Amidah* for *Chagim* (Chapter 7). The first paragraph, *Attah v'chartanu* (You have chosen us) is identical to *Attah v'chartanu* for *Chagim* (page 70). The second paragraph, *Vatiten lanu* (And You have given us) is similar to *Vatiten lanu* for *Chagim* (page 70), but reflects Rosh haShanah themes and concepts.

The next two paragraphs, namely, *Umi-p'nei chata-einu* (But because of our sins) and, on *Shabbat*, *Uvyom haShabbat* (And on the Sabbath day), are identical to the corresponding prayers in the *Amidah* for *Chagim* (pages 72 and 73).

The fifth paragraph, beginning *Uvachodesh ha-sh'vi-i* (And in the seventh month), is Numbers 29:1–2; it corresponds to the other sacrificial offerings listed on pages 73 and 74. On *Shabbat*, this section of the *Amidah* is concluded with *Yis-m'chu v'malchu-t'cha* (They shall rejoice in Your kingdom), exactly as on *Chagim*.

Three Intermediate *B'rachot*

Up to now, the Rosh haShanah Additional Service *Amidah* appears to be all but identical to the corresponding *Amidah* for *Chagim*. However, at this point it takes on its totally unique structure. Three lengthy *b'rachot* now follow. They are termed *Malchuyot* (Kingship), *Zichronot* (Remembrances), and *Shofarot* (*Shofar* Blasts) because these are the themes of the respective *b'rachot*. The structure of each of these *b'rachot* is shown below:

Opening liturgical poem
Ten Biblical verses, consisting of:
Three verses from the *Torah*
Three verses from *T'hillim*
Three verses from the Prophets
One verse from the *Torah*
Closing liturgical poem

The opening liturgical poems (in Hebrew: *piyutim*) have been attributed to Rav who lived in Babylonia in the third century C.E.

Opening Liturgical Poems

Malchuyot (Kingship)	*Aleinu l'shabbe-ach laAdon hakol* ... (It is our duty to praise the Lord of all ...)
Zichronot (Remembrances)	*Attah zocher ma-asei olam* ... (You remember the deeds of the world ...)
Shofarot (*Shofar* Blasts)	*Attah nigleita ba-anan k'vodecha* ... (You revealed Yourself in Your clouds of glory ...)

The opening *piyut* for the *Malchuyot* (Kingship) *b'rachah* is the *Aleinu* prayer (page 133), recited toward the end of every service. However, there is one difference, the final verse, beginning *V'ne-emar, v'hayah Adonai l'Melech al kol ha-aretz* (And it is said: The Lord will be King over all the earth) (Zech. 14:9) is not found in the *Musaf Amidah*.

Turning now to *Zichronot* (Remembrances), the opening liturgical poem, beginning *Attah zocher* (You remember), describes how God recalls and analyzes our deeds.

The *Shofarot* (*Shofar* Blasts) *b'rachah* begins with a *piyut* describing the giving of the *Torah* on Mount Sinai, accompanied by *shofar* blasts.

Ten Biblical Verses

Malchuyot (Kingship)	
Three verses from the *Torah*	Exodus 15:18, Numbers 23:21, Deuteronomy 33:5
Three verses from *T'hillim*	Psalms 22:29, 93:1, 24:7–10
Three verses from the Prophets	Isaiah 44:6, Obadiah 1:21, Zechariah 14:9
One verse from the *Torah*	Deuteronomy 6:4
Zichronot (Remembrances)	
Three verses from the *Torah*	Genesis 8:1; Exodus 2:24; Leviticus 26:24
Three verses from *T'hillim*	Psalms 111:4, 111:5, 106:45
Three verses from the Prophets	Jeremiah 2:2, Ezekiel 16:60, Jeremiah 31:19
One verse from the *Torah*	Leviticus 26:45
Shofarot (*Shofar* Blasts)	
Three verses from the *Torah*	Exodus 19:16, 19:19, 20:15
Three verses from *T'hillim*	Psalms 47:6, 98:6, 81:4–5, 150:1–6
Three verses from the Prophets	Isaiah 18:3, 27:13; Zechariah 9:14-15
One verse from the *Torah*	Numbers 10:10

The 3–3–3–1 pattern is not strictly followed in any of the three intermediate *b'rachot*. In *Malchuyot*, the first verse from the *Torah* (Exod. 15:18) is actually the last part of *Aleinu*, the opening liturgical poem. Also, the third excerpt from *T'hillim* is not a single verse but rather four verses (Ps. 24:7–10).

In *Zichronot* the final verse from the *Torah* (Lev. 26:45) is part of the closing liturgical poem.

In *Shofarot* there are four excerpts from *T'hillim*. First come two single verses (Ps. 47:6 and 98:6), then follow two verses from Psalm 81 (81:4–5). Finally, all six verses of Psalm 150 appear here. Again, the final verse from the *Torah* (in this case Num. 10:10) is part of the closing liturgical poem.

Closing Liturgical Poems

Malchuyot (Kingship)	*Eloheinu Velohei avoteinu, m'loch al kol ha-olam kulo ... Baruch Attah Adonai, Melech al kol ha-aretz, M'kadaish [haShab-bat v'] Yisra-el v'Yom haZikaron* (Our God and God of our fathers, rule over all the entire world ... Blessed are You, O Lord, King of the whole world, Who sanctifies [the Sabbath and] Israel and the Day of Remembrance)
Zichronot (Remembrances)	*Eloheinu Velohei avoteinu, zochrenu b'zichron tov l'fanecha ... Baruch Attah Adonai, Zocher habrit* (Our God and God of our fathers, remember us with a favorable remembrance before You ... Blessed are You, O Lord, Who remembers the covenant)
Shofarot (*Shofar* Blasts)	*Eloheinu Velohei avoteinu, t'ka b'shofar gadol l'cherutenu ... Baruch Attah Adonai, Shome-a kol t'ru-at ammo Yisra-el b'rachamim* (Our God and God of our fathers, sound the great *shofar* for our free-dom ... Blessed are You, O Lord, Who hears the sounds of the *shofar* of His people Israel in mercy)

Each of these closing *piyutim* (liturgical poems) starts with the words *Eloheinu Velohei avoteinu* (Our God and God of our fathers). Parts of these liturgical poems, like those of the opening *piyutim*, are found in other parts of the *Siddur*.

The closing *piyut* of the *Malchuyot* (Kingship) *b'rachah* starts with the words *Eloheinu Velohei avoteinu, m'loch al kol ha-olam kulo* (Our God and God of our fathers, rule over all the entire world). The *b'rachah* concludes with a Rosh haShanah version of the prayer that concludes the *K'dushat haYom* part of each *Shabbat Amidah*, namely, *Eloheinu Velohei avoteinu, r'tzei vimnuchatenu* (Our God and God of our fathers, accept our rest)—see page 30.

The first half of the closing *piyut* for *Zichronot* (Remembrances), beginning *Eloheinu Velohei avoteinu, zochrenu b'zichron tov l'fanecha* (Our God and

God of our fathers, remember us with a favorable remembrance before You), now also forms part of the Preliminary Morning Service (page 228). The *b'rachah* ends *Baruch Attah Adonai, Zocher habrit* (Blessed are You, O Lord, Who remembers the covenant).

Finally, the *Shofarot* (*Shofar* Blasts) *b'rachah* concludes with the *piyut Eloheinu Velohei avoteinu, t'ka b'shofar gadol l'cherutenu* (Our God and God of our fathers, sound the great *shofar* for our freedom). The first sentence (minus the introductory *Eloheinu Velohei avoteinu*) is taken from the first sentence of the tenth *b'rachah* of the weekday *Amidah, T'ka b'shofar gadol l'cherutenu* (Sound the great *shofar* for our freedom) (page 52). The next three sentences, beginning *v'karev p'zureinu* (and gather our scattered people together), are also to be found at the end of the paragraph *Umi-p'nei chata-einu* (But because of our sins) that begins the Intermediate *B'rachah* of the *Musaf Amidah* for *Chagim* (page 72).

Additions during the Repetition of the *Amidah*

When the *Amidah* is repeated by the Reader, additional material is inserted into every one of the nine *b'rachot* of the Rosh haShanah *Musaf Amidah;* much of this material consists of *piyutim* (liturgical poems). Unfortunately, this material goes far beyond the scope of this book, "The Structure of the *Siddur.*" After all, the basic *Amidah* for Rosh haShanah and Yom Kippur appears in some *Siddurim*, but the Reader's Repetition is found only in a *Machzor* (Festival Prayer Book).

The reader who is curious about the structure of the service on Rosh haShanah and Yom Kippur will have to wait for the publication of a future book, entitled "The Structure of the *Machzor.*"

Appendix A
Sources

The material in this book that relates to the structure of the *Siddur* is original. That is, all the diagrams and accompanying explanatory text are my own unaided work.

Much of the rest of the material, particularly the "For the Maven" sections, can be described as synagogue general knowledge. For example, most regular worshippers know from experience the four occasions when three *Sifrei Torah* are read (page 184). The origin of other "For the Maven" material has proved harder for me to trace. For instance, I simply cannot recall where I first learned the *YaKN'HaZ* acronym for *Kiddush* on Festivals (page 118). It was probably from one of my teachers, but I cannot remember from whom it was or when. Similarly, I recall reading somewhere about the two forms of the *b'rachah* to say before reciting *Hallel* (page 152). What I cannot remember, however, is where I saw it.

In order to give credit as accurately as I can, I have reread the commentaries in the three annotated *Siddurim* I have used the most, namely:

[ArtScroll]   "The Rabbinical Council of America Edition of The ArtScroll *Siddur.*" New York: Mesorah Publications, 1990.

[Birnbaum]   "*Ha-Siddur Ha-Shalem*, Daily Prayer Book, Translated and Annotated with an Introduction by Philip Birnbaum." New York: Hebrew Publishing Company, 1949.

[Hertz]   "The Authorized Daily Prayer Book of the United Hebrew
               Congregations of the British Empire, Revised Edition, with
               Commentary by the Late Chief Rabbi (Dr. J. H. Hertz,
               C.H.)." London: Shapiro Vallentine & Co., 1946.

Where I believe that one of those three *Siddurim* is the source, the name of the *Siddur* appears in brackets in the text. For the rest, I would be grateful for any assistance in giving attribution appropriately. I will rectify matters in a future edition.

In this book I describe the structure of the *Siddur* and how the prayers relate to one another; I have devoted only a sentence or two to the contents of each prayer. For those readers who are interested in learning more about the contents of the individual prayers, I strongly recommend "To Pray as a Jew" by Rabbi Hayim Halevy Donin, New York: Basic Books, Inc., 1980.

Other excellent sources include "Encyclopedia Judaica," 16 Volumes, Jerusalem: Keter Publishing House Ltd., 1972; "Jewish Worship" by Abraham E. Millgram, Philadelphia: Jewish Publication Society, 1975; and "Jewish Liturgy: A Comprehensive History" by Ismar Elbogen, Philadelphia: Jewish Publication Society, 1993.

Appendix B
Cross References to
Siddurim

The subject of this book is the **structure** of the *Siddur*. Readers who are interested in the **contents** of a specific prayer should consult a *Siddur*. To assist, this Appendix lists the page numbers for specific prayers in three of the more popular *Siddurim*, namely, the ArtScroll *Siddur*, *Ha-Siddur Ha-Shalem* by Philip Birnbaum, and *Siddur Sim Shalom*.

Chapter 4. The Structure of *B'rachot*

Page	Section	ArtScroll	Birnbaum	Sim Shalom
17	Short Form *B'rachah* (*Hamotzi*)	224	773	726
18	Short Form *B'rachah* (*Kiddush* for *Shabbat* Evening)	360	289	726
19	Long Form *B'rachah* (*Kiddush* for *Shabbat* Evening)	360	289	726
20	Long Form *B'rachah* (*Havdalah*)	618–620	551	700
25	*Mitzvah* Form *B'rachah* (Before Lighting *Shabbat* Candles)	296	221	717
26	*Mitzvah* Form *B'rachah* (Before Counting the *Omer*)	284	637	237
26	*Mitzvah* Form *B'rachah* (Before Taking the *Lulav*)	630	677	379

Chapter 5. The Structure of the *Shabbat Amidah*

Page	Prayer	ArtScroll	Birnbaum	Sim Shalom
27	*Shabbat Amidah*	338–346, 420–430, 462–474, 514–522	265–273, 349–359, 391–405, 449–459	296–302, 354–364, 430–440, 486, 490, 496–502, 574–584
28	First Section of the Basic *Shabbat Amidah*: Praises	338, 420–422, 462–464, 514–516	265–267, 349–353, 391–393, 449–453	296, 354, 358, 430, 434, 486, 496, 574, 578
29	First *B'rachah*	338, 420, 462, 514	265, 349, 391, 449–451	296, 354, 430, 486, 574

Page	Prayer	ArtScroll	Birnbaum	Sim Shalom
29	Second *B'rachah*	338, 420–422, 462, 514–516	265, 349–351, 391–393, 451	296, 354, 430, 486, 574
29	Third *B'rachah*	338, 422, 464, 516	267, 353, 393, 453	296, 358, 434, 496, 578
30	Second Section of the Basic *Shabbat Amidah*: *Shabbat* Themes	340, 424, 466–468, 516–518	267, 353, 395, 453	298, 358, 434–436, 578
30	Fourth *B'rachah*: Evening Service	340	267	298
31	Fourth *B'rachah*: Morning Service	424	353	358
32	Fourth *B'rachah*: Additional Service	466–468	395	434–436
33	Fourth *B'rachah*: Afternoon Service	516–518	453	578
34	Third Section of the Basic *Shabbat Amidah*: Thanksgiving	342–344, 426–430, 470–472, 518–522	267–269, 353–359, 399–403, 453–457	298–302, 358–364, 436–440, 500–502, 578–582
34	Fifth *B'rachah*	342, 426, 470, 518	267, 353–355, 399, 453–455	298, 358–360, 436, 500, 578–580
35	Sixth *B'rachah*	342–344, 426–428, 470–472, 520–522	269–271, 355–357, 399–401, 455–457	300, 360–362, 436–438, 500–502, 580–582
35	Seventh *B'rachah*	344, 428–430, 472, 522	271, 359, 403, 457	302, 362–364, 438–440, 502, 582
36	Personal Prayers	344–346, 430, 472–474, 522	271–273, 359, 403–405, 451	302*, 364*, 440*, 502–504*, 584*

* The item in this *Siddur* differs significantly from the description in this book.

Page	Prayer	ArtScroll	Birnbaum	Sim Shalom
37	Additions	338–346, 420–430, 462–474, 514–522	265–273, 349–359, 391–405, 449–459	296–302, 354–364, 430–440, 486, 490, 496–502, 574–584
37	Additions to First *B'rachah*	338, 420, 462, 514	265, 349, 391, 449–451	296, 354, 430, 486, 574
38	Additions to Second *B'rachah*	338, 420–422, 462, 514–516	265, 349–351, 391–393, 451	296, 354, 430, 486, 574
39	Additions to Third *B'rachah*	338, 422, 464, 516	267, 351–353, 393, 451–453	296, 356–358, 432–434, 490, 576–578
40	Additions to Fourth *B'rachah*: Additional Service on *Shabbat Rosh Chodesh*	466–468	397–399	496–498
42	Additions to Fifth *B'rachah*	342, 426, 470, 518	267–269, 399, 453–455	298, 358–360, 500, 578–580
43	Additions to Sixth *B'rachah*	342–344, 426–428, 470–472, 520–522	269–271, 355–357, 399–403, 455–457	300, 360–362, 436–438, 500–502, 580–582
44	Additions to Seventh *B'rachah*	344, 428–430, 472, 522	271, 359, 403–405, 457–459	302, 362–364, 438–440, 502, 582

Chapter 6. The Structure of the Weekday *Amidah*

Page	Prayer	ArtScroll	Birnbaum	*Sim Shalom*
45	Weekday *Amidah*	98–118, 234–248, 266–278	81–97, 159–175, 199–211	106–120, 168–186, 210–220
46	First Section of the Basic Weekday *Amidah*: Praises	98–102, 234–236, 266–268	81–85, 159–163, 199–201	106, 110, 168, 172, 210
47	Second Section of the Basic Weekday *Amidah*: Petitions	102–108, 236–242, 268–274	85–89, 163–167, 201–205	110–114, 172–178, 212–216
48	Six Requests for Personal Well-Being (*B'rachot* 4 through 9)	102–104, 236–238, 268–270	85–87, 163–165, 201–203	110–112, 172–174, 212–214
49	Fourth *B'rachah*	102, 236, 268	85, 163, 201	110, 172, 212
49	Fifth *B'rachah*	102, 236, 268	85, 163, 203	110, 172, 212
49	Sixth *B'rachah*	102, 236, 268	85, 163, 203	110, 172, 212
50	Seventh *B'rachah*	102, 238, 270	85, 163, 203	110, 172, 212
50	Eighth *B'rachah*	104, 238, 270	87, 163–165, 203	112, 174, 212
50	Ninth *B'rachah*	104, 238, 270	87, 165, 203	112, 174, 214
51	Six Requests for National Well-Being (*B'rachot* 10 through 15)	106–108, 238–242, 270–272	87–89, 165–167, 203–205	112–114, 174–178, 214–216
52	Tenth *B'rachah*	106, 238, 270,	87, 165, 203	112, 174, 214
52	Eleventh *B'rachah*	106, 240, 270,	87, 165, 203	112, 174, 214

Page	Prayer	ArtScroll	Birnbaum	Sim Shalom
52	Twelfth *B'rachah*	106, 240, 270–272	87, 165, 205	112, 176, 214
53	Thirteenth *B'rachah*	106, 240, 272	87–89, 165, 205	112, 176, 214
53	Fourteenth *B'rachah*	108, 240, 272	89, 167, 205	114, 176, 214
54	Fifteenth *B'rachah*	108, 242, 272	89, 167, 205	114, 176, 216
54	Last Petition (Sixteenth *B'rachah*)	108–110, 242, 272–274	89, 167, 205	114, 178, 216
55	Third Section of the Basic Weekday *Amidah*: Thanksgiving	110–116, 242–248, 274–276	89–95, 169–173, 205–209	114–120, 178–184, 216–220
56	Personal Prayers	118, 248, 276–278	95–97, 175, 211	120, 184–186, 220
56	Additions	98–118, 234–248, 266–278	81–97, 159–173, 199–211	106–120, 168–186, 210–220
56	Additions to First, Second, and Third *B'rachot*	98–102, 234–236, 266–268	81–85, 159–163, 199–201	106–110, 168–172, 210
57	Additions to Fourth *B'rachah*	102, 236, 268	85, 163, 201	110, 172, 212
58	Additions to Seventh *B'rachah*	102–104, 238, 270	87, 163, 203	110, 172, 212
58	Additions to Eighth *B'rachah*	104, 238, 270	87, 163–165, 203	112, 174, 212
59	Additions to Ninth *B'rachah*	104, 238, 270	87, 165, 203	112, 174, 214
59	Additions to Eleventh *B'rachah*	106, 240, 270	87, 165, 203	112, 174, 214

Page	Prayer	ArtScroll	Birnbaum	Sim Shalom
60	Additions to Fourteenth *B'rachah*	108, 240, 272	89, 167, 205	114, 176, 214
61	Additions to Sixteenth *B'rachah*	108–100, 242, 272– 274	89, 167– 169, 205	114, 178, 216
61	Additions to Seventeenth *B'rachah*	110, 242– 244, 274	89–91, 169, 205– 207	114–116, 178, 216
62	Additions to Eighteenth *B'rachah*	112–116, 244–246, 274–276	91–95, 171–173, 207–209	116–120, 180–184, 216–220
63	Additions to Nineteenth *B'rachah*	116, 246– 248, 276	95, 173, 209–211	120, 184, 220
65	*Havinenu*	—	97	228–230

Chapter 7. The Structure of the *Amidah* for Festivals

Page	Prayer	ArtScroll	Birnbaum	Sim Shalom
68	*Amidah* for *Chagim*	660–670, 674–692	585–597, 609–625	304–312, 366–376, 456–476, 586–594
69	Intermediate *B'rachah* for *Chagim*	662–666, 678–688	589–593, 613–621	304–308, 370–372, 462–470, 588–592
70	Intermediate *B'rachah* for Evening, Morning, and Afternoon Services	662–666	589–593	304–308, 370–372, 588–592
72	Intermediate *B'rachah* for Additional Service	678–688	613–621	462–470
73	Sacrificial Offerings	680–686	615–619	466–467

Page	Prayer	ArtScroll	Birnbaum	*Sim Shalom*
75	*Amidah* for *Chol haMo-ed*	110, 244, 274, 342, 426, 518, 674–692	89–91, 169, 205–207, 267–269, 353–355, 453–455, 609–625	114, 178, 216, 298, 360, 456–476, 580
76	*Amidah* for *Rosh Chodesh*	110, 244, 274, 342, 426, 466–468, 518, 644–652	89–91, 169, 205–207, 267–269, 353–355, 397–399, 453–455, 575–583	114, 178, 216, 298, 360, 486–504, 580
77	Intermediate *B'rachah* for Weekday Additional Service on *Rosh Chodesh*	646–648	577–579	492–494
78	Prayer for Rain and Prayer for Dew	702–704, 704–708	633–635, 697–701	478–480, 482–484
79	Additions to First *B'rachah*	702, 704–706	633, 697	—
80	Additions to Second *B'rachah*	702–704, 706–708	633–635, 697–701	478–480, 482–484
82	*Birkat Kohanim*	692–700	625–631	470–474
84	Changes to Fifth *B'rachah*	692	625–627	470
85	Changes to Sixth *B'rachah*	692–700	627–631	470–472
86	*Y'hi Ratzon Mi-l'fanecha*	694	627	—
86	Summoning the *Kohanim*	694	627	472
87	*B'rachah* of the *Kohanim*	694	627	472
88	*Birkat Kohanim*	696–698	627–629	474
89	*Adir Bamarom*	700	631	474

Chapter 8. The Structure of *K'riat Sh'ma*

Page	Prayer	ArtScroll	Birnbaum	*Sim Shalom*
91	*K'riat Sh'ma*	84–96, 256–266, 330–336, 406–420	71–81, 191–199, 257–263, 335–349	96–104, 200–208, 279–292, 340–352
93	*Ba-r'chu*	84, 256, 330, 406	71, 191, 257, 335	96, 200, 279, 340
94	*B'rachot* before *K'riat Sh'ma*: Morning Service	84–90, 406–414	71–75, 337–343	96–98, 340–346
94	First *B'rachah* before *K'riat Sh'ma*: Morning Service	84–88, 406–412	71–73, 337–343	96–98, 340–344
95	*K'dushah d'Yotzer*	84–88, 408–412	71–73, 337–341	96–98, 340–344
96	*Hame-ir La-aretz*	84–86, 408	71, 337	96, 342–344
97	*Hakol Yoducha*	408	337–339	340
97	*El Adon*	410	339	342
98	*La-El Asher Shavat*	410–412	339–341	342
98	*Titbarach Tzurenu*	86–88, 412	71–73, 341	96–98, 344
99	Second *B'rachah* before *K'riat Sh'ma*: Morning Service	88–90, 412–414	73–75, 343	98, 346
100	*B'rachot* before *K'riat Sh'ma*: Evening Service	256–258, 330	191, 257	200, 280–282
100	First *B'rachah* before *K'riat Sh'ma*: Evening Service	256–258, 330	191, 257	200, 280
100	Second *B'rachah* before *K'riat Sh'ma*: Evening Service	258, 330	191, 257	200, 282
101	The *Sh'ma*	90–94, 258–260, 330–334, 414–416	75–77, 193–195, 257–261, 343–345	100–102, 202–204, 284–286, 346–348

Page	Prayer	ArtScroll	Birnbaum	*Sim Shalom*
101	First Paragraph of the *Sh'ma*	90–92, 258, 330–332, 414	75, 193, 257–259, 343–345	100, 202, 284, 346
101	Second Paragraph of the *Sh'ma*	92, 260, 332, 414–416	77, 193, 259, 345	100–102, 202, 286, 348
102	Third Paragraph of the *Sh'ma*	94, 260, 332–334, 416	77, 193–195, 259–261, 345	102, 204, 286, 348
103	*B'rachot* after *K'riat Sh'ma*: Morning Service	94–96, 416–420	77–81, 347–349	102–104, 350–352
103	First and Only *B'rachah* after *K'riat Sh'ma*: Morning Service	94–96, 416–420	77–81, 347–349	102–104, 350–352
104	*B'rachot* after *K'riat Sh'ma*: Evening Service	260–266, 334–336	195–199, 261–263	204–208, 288–292
104	First *B'rachah* after *K'riat Sh'ma*: Evening Service	260–262, 334	195, 261	204, 288–290
104	Second *B'rachah* after *K'riat Sh'ma*: Evening Service for *Shabbat* and Festivals	334–336	261–263	292
104	Second *B'rachah* after *K'riat Sh'ma*: Evening Service for Weekdays	262–264	197	206
106	Third *B'rachah* after *K'riat Sh'ma*: Evening Service for Weekdays	264–266	197–199	206–208

9. The Structure of Commonly Occurring Components

Page	Prayer	ArtScroll	Birnbaum	*Sim Shalom*
107	*Havdalah*	618–620	551	700
108	Biblical Verses	618	551	700
109	First *Havdalah B'rachah*	618	551	700
109	Second *Havdalah B'rachah*	618	551	700
110	Third *Havdalah B'rachah*	618	551	700
111	Fourth *Havdalah B'rachah*	620	551	700
112	*Kiddush*	348–350, 360, 492, 656–658	277, 289, 423, 597–599, 631	318, 726, 734, 742–744, 746, 748, 752
114	Biblical Verses	360, 492, 656	289, 423, 597, 631	726, 734, 742, 746, 748, 752
115	*B'rachah* over Wine, Other Liquids, or Bread	348, 360, 492, 658	277, 289, 423, 597, 631	318, 726, 734, 742, 746, 748, 752
116	Long Form *B'rachah*	348–350, 360, 658	277, 289, 597–599	318, 726, 742, 748
117	*Havdalah B'rachot*	658	599	320, 744, 748
117	*Shehecheyanu*	658	599	320, 744, 748

Page	Prayer	ArtScroll	Birnbaum	Sim Shalom
119	*K'dushah*	84–88, 100, 154–156, 236, 408–412, 422, 464, 504–506, 516, 596–598, 646, 662, 676	71–73, 83–85, 131–133, 161–163, 337–341, 351, 393, 439–441, 451–453, 537–539, 575–577, 587–589, 609–613	96–98, 108, 156–158, 170, 340–344, 356, 368, 432, 458–460, 488–490, 560–564, 576, 588, 684–686
120	The Structure of the *K'dushah*	100, 236, 422, 464, 516, 646, 662, 676	83–85, 161–163, 351, 393, 451–453, 575–577, 587–589, 609–613	108, 170, 356, 368, 432, 458–460, 488–490, 576, 588
122	Introductory Sentence	100, 236, 422, 464, 516, 646, 662, 676	83, 161, 351, 393, 451, 575, 587, 609	108, 170, 356, 368, 432, 458, 488, 490, 576, 588
123	Components of the *K'dushah*	100, 236, 422, 464, 516, 646, 662, 676	83–85, 161–163, 351, 393, 451–453, 575–577, 587–589, 609–613	108, 170, 356, 368, 432, 458–460, 488–490, 576, 588
124	*Kaddish Shalem*	156–158, 252, 278, 348, 430–432, 474, 524, 598–600, 642	133–135, 183, 211–213, 275, 361, 405, 461, 541	158–160, 194, 222, 316, 392, 506, 596, 688

Page	Prayer	ArtScroll	Birnbaum	*Sim Shalom*
128	*Chatzi Kaddish*	82, 138, 234, 266, 336, 506	69, 117, 123, 159, 199, 263, 335, 373, 389, 441, 449	94, 126, 146, 166, 208, 294, 338, 390, 408, 428, 564, 572, 682
129	*Kaddish d'Rabbanan*	52–54, 328, 480	45–47, 255, 411	20, 274
130	*Kaddish Yatom*	56, 160, 254, 280–282, 322, 352, 368, 482, 528, 610	49–51, 137, 185–187, 215, 219, 249, 279, 299–301, 413–415, 463	52, 162, 198, 226, 268, 294, 324, 512, 524, 600, 698
131	*Kaddish l'It-chad'ta*	800	737–739	—
132	*Uva l'Tziyon/V'Attah Kadosh*	154–156, 504–506, 596–598	131–133, 439–441, 537–539	156–158, 560–564, 684–686
133	*Aleinu*	158–160, 252–254, 280, 350, 480–482, 526–528, 608–610	135–137, 185, 213–215, 277–279, 413, 461–463	160–162, 196, 224, 320–322, 510, 598, 696
133	Missing Verse	158, 252, 280, 350, 480, 526, 608	135, 185, 213, 277, 411, 461	160, 196, 224, 320, 510, 598, 696
135	*Tachanun*	124–136, 250–252	103–105, 105–117, 181–183	128–136, 192–194
135	Short Version of *Tachanun*	132, 136, 250–252	103–105, 181–183	132–136, 192–194

Page	Prayer	ArtScroll	Birnbaum	Sim Shalom
137	Long Version of *Tachanun*	124–136	105–117	128–136, 192–194
138	Seven Lengthy Paragraphs of Elegies and Lamentations	124–132	105–113	128–132*
138	Responsive Series of Entreaties	134	113–115	—
140	*Ashrei*	66–68, 150–152, 232, 390–392, 456–458, 502–504	57–59, 127–129, 157–159, 319–321, 383–387, 437–439	80–82, 152–154, 164–166, 420–422, 558–560
141	*Avinu Malkenu*	120–122	97–101, 175–179	124–126, 188–190
142	*Yigdal, Adon Olam*	12–14, 352	11–13, 281–283, 423	6, 326, 514
143	Chanukah and Purim	112–114, 244–246, 274–276, 342–344, 428, 470, 520, 782–784, 786–788	91–93, 171–173, 207–209, 269–271, 401, 581, 709–711, 725–729	116–118, 180–182, 218, 242, 300, 362, 438, 500, 582
144	Structure of Liturgy for Chanukah and Purim	782–784, 786–788	709–711, 725–729	242, —
144	*B'rachot* before Kindling Chanukah Lights and Reading the *M'gillah*	782, 786	709, 725	242, —
145	Structure of Remainder of Chanukah Liturgy	782–784	709–711	242
146	Structure of Remainder of Purim Liturgy	786–788	727–729	—

* The item in this *Siddur* differs significantly from the description in this book.

Chapter 10. The Structure of Components from the Psalms

Page	Prayer	ArtScroll	Birnbaum	*Sim Shalom*
148	Psalm of the Day	162–168, 488	139–147, 419–421	22–34
149	Psalms for Special Days	54, 82, 170–174, 282, 368, 406, 488, 530–532	49, 147–151, 215–219, 281, 299, 421, 465–467, 473	34–44, 50–52, 676
150	*Hallel*	632–642	565–573	380–388
152	B'rachah before Reciting *Hallel*	632	565	380
153	Psalm 113	632	565–567	380
153	Psalm 114	632–634	567	380
153	Psalm 115	634–636	567–569	382
154	Psalm 116	636–638	569	384
154	Psalm 117	638	571	386
155	Psalm 118	638–640	571–573	386–388
156	B'rachah after Reciting *Hallel*	640–642	573	388
157	*P'sukei d'Zimrah* and its Psalms	54–82, 368–404	49–69, 299–335	50–94, 334–338
158	Introductory Psalm to *P'sukei d'Zimrah*	54–56, 368	49, 299	50–52
158	B'rachah before Reciting *P'sukei d'Zimrah*	58–60, 370	51, 301	54
159	Lengthy Succession of Biblical Verses, Mainly from the Psalms	60–80, 370–400	51–69, 301–329	54–94
160	I Chronicles 16:8–36	60–62, 370–372	51–53, 301–303	54–58
160	Eighteen Excerpts from the Psalms	62–64, 372–374	53–55, 303–305	58

Page	Prayer	ArtScroll	Birnbaum	Sim Shalom
160	Psalm 100	64	55	60
161	Nine Psalms (*Ashkenazi* Liturgy) / Fourteen Psalms (*Sephardi* Liturgy)	374–388	305–317	60–80
161	Verses Primarily from the Bible	64–66, 388–390	55–57, 319	80
162	Five *Halleluyah* Psalms	70–74, 392–396	59–65, 321–325	82–88
162	Three Doxologies from the Psalms	74, 396	65, 327	90
163	Three Biblical Passages	74–80, 396–400	65–69, 327–329	90–92
163	Three Biblical Verses	80, 400	69, 331	94
163	*Nishmat*	400–402	331–333	334–336
165	Beginning of the Morning Service Proper	404	333–335	336
165	*B'rachah* after Reciting *P'sukei d'Zimrah*	82, 404	69, 335	94, 338
166	Other *Shabbat* Psalms	530–542, 592–594, 608	465–475, 535, 549	34, 666–680, 694
167	*Ba-r'chi Nafshi* and the *Shir haMa-alot* Psalms	530–542	465–475	34, 666–680
168	Psalms before the Saturday Evening Service	592–594	535	—
168	Psalm at the End of the Saturday Evening Service	592–594	549	694

Chapter 11. The Structure of *K'riat haTorah*

Page	Prayer	ArtScroll	Birnbaum	Sim Shalom
169	*K'riat haTorah*	138–146, 432–460, 508–512, 672, 758–760, 810–814	117–127, 361–389, 443–449, 601–607, 703–707	136–150, 394–426, 516–524, 548–552, 566–570
173	Before Opening the Ark	138, 432	117, 361–363	136, 394
174	On Opening the Ark	138, 432, 508	119, 363, 443	138, 394, 566
174	In Front of the Ark	140, 434–436, 508	119–121, 363–365, 443	394–398
176	*B'rich Sh'mei*	140, 436, 508	119–121, 365, 443	396–398
176	On Taking the Scroll	140, 436, 508	121, 365, 445	138, 398, 566
177	Procession I	140, 436–438, 508	121, 365–367, 445	138–140, 398–400, 566
178	On Unrolling the Scroll	142, 438–440, 510	121, 367–369, 445	140, 400, 568
180	Structure of Each *Aliyah*	142, 440, 510	123, 369, 445–447	140–142, 400–402, 568
181	Additional *B'rachot*	142–144, 444	123, 369	142, 402
182	*Misheberach*	442–444	371	142–144, 402–408
183	After Prescribed Readings	138	123, 373	146, 408

Page	Prayer	ArtScroll	Birnbaum	Sim Shalom
185	On Raising the Scroll	146, 444, 510	125, 373, 447	146, 410, 570
186	Reading from the Prophets	446–448	373–377	410–412
187	Prayers before Returning Scroll to the Ark	146, 448–458, 810–814	125, 377–387, 601–607	146–148
188	Prayers before Returning Scroll to the Ark: *Shabbat* Morning	448–458, 810–814	377–387, 601–607	412–422
189	Prayers for Scholars, Congregation, Government, and Israel	448–450	377–379	412–416
191	*Birkat haChodesh*	452	381	418
193	The Structure of *Yizkor*	810–814	601–607	516–524
195	Prayer for Martyrs	454–456	383	420
196	Prayers before Returning Scroll to the Ark: Festivals	456–458, 672, 810–814	383–387, —, 601–607	420–422, —, 516–524
197	Prayers before Returning Scroll to the Ark: Mondays and Thursdays	146	125	146–148
198	On Taking the Scroll	148, 458, 512	125–127, 387, 447	150, 422, 570
198	Procession II	148, 458–460, 512	127, 387–389, 447	150, 424, 570
199	In Front of the Ark	148, 460, 512	127, 389, 449	150, 426, 570
200	*Torah* Reading on *Simchat Torah*	758–760	703–707	548–556
200	*Hakafot*	758–760	703–707	548–552
201	*Torah* Reading	—	—	552–556*

* The item in this *Siddur* differs significantly from the description in this book.

Chapter 12. The Structure of the Afternoon Service

Page	Prayer	ArtScroll	Birnbaum	Sim Shalom
203	Afternoon Service	232–254, 502–586	157–187, 437–533	164–198, 558–680
205	Va-ani T'filati	506	443	566
205	Tzidka-t'cha	524	459	584
206	Pirkei Avot	544–586	477–533	602–665

Chapter 13. The Structure of *Kabbalat Shabbat*

Page	Prayer	ArtScroll	Birnbaum	Sim Shalom
207	Kabbalat Shabbat	308–328	237–255	254–272, 682–702
208	Six Psalms	308–314	237–243	254–260
209	Ana b'Ko-ach	314	243	—
209	L'chah Dodi	316–318	243–247	262–264
210	Psalms 92 and 93	320–322	247–249	266–268
210	Bameh Madlikin	322–328	251–255	270–272*

* The item in this *Siddur* differs significantly from the description in this book.

Chapter 14. The Structure of the Evening Service

Page	Prayer	ArtScroll	Birnbaum	Sim Shalom
213	Evening Service	256–282, 308–352, 592–594, 594–610	237–283, 535, 537– 551	254–326, 682–700
215	Evening Service for *Shabbat* and *Chagim*	308–352	237–283	254–326
216	Biblical Verses	336	263	294
217	*Va-y'chulu*	346	273	314
218	*B'rachah Me-ein Sheva*	346–348	273–275	314
219	Evening Service for Weekdays	256–282, 594–610	191–219, 537–551	200–226, 682–700
220	*V'Hu Rachum*	256	191	200
221	Section after *Amidah*, Saturday Evening	594–610	537–551	682–700
222	*P'sukei B'rachah*	600–610	541–549	690–694

Chapter 15. The Structure of the Preliminary Morning Service

Page	Prayer	ArtScroll	Birnbaum	Sim Shalom
223	Preliminary Morning Service	2–54	3–47	2–20
225	Structure of *Birchot haShachar*	18–54	3–47	10–20
226	List of Fifteen *B'rachot*	18–20	15–17	10
227	*Hama-avir Shenah*	20	17–19	10–12
227	*Y'hi Ratzon Mi-l'fanecha*	20	19	12
228	*Zochrenu b'Zichron Tov*	22–24	19–23	—
229	*L'Olam Y'hei Adam*	26–28	23–25	12–14
230	*Attah Hu ad Shelo*	28	25	14
230	*Attah Hu Adonai Eloheinu*	28	25	14
230	*Korbanot*	30–42	27–37	—
231	Obligatory Talmudic Passages	42–52	37–45	—
231	*Y'hi Ratzon Mi-l'fanecha*	52	45	18

Chapter 16. The Structure of the Morning Service

Page	Prayer	ArtScroll	Birnbaum	Sim Shalom
233	Morning Service	2–174, 369–461	3–151, 299–390	2–162, 334–426
235	Psalm 20	152	131	154
236	Concluding Material	158–174	135–151	160–162, 22–52

Chapter 17. The Structure of the Additional Service

Page	Prayer	ArtScroll	Birnbaum	Sim Shalom
237	Additional Service	462-488, 644-652, 674-692	391–423, 575-583, 609-625	428-440, 456-476, 486-504
239	Hoshanot	726–756	679–696	530–547
240	Acrostic Hymn Sets	726–740	679–686	531–537
242	Ani Vaho	734, 736, 738, 740	683, 684, 685, 686	534, 536, 542, 543
242	Hoshiah et Amecha	736, 740, 754	684, 686, 696	535, 538, 546
243	Ein Keloheinu	476	407	508
243	Talmudic Passages	476–478	407–411	508*
244	Hymn of Glory	484–486	415–419	46–50

Chapter 18. The Structure of the *Amidah* for the Additional Service on Rosh haShanah

Page	Prayer	ArtScroll	Birnbaum	Sim Shalom
245	Amidah for the Additional Service on Rosh haShanah	—	—	—
246	Attah V'chartanu	—	—	—
247	Three Intermediate B'rachot	—	—	—
248	Opening Liturgical Poems	—	—	—
249	Ten Biblical Verses	—	—	—
250	Closing Liturgical Poems	—	—	—
251	Additions during the Repetition of the Amidah	—	—	—

Index to Prayers

Subject Index

About the Author

Stephen R. Schach is an associate professor of Computer Science at Vanderbilt University in Nashville, Tennessee. He is also a software engineering consultant. Dr. Schach has published over 80 technical papers, given numerous seminars, and written four other books, including *Classical and Object-Oriented Software Engineering*, Third Edition, which is used as a college textbook. He has also presented a number of lectures on the structure of the Jewish religious service. Dr. Schach obtained his Ph.D. at the University of Cape Town. He now lives in Nashville with his wife, Sharon, and their two children.